TIKTOK AND YOUTH CULTURES

TIKTOK AND YOUTH CULTURES

BY

CRYSTAL ABIDIN
Curtin University, Australia

emerald
PUBLISHING

United Kingdom – North America – Japan – India
Malaysia – China

Emerald Publishing Limited
Emerald Publishing, Floor 5, Northspring, 21-23 Wellington Street,
Leeds LS1 4DL

First edition 2025

Reprints and permissions service
Contact: www.copyright.com

British Library Cataloguing in Publication Data
A catalogue record for this book is available from the British Library

ISBN: 978-1-80117-531-9 (Print)
ISBN: 978-1-80117-528-9 (Online)
ISBN: 978-1-80117-530-2 (Epub)

INVESTOR IN PEOPLE

To Katie Warfield,
for showing me the life hack that I randomly saw one day,
that is now an unconscious standard practice in my life

&

Acacia,
my Shy Little Frog

CONTENTS

LIST OF FIGURES AND TABLES

Chapter 2

Chapter 3

Chapter 4

Chapter 5

Appendix

PREFACE: WHY WRITE A BOOK ON TIKTOK?

I write this book as a digital anthropologist of internet celebrity, influencer cultures, and social media pop cultures, having focused for more than a decade on the Asia Pacific region at large. To put it plainly, it is my job to understand how internet celebrities operate online, their function in society and their impact on the media. In a world of ever-changing technology and trends, this is a fast-paced dynamic field. My research is constantly evolving to understand how the latest social media trends relate to the experiences of everyday people and how adverse consequences could be mitigated. For instance, my research has previously contributed to understanding how a specific genre and tier of internet celebrities known as 'influencers' have shaped public conversations and perceptions about anti-racism, LGBTQ rights, sexuality education, political participation, misinformation and grassroots activism. And as these prolific users have grown up and grown old on the internet, moving across spaces and places as older platforms retire and newer ones emerge, my research has naturally followed their trajectory into spaces like TikTok.

This brief biographical preamble is important for the reader to understand where this book is 'coming from'. This book is not a comprehensive study of TikTok and its parent company ByteDance; several journalists in the market have provided investigative reportage on this topic. This book is also not an overview of how TikTok works, and the impact of its structure and culture on our society; a scholarly inquiry into TikTok as a platform is already on the scholarly market. Instead, this book is written by a digital anthropologist who specialises in internet celebrity, and who is investigating the youth vernacular cultures of TikTok. In academia, this sort of framing can be understood as Standpoint Theory. In plain speech, this refers to the fact that all studies and analyses of society come from *particular* perspectives, as informed by the *particular* vantage points to which we are privy, which are in turn shaped by the *particular* ways that our bodies interface with the world. For instance, as a mixed-race Asian woman, who grew up alongside emerging technologies and internet cultures in the 1990s, who has long been immersed in inter-Asia multicultural family settings, and who lives in Australia and routinely travels across the Asia Pacific for research, I am bound to perceive society and social issues via my specific biographical lens. This acknowledgement of my 'in-built' or implicit preferences as a scholar allows me to be reflexive about why and how some issues seem to 'stand out' more, be more legible or appear to be more meaningful for study. It also impacts the types of scholarly questions I ask about the world.

In a similar vein, given my scholarly interests and expertise as a digital ethnographer, this book privileges perspectives from the grassroots, from the ground, from the people. Specifically, this book looks at how different types of youth cultures unfold on TikTok. It focuses on how the design and features of an app like TikTok encourage us to commit to certain practices online, generating relatively recognisable templates and platform norms over time, and what impacts these might have on groups of users and the spaces we inhabit.

While some readers may think that TikTok and its cultures is a playground that only young people engage in, many of its principles and practices are evidencing a much wider penetration in digital cultures and society in general.

TikTok has become a critical conduit for channelling and suppressing attention online, how users enact personal agency and choice to circumvent the limitations and restrictions of social media platforms and how impression management on the internet has become pervasive in the wider society. It is also the site where 'under the radar' strategies are being honed, understandings of how 'algorithms' work are being questioned and challenged, and where 'touchy issues' – such as racism, colonialism, sexism, self-harm – are being discussed in ways that invite participation from a wide group of users. From teenagers using the app to organise climate change marches, to prospective small business owners crafting immaculate content to advertise their wares, and even politicians using TikTok to campaign and address their citizens, TikTok cultures have now impacted almost every avenue in society. And if the reader needs any more convincing, the swift 'adoption' of TikTok's short-video format and its various content creation and sharing features by older, more established apps – Reels on Instagram, Shorts on YouTube, Highlights on WhatsApp – tells us that perhaps imitation is the highest form of flattery.

A brief note on methods: My longitudinal study of TikTok and its associated apps began in 2017 as I followed the uptake of its sister-app Douyin among my East Asian internet celebrity informants, witnessed users on the short-video app Dubsmash migrate to rival app Musical.ly, observed the acquisition of Musical.ly by Douyin's parent company Byte-Dance and followed the eventual launch of TikTok on the international stage. These longer term chronological observations have guided my analyses throughout the book, focused especially on voices and perspectives from the people I study throughout the Asia Pacific region. For this reason, I like to think of the work in these pages as early origin stories from the Global South, providing alternative accounts of TikTok's rise through oral histories from the ground, at times juxtaposed against the popular media headlines proliferating from American media.

The data recorded and detailed in this book come from three main sources. Firstly, I conducted an intensive digital ethnography on TikTok from June 2019 to December 2021, comprising 1–2 hours of online immersion and systematic notetaking daily (on weekdays) based on culturally informed observations, as well as the curation of specific case studies for content analyses. This was then supplemented by follow-up digital ethnography from July 2022 to January 2023. Second, I conducted in-person and online personal interviews with influencers, internet celebrities and the managerial and administrative staff of digital media firms (e.g. influencer incubators, talent management companies, digital advertising firms, technological start-ups) across the Asia Pacific region who were early adopters in the 'Asian wave' of TikTok's uptake. Third, I committed to anthropological participant observation of various industry events involving the use of TikTok for content creation and curation, touring fieldsites in Hong Kong, Tokyo, Seoul, Shanghai and Singapore to witness the practices firsthand. Several informants in my study were interviewed on several occasions throughout the years, thus where possible, I timestamp our interviews to indicate the temporal context of their opinions and thought. Such a methodological practice is crucial especially as TikTok and global impressions of it have evolved very quickly during the few years that this research was undertaken, and I aim to reflect the progression and evolution of my informants' accounts where possible.

Although this book is based on in-depth and rigorous academic research, in the spirit of maintaining open access to scholarly inquiry, it is written in plain speak for a general audience. Academics tend to refer to such works as 'public scholarship', inviting conversation, reflections and sometimes even scrutiny from the general public as they engage with our work. I hope that the research documented and discussed in this book will provide the reader with some insight into the youth cultures on TikTok, whether you are a seasoned Tik-Toker, closet lurker or new to the world of short video apps.

In this vein, please allow me to share that in October 2020, I founded the TikTok Cultures Research Network – a research portal focused on studying TikTok cultures from a variety of qualitative research methodologies. Our Network provides and facilitates the production of scholarly resources, research projects and events that connect networks of qualitative scholars of various disciplines from around the world. The initiatives, events and projects that I have spearheaded through the Network also inform the insights in this book. You might like to find out more at TikTokCultures.com.

In a time where readers are spoilt for choice, feeling fatigued from content saturation, or preferring a variety of digital formats to the traditional book, I thank you for your interest in this text. A humble request: Wherever you are in the world, whenever you happen to be reading this text, I would love to hear from you. Which side of TikTok do you live on? Can we swap links to our favourite posts of the week? What TikTok-related issues are unfolding where you are? Future me would love to know – I am generally @wishcrys on the internet <3

Yours,
Crystal Abidin aka wishcrys

ACKNOWLEDGEMENTS

I would like to publicly acknowledge and thank all the informants, participants and interviewees whom I have met throughout the fieldwork for this book. I appreciate your generosity and trust in responding to cold call correspondence, meeting with a stranger for long chats in your offices and cafes, and in some instances even inviting me into your homes and to travel with you to various cities. As an anthropologist, these relationships are one of the most precious things to nurture in my work, and I am ever so grateful for having the opportunity to hear your stories and learn about your lives. I am especially thankful to Kathy Chan and the crew at New Service Concepts (NSC) and Althea Lim and the crew at Gushcloud International for the years of friendship, your kindness in brokering new networks and conversations on my behalf, and for being nourishing human beings in general. Thank you also to the many informants who spoke to me on the condition of anonymity and whose insights are documented in the pages of this book.

The fieldwork for this project and several seed projects that developed ideas for this book were funded by several schemes: the Discovery Early Career Researcher Award (DECRA) from the Australian Research Council (DE190100789); a Tencent Research Bursary; the Strategic Research Investment scheme from the Faculty of Humanities at Curtin University; the

Creative-Critical Imaginations Seed Funding from MCASI Research & Creative Production Committee at Curtin University; and the Rapid-Response Grants on COVID-19 grant from the Social Science Research Council (SSRC) and Wenner-Gren Foundation.

In the process of conducting research and developing this project, I was invited to present portions of the book at various events, and thank the organisers for hosting me and for the invigorating Q&A sessions: Keynote at the Curtin Singapore ASEAN Lecture (2021); Keynote at Digital Trans formations for HUMlab at Umeå University (2021); Keynote for the Anthropological Society of Western Australia Wilson-Locke Lecture (2021); Keynote for the fifth New Media Studies National Congress in Turkey (2021); Keynote for the Connected Learning Summit (2021); Plenary at the Inter-Asia Cultural Studies Society Conference (2021); Panel at the 'Racialisation and the Media from Television to Twitter' event by Oxford University (2021); Roundtable at the International Journal of Screendance Online Symposium (2021); Public dialogue for ANU Policy Forum & Learning Communities (2020); and Research seminar at the Communication and Media Research Speaker Series at University of Zurich (2021). I was also given the opportunity to invite postgraduate students to engage with some of my ideas in two master classes, hosted by the Department of Communications & New Media at National University of Singapore (2021), and the 'Global Communication in a Digital Age' MA Programme at RMIT (2021). Finally, I would like to acknowledge the organisers and audience members at the very first presentations from my pilot studies on short video app cultures and TikTok: The ACAT seminar series for the Centre for Culture and Technology (CCAT) at Curtin University (2020), and The 'Open Literacy: Digital Games, Social Responsibility and Social Innovation' event at Curtin University (2019).

At Emerald Publishing, I am indebted to a long list of crew members, but am especially grateful to Kimberly Chadwick for first endorsing this project, and to Iram Satti and Lydia Cutmore for seeing the book to completion – the care work and empathy we have shared regarding newborns, pandemics, illnesses, grief and all of life's exciting contingencies are memorialised in Too Many email chains, and you have my eternal gratitude.

The incisive illustrations were commissioned and directed by me, and created by a very talented group of art Research Assistants. I am ever so grateful to have the artwork come to life thanks to River Juno, Ardine Keyla, and Phoebe Tan.

Snippets of the writing in this book have been previously published. I thank the outlets and editors for permitting the reuse of these texts. Selections of Chapter 1 were previously published in Abidin, Crystal and Jin Lee. 2023. 'K-pop Tik-Tok: TikTok's expansion into South Korea, TikTok Stage, and Platformed glocalization'. *Media International Australia* 188(1): 86–111. Selections of Chapter 2 were previously published in Abidin, Crystal. 2021. 'Making Sense of Our Digital Lives: A Graphic Conceptual Glossary of the New Ways Attention Is Being Baited, Generated, and Played with Online by Influencers'. *Commonplace,* 2 December 2021. Selections of Chapter 3 were previously published in Zhao, Xinyu, and Crystal Abidin. 2023. 'The "Fox Eye" challenge trend: Anti-racism work, platform affordances, and the vernacular of gesticular activism on TikTok'. *Social Media + Society* 9(1): 1–16. Selections of Chapters 2–4 were previously published in Abidin, Crystal. 2021. 'Mapping Internet Celebrity on TikTok: Exploring Attention Economies and Visibility Labours'. *Cultural Science Journal* 12(1): 77–103.

My trusty Research Assistants D. Bondy Valdovinos Kaye, Darcy Morgan, Yu Ting Poh, Janey Umback and Xinyu (Andy) Zhao supported this longitudinal project through various data collection, data sorting and referencing contributions, and the book would not have been possible without them. I would also like to thank my collaborators on various TikTok projects. Jin Lee, Arantxa Vizcaíno-Verdú and Meg Jing Zeng: It has been wonderful to swap brain foods and brain farts with you.

   To my wider collegial community in academia, I want to take a moment to partake in a little public vulnerability and acknowledge that finishing this project was a great challenge for me. As the pandemic wore on, many of us had to prematurely truncate fieldwork and projects, and conjure creative pivots to sustain our work. The trying few years that followed saw academic job losses at shocking levels, as so many of our colleagues found themselves in greater insecurity in an already precarious industry. There were days when it made no sense to sit at a laptop to type words, when it felt like the world was falling apart, and when I had lost many loved ones in succession to various illnesses. Among these, our academic community had to bid farewell to Dr Katie Warfield – a luminary in the field of digital media studies, a brilliant writer, a generous mentor, a kind friend and really an impeccable specimen of a human being. It was difficult to work through the grief of losing a very treasured friend who was close to my heart, and even more frustrating still to feel so far away and separate from our special crew of found family amidst the halt on international travel. During this very bewildering time, I am immensely grateful for many colleagues-turned-friends who have been guiding lights and soothing comforts to me and for those around us: Kath Albury, Paul Byron, Stefanie Duguay, Natalie Ann Hendry, Amelia Johns, Gabriel Pereira, Brady Robards, Katrin Tiidenberg, César Albarrán Torres – from the bottom of my heart, thank you. To Christina Chau, Natalie Pang, Gabriele de Seta and Meg Jing Zeng: Thank you for being my voices of reason during this pandemic season.

At Curtin University, I thank the wonderful colleagues and friends in the Discipline of Internet Studies, known affectionately as 'the corridor'. At the School of Media, Creative Arts and Social Inquiry (MCASI), thank you to Mike Kent, Lynda Durack, Gaylene Galardi, Cherie Galvin, Andrew McLean for supporting the unseen logistics and administrative work that allows all the research that we do to come to fruition. Thank you also to Umberto Ansaldo who was very supportive and trusting of my ambitious plans during the period when the research for this book was undertaken. At the Research Office, thank you to Melanie McKee, Mandy Downing, Felicity Kamid, Robyn Kenneally and Joanne McEwan for supporting the arduous processes of the many grant applications. At the Faculty of Humanities, thank you to Tim Pitman for seeing the potential in me and my research, and for your collegiality and friendship. Most importantly, thank you to Michael Keane for being the first mentor to trust in my wild ambitions to host the first TikTok academic event on a shoestring budget (we have since hosted or co-hosted another ten!), to launch a research group (we are now the TikTok Cultures Research Network) and for role-modeling what it means to advocate for junior scholars.

Finally, the finishing touches to this book were prematurely 'interrupted' by the (early!) arrival of my precious little human. I write these acknowledgements as she is peacefully asleep and drooling in my lap. I thank our Shy Little Frog for being patient with me in the moments when I was multitasking in life, and thank Sherm for being the best Duet partner ever.

1

ORIGIN STORIES AND PLATFORM WARS

Amid the news coverage and frenzy surrounding the emergence of TikTok, it might appear as if the app turned up in our lives overnight and ushered in the concept of 'short videos' into our lives forever. After all, since TikTok emerged in the international market in 2017, its competitors swiftly rolled out short story features such as Reels on Instagram in 2020 and Shorts on YouTube in 2021. But all origin stories are contextual and political, depending on one's vantage point. In this section, we explore some of these stories.

PREDECESSOR ORIGIN STORIES

In following the English language media coverage on TikTok throughout the course of my fieldwork, it became evident that there were primarily three origin stories that attempted to explain the rise of TikTok in relation to predecessor platforms Vine, Dubsmash, and Musical.ly.

Vine (2013) to TikTok

In the popular media discourse about TikTok, Vine is often credited as 'one of the first social media apps to make the short form video both mainstream and accessible'.[1] Vine – an American short video app that features 6-second video clips that automatically play in a loop, also described as 'a GIF with audio'[2] – was first launched in 2012 and acquired by American micro-blogging platform Twitter in the same year. At its peak around 2013–2014, Vine reportedly boasted over 200 million viewers monthly and over 1.5 billion 'loops' daily.[3] It was responsible for launching the careers of professional 'Viners' and Vine Influencers who would go on to live in collectives (shared apartments or houses) to focus on making collaborative content.[1]

That was until the American ephemeral photo messaging app Snapchat introduced the 10-second video-messaging feature in late 2012,[4] and the American photo-sharing app Instagram introduced the 15-second Story feature in 2013.[2] Twitter shuttered Vine in 2016, but in the years after its closure, Vine would continue to be lauded for conditioning social media users for the arrival of TikTok in 2017.[5] After all, many prolific Viners had swiftly immigrated onto TikTok and quickly established themselves there among old and new followers.[6]

Dubsmash (2014) to TikTok

Another origin story ties TikTok's success to Dubsmash. German video selfie app Dubsmash became an instant success across Europe when it was founded in 2014.[7] The app allowed users – known as 'Dubsmashers' but more affectionately called 'Dubbers' – to lip-sync, act, and dance to a library of audio clips including dialogue and dance in 10-second clips. It was the norm for these to be filmed with front-facing cameras, selfie-style. When it took off in the United States, Dubsmash became popular among Black and Latino teens, who primarily used uploaded sounds from 'unlicensed content, namely TV and film sound clips'[7]; this would later prompt in-app 'take-down notice[s]'.[7]

In 2017, when TikTok's parent company ByteDance acquired Musical.ly (see below) to launch TikTok in the international market, its rapidly rising popularity around the world saw Dubsmash struggling to maintain its market. Shortly after, in the same year, Dubsmash was prompted to update and relaunch, specifically to compete with the burgeoning TikTok market.[8] The app recuperated some of its market to the tune of 1 billion views monthly,[8] and at its peak it was considered second to TikTok in the US market.[8] Dubsmash was acquired by American discussion board website Reddit in 2020.

However, it was around this time that TikTok's global success instigated several social media platforms to introduce short video features[9] – like Instagram's 'Reels' or video-sharing platform YouTube's 'Shorts' – and Reddit eventually decided to similarly 'integrate its video creation tools' onto its platform.[10] It was announced that Dubsmash would be shuttered in 2022.[10] While many of Dubsmash's legacy norms would eventually find their way onto TikTok, especially head bops, point-of-view acting, and the promotion of new music for music labels,[11] the social memory of the app seemed to be outshined by TikTok. Dubsmash has been described in the news as a 'short-form TikTok-like video platform',[10] despite actually predating and preceding it, and evaluated as 'an earlier and ultimately much less successful version of TikTok'.[12]

Musical.ly (2014) to TikTok

Perhaps the most prominent origin story of TikTok takes root in Musical.ly, a lip-syncing video-creation and sharing platform where users – known as 'Musers' – act or, more prominently, perform dances with hand gestures set to a library of available music in 15-second videos. China-based Musical.ly was founded in 2014 but became especially popular with tweens and teenagers in the United States to the extent that some of its most popular Musers and Musical.ly Influencers were 13-year-olds clinching merchandising deals[13] and boasting 20 to 30 million fans.[14] At its peak, there were over 60 million Musers in the United States and Europe alone,[15] and the app was ranked first in downloads in the app store in the United States and 18 countries worldwide.[16] Singers like Selena Gomez would launch Musical.ly specific campaigns to promote their new music,[13] and the platform was noted for being 'one of the few apps to come out of China to become a smash hit in the US'.[13]

After launching its Chinese predecessor sister app Douyin for the domestic market in 2016, in 2017 ByteDance acquired Musical.ly, migrated all of the latter's accounts over in 2018, and rebranded and relaunched Musical.ly as TikTok for the international market.[14] Douyin and TikTok would continue to be 'parallel platforms', sharing 'many similarities in terms of appearance, functionality, and platform affordances' despite being in 'radically different markets' and being 'governed by radically different forces'.[17] Musical.ly's early culture of platform-specific niche inside jokes and music memes[18] was observed to continue on TikTok.[14]

In addition to Vine, Dubsmash, and Musical.ly, a handful of other short video apps were launched as potential competitors to TikTok. They include the likes of Vine's successor 'Byte' launched in 2020[19] and acquired by competitor short-video app Clash in 2021;[20] Facebook's 'Lasso' launched in 2018 and shuttered in 2020;[21] and American short video app Triller launched in 2020.[22]

SHORT VIDEO APPS IN THE ASIA–PACIFIC REGION

Turning to the Asia–Pacific region more specifically, short video app cultures have had a longer history – from as early as 2011 – and are an especially thriving ecology in Mainland China. My brief survey of some of the most prominent and popular apps in the region – by press mentions and user base – reveal at least 27 of such short video platforms that were launched between 2011 and 2020. In the table below (see Table 1), I document the year each app was launched, their parent companies, and brief details about former ownership or subsidiaries where applicable. While many of these apps are popular across more than one country in the Asia–Pacific region, I also detail the primary country market in which the app was most used. In broad strokes, these can be broken into four markets – Mainland China, East Asia, India, and South East Asia – but this section will focus on the first.

Pre-Douyin

According to my digital ethnography surveying the landscape of platforms in East Asia, prior to the launch of Douyin in 2016, there were six main short video apps of prominence in the Mainland Chinese market. The earliest iteration of these appears to be Miaopai, a short video app by Yixia Technology, which had three incubation bases in Shanghai, Chengdu, and Xi'an, with an ethos of supporting local content creators. The app offered more than 30 different music-video styles that

Table 1. A List of Short Video Apps Popular in the Asia–Pacific Region From 2011–2022, Organised by Chronology. Compiled by Author and Research Team, December 2020.

Year Launched	App, Parent Company	Primary APAC Country Markets
2011	Miaopai, Sina Weibo & Miaopai (prev. Yixia Tech)	Mainland China
2012	Kuaishou, Beijing Kuaishou Tech Co.	Mainland China (Tiers 3 and 4, Rural, Indonesia, Philippines, South Korea, Thailand)
2013	Vine, Twitter	Japan
	Weishi, Tencent	Mainland China
	Viva Video, Qu Video Inc.	Mainland China
2014	Meipai, Meitu	Mainland China
	Roposo, InMobi Glance Digital Pvt Ltd (Prev. Relevant E-Solutions Pvt Ltd)	India
2015	Xiaokaxiu, Yixia Technology	Mainland China
2016	Cheez, KakaoTalk	South Korea
	Douyin, ByteDance	Mainland China (Tier 1 and 2 cities)
	Douyin Huoshan (prev. Vigo Video), ByteDance	Mainland China
	Pear Video, Pear Video	Mainland China
	VMate, UC Web (subs. Alibaba Group)	India (rural)
2017	Chingari, Chingari	India
	Haokan Video, Baidu	Mainland China

Table 1. (*Continued*)

Year Launched	App, Parent Company	Primary APAC Country Markets
	Likee, Joyy Inc & Bigo	India
	Nani, Baidu	Mainland China
	Ookbee U, Ookbee & Tencent	Thailand
	TikTok, ByteDance	Australia, Cambodia, Indonesia, Japan, Malaysia, Singapore, South Korea, Thailand, Vietnam
	Tudou, Youku Tudou Inc	Mainland China
	Xigua Video, ByteDance	Mainland China
2018	Aidong, Sina Weibo	Mainland China
	Lu Ke, Alibaba	Mainland China
	Quanmin Video, Baidu	Mainland China
2019	Reels, Instagram	Australia, India, Japan
2020	Mitron, Mitron	India
	YouTube Shorts, Google	India

users are able to adopt as audio–visual templates to record and post short clips. Various Influencer and *wanghong* company reps whom I interviewed throughout the course of my fieldwork inform me that even in its early stages, up to 500 to 600 mainstream entertainment celebrities (from television, film, and the music industries) were using Miaopai to interact with fans. The user demographic on the app mainly comprised top celebrities, media stars, and microbloggers.

In contrast to this relatively upmarket market segment on Miaopai, the launch of Kuaishou in 2012 primarily catered to

users in the Tier 3 (i.e. gross domestic product [GDP] of
US$18–67 billion) and Tier 4 (i.e. GDP below US$17 billion)
cities and rural areas in Mainland China. Kuaishou, which
would eventually become the largest competitor to Douyin in
China, was better known for its vernacular and mundane
content, often offering a glimpse into life in the outskirts of
China. The platform algorithms do not appear to favour
'glamorous' content but focuses instead on promoting and
important rural produce into urban areas to square nicely
with China's push to invigorate its rural economy.

In this vein, Weishi was launched in 2013 to similarly focus
on advertising and commerce. Specifically, the app incenti-
vised users with case rewards to encourage spending more
time on the platform.[23] According to observations from digital
ethnography conducted by my team and I, ads on the platform
claim that users who watch videos on Weishi for seven
consecutive days were able to earn rewards of up to RMB88
(USD12.3). The commercial baseline of Weishi is also
underscored in its partnership and app-pairing with WeChat
and QQ wallets, allowing viewers to withdraw money via
either account. As part of their integration with Tencent,
Weishi users are also able to cross-post short videos under 30
seconds to the 'Moments' feature (similar to 'Stories' on
Instagram) on WeChat, which otherwise only limits posts to
10 seconds.

As the popularity of short video apps developed alongside
advertising and commercial potentials, the next wave of apps
focused especially on visual cultures. These include Viva (est.
2013), which focused on fine-tuning the aesthetics of short
videos through its in-app features, and Xiaokaxiu (est. 2015),
which became popular for encouraging lip-syncing and acting
trends and the proliferation of more original content. But
perhaps the most successful of this wave of short video apps
was Meipai, which went globally viral after its launch in

2014. In the English language media, Meipai was often referred to as an Instagram-like platform but for video, for allowing users the use of an extensive repertoire of video-editing features, filter templates, special effects, and sharing options. Above and beyond being a short video production and publishing app, it was also widely used as a video-messaging app that was highly interactive. Its most attractive offerings were template effects that allowed users to touch up blemishes on their faces, slim their faces, sharpen jawlines, whiten complexions, and even elongate legs.

As the top short video app during its time, Meipai quickly attracted throngs of *wanghong* (loosely translated as Chinese internet celebrity) and Key Opinion Leaders (KOL) – who were generally understood as Influencers – and advertisers and saw a rapid influx of sponsored posts. To this end, a new set of rules and regulations was introduced to govern this emerging market via 'The M Plan', which subsequently saw massive censorship campaigns being imposed from 2018. This was the pivot on which many *wanghong* and KOL switched over to Douyin when it was launched in 2016. At the time of writing, Meipai is no longer as active in the market.

The ByteDance's Triplet

Douyin was one of the first short video platforms to be launched by ByteDance in 2016.[24] In its infancy, its parent company invested in innovative marketing strategies to promote the app and on-board clients and sponsors for advertising revenue. For instance, in 2017 Douyin launched various hashtag challenges to instigate viral trends and encourage sales on the app, partnering with the likes of luxury brand Michael Kors for their 'City Catwalk Event'. It also introduced 'splash ads', where 3–5-second full-screen ads were displayed to users the moment they opened the app, and 'newsfeed ads', where short advertising videos of 15–60 seconds would auto-play when users scroll past them on their feed. Market research found that users were more likely to finish watching vertical ads on mobile platforms in such a format, than horizontal ads.

By 2019, the increase in transaction volume on short-video platforms was three times as much of that on Weibo, signalling a clear shift from text-based marketing to short video-based marketing. And by 2020, Douyin had reached over 400 million daily active users, which is almost half of China's online population, thus solidifying its status as a mature social e-commerce platform. Based on observations from our digital ethnography and our study of the in-app promotions of features – where its strongest competitor Kuaishou relied primarily on livestreaming sessions to generate revenue – Douyin derived revenue mainly from advertising. And unlike Kuaishou's focus on the Tier 3 and 4 cities, Douyin targeted those in Tier 1 (i.e. GDP of over US\$300 billion) and Tier 2 (i.e. GDP of US\$68–299 billion) cities.

It is noteworthy that ByteDance's initial strategic focus on short video formats encompassed a triple-app approach. Where Douyin's contents were geared towards music and entertainment from the onset, the company launched the companion app Douyin Huoshan in the same year to focus more on work and daily life. This genre specialisation was effective in luring over some users from Kuaishou, as Douyin Huoshan's base of slightly older users eventually began to produce content and initiate trends similar to those from the former.

The third app in ByteDance's triplet of short video platforms is Xigua Video, initially launched as Toutiao Video in 2016 and later merged and renamed.[25] Xigua Video specialised in longer-form video content, including films and TV episodes, but also offered short video clips and livestream features. At the time of writing, ByteDance has merged Toutiao Video and Xigua Video into Douyin.

Post-Douyin

The successful uptake of short video as a format on social media saw the entry of several other competitor apps, such as Pear Video (est. 2016) which focused on news; Tudou (est. 2006) which pivoted from long-form to short-form video in 2017; Aidong (est. 2018) which was launched by Weibo to compete with Douyin after it disabled the cross-platform feature for Weibo users to link to their Douyin accounts; and Lu Ke (est. 2018) which was a lifestyle platform for users to share product reviews.

In response to ByteDance's success with Douyin, tech company Baidu launched a three-pronged strategy of three short video apps. They include Haokan Video (est. 2017) which focused on short videos and livestreams across multiple categories and which also uses cash rewards to lure in more users; Nani (est. 2017) which supports short videos of up to 15-seconds, including the use of in-app stickers and beauty filters; and Quanmin Video (est. 2018) which is the most similar in interface to Douyin, with its full-screen video feed and livestreaming features. Although Baidu's trio of short video apps were moderately successful, they paled in comparison to Douyin, whose primary competitor in the Chinese market remains Kuaishou.

Other Markets

Outside of the Mainland Chinese market, a string of other short video apps were making waves in the Asia–Pacific region. In East Asia, Kuaishou (est. 2012) and Cheez (est. 2016) were popular in South Korea while Vine (est. 2013) was widely adopted across Japan until it shuttered in 2017. When TikTok was launched in 2017, it also eventually grew to be popular in both countries although Instagram's launch of its Reels feature (est. 2019) emerged as a strong competitor. At that time, Reels enabled users to record videos of up to 15 seconds long and overlay popular music, filters, and special effects over them. It is differentiated from its predecessor Instagram Stories within the app's ecology, by offering several editing capabilities, including augmented reality (AR) effects, speed controls, and the option to align multiple clips for cleaner transitions. Reels can also be shared on Instagram's Explore Page, Stories, and Feed.

In India, the two popular short video apps pre-dating TikTok include Roposo (est. 2014) that allows users to create and share short videos, and also share WhatsApp statuses; and VMate (est. 2016) which primarily boasts a rural userbase. At the time of TikTok's entry into the Indian market, Chingari (est. 2017) was the top competitor of the app, and Likee (est. 2017) was once known as the breakout app of the year in the market. Amid controversies, including both temporary and permanent bans on TikTok in India, Indian-based Mitron (est. 2020) was observed to be performing well as an alternative to TikTok.

In Southeast Asia, Kuaishou was found to be especially popular in Indonesia, Philippines, and Thailand. TikTok entered the market to a resounding success in the region and fared well especially in Cambodia, Indonesia, Malaysia, Singapore, Thailand, and Vietnam. In Thailand, another short video app, Ookbee U (est. 2017) was a popular companion to TikTok and was used by locals mainly to uncover talents involved in writing, music, and scripting.

EMERGENT GLOBAL INTEREST

By December 2020, the interest in TikTok worldwide was beginning to rise rapidly. At that time, Google Trends suggested that the top 4 topics related to searches on TikTok were 'Ban', 'Dance', 'Watermark', and 'Viral video'. These correspond to the four key issues surrounding TikTok, including temporary and permanent bans by various governments; the dominant vernacular of dance trends as TikTok's iconic offering; rampant cross-posting of TikTok's watermarked videos on other apps like Instagram's Reels and the overnight internet celebrities being churned out en masse from TikTok virality. 2020 can be said to be the year that TikTok became mainstream. A brief overview of the key issues covered by prominent media outlets demonstrates this in the next section.

In the table below (see Table 2), I summarise the key corporate and vernacular milestones in TikTok's development from 2017–2020. 'Corporate milestones' refer to developments originating from ByteDance, with reportage primarily stemming from the TikTok Newsroom and TikTok's regional offices. 'Vernacular milestones' catalogue the coverage that was most popular and prominent in the media, including reactions to ByteDance's corporate actions and ethos, notable pitfalls and concerns from various governments, and some of the most discussed controversies pertaining to TikTok's impact on specific demographics and geolocations.

Four of the key issues in the year TikTok became mainstream inform the selection of case studies featured in the rest

Table 2. Corporate and Vernacular Milestones in TikTok's Development in 2020. Table by Author and Research Team, December 2020.

2020	Corporate Milestones	Vernacular Milestones
Jan	• Launch of expanded and more comprehensive Community Guidelines, including 10 distinct categories of violations[26]	• US military branches block access to TikTok amid Pentagon warning.[27] • Security flaw found in TikTok app which lets hackers use text messages to control accounts.[28]
Feb		• Transportation Security Administration bans employees from using TikTok.[29] • Reddit CEO: TikTok is 'fundamentally parasitic'.[30]
Mar	• Appointment of new Chief Information Security Officer to cater to growing global community[31] • WHO features on TikTok landing page, creates TikTok account, conducts first livestream amid COVID-19[32]	• TikTok accused of filtering out videos from 'ugly, poor and disabled users'.[33]
Apr	• Pledge of USD$250M for COVID-19 relief efforts (frontline medical workers, educators, local communities), USD$25M in ads for public health information delivery, USD$100M in ad credits for businesses to rebuild[34]	

Table 2. *(Continued)*

2020	Corporate Milestones	Vernacular Milestones
	• Introduction of 'Family Pairing' function to link parent–teen accounts for privacy settings[35]	
May	• Launch of TikTok Youth Portal to provide digital literacy around digital safety for teens[36] • Appointment of new Chief Executive Officer to lead growth of global community[37]	• TikTok accused of breaking privacy promises for children.[38] • US republicans pressure TikTok for information on use of kids' data and ties to Beijing.[39] • Google deletes millions of negative TikTok reviews.[40]
Jun	• Partnership with WePROTECT Global Alliance to combat online child sexual exploitation and abuse[41] • Joins EU Code of Practice on discrimination to combat spread of falsehoods online[42]	• TikTok apologises after being accused of censoring '#BlackLifeMatters' posts.[43] • TikTok 'played' by K-pop fans and TikTok users who disrupted Tulsa rally.[44] • India bans TikTok.[45]
Jul	• Launch of USD$200M Creator Fund in the United States[46]	• Indian TikTokers struggle with ban.[47] • Japan proposes ban on TikTok.[48] • TikTok sued by Triller over patent infringement.[49]
Aug	• Launch of information hub and official Twitter account in response to Trump Administration's executive order on ban[50]	• Trump orders ByteDance to sell TikTok in the United States.[53] • Microsoft considers potential TikTok purchase in the United States.[54]

(Continued)

Table 2. *(Continued)*

2020	Corporate Milestones	Vernacular Milestones
	• Partnership with UnitedMasters to distribute music to other streaming platforms[51] • Sued US Administration's TikTok ban[52]	• Class Action Lawsuit against TikTok for 'stealing' kids' data and sending it to China.[55] • Trump issues executive order to ban US transactions with WeChat and TikTok.[56] • TikTok investigated by France's data watchdog.[57] • Profile of one US politician's use of TikTok to engage with Gen Z.[58] • Walmart considers potential TikTok purchase in the United States.[59]
Sep	• Launched #TikTokFashionMonth, including runway livestreams and musical performances[60] • Launched marketing partner programme for advertisers[61] • Banned ads for fasting apps and restrictions on promotion of negative body image[62] • Proposed global coalition to protect users from harmful content, via Memoradum of Understanding[63] • Launched in-app guide to 2020 US Elections, offering candidate information[64]	• TikTok says 'dark web' is response for viral suicide video.[65] • TikTok to be owned by new company 'TikTok Global' with HQ in the United States, with 12.5% stake by Oracle, 7.5% stake by Walmart, and the majority stake by ByteDance.[66]
Oct	• Partnered with OpenSlate to enhance brand safety[67]	

Table 2. *(Continued)*

2020	Corporate Milestones	Vernacular Milestones
	• Added clarity to content removals due to violations, with ability to appeal decision[68] • Partnered with Shopify to allow merchants to access TikTok For Business Ads Manager from Shopify dashboard[69]	• Pakistan blocks TikTok for 'immoral and indecent' content.[70] • Pakistan lifts TikTok ban after 10 days.[71] • TikTok ban in the United States halted by judge.[72]
Nov	• Signed agreement with Sony Music Entertainment to roster artists and songs on TikTok[73] • Launched 'Shop Black Businesses' online hub[74] • Introduced photosensitivity feature in the United Kingdom to protect people from epilepsy[75]	• ByteDance given 1 week to sell TikTok in the United States.[76] • Viral TikTok videos showcase drug cartel culture.[77]
Dec		• US Appeals Court schedules hearing on TikTok ban.[78] • TikTok is upending workplace social media policies.[79] • Viral TikTok calls out social media trends that 'colonised and whitewashed' Black culture.[80]

of the book. Firstly, concerns around TikTok's ownership and ByteDance's autonomy in the United States helped shape the emergence of diaspora and migrant voices who took leadership on TikTok to educate their audiences (see Chapter 2). Secondly, the bans and blocks on TikTok in various parts of the world instigated some creative circumvention strategies by users who worked to maintain their access to and visibility on the app (see Chapter 3). Thirdly, the platform's campaigns for safety, especially around children and minors, grew in tandem with the rise of call-out cultures by users with social justice causes and who were involved in social movements that organically took root on TikTok (see Chapter 4). Finally, TikTok's in-app campaigns for businesses, and the eventual launch of the Creator Fund, saw the rise of small business and marketplace cultures, as artists and merchants began to on-board the platform (see Chapter 5).

To situate how this emergent global interest in TikTok developed, the next few sections draw on my original ethnographic fieldwork and personal interviews with some of the early adopters of TikTok in the Asia–Pacific region.

Just a Chinese Market

After some years of using and observing how Vine, Dubsmash, and Musical.ly generated specific forms of internet celebrity, my ethnographic research on TikTok formally began in 2019 as I followed the lead of my long-term informants, who began to turn their attention to the platform. When I first commenced a round of personal interviews in early-2019, the Influencers, digital agencies, and start-ups I had spoken to seemed to unanimously refer to TikTok as just a 'Chinese app'; this was a gentle but loaded placeholder for an array of sentiments. One founder of a start-up indicated that apps from the Chinese market were 'a dime a dozen' and that it would be too effortful to pursue every new entrant of the market as a potential platform for digital advertising.

Another Influencer lamented that their Chinese followers had a particular appetite for fast-moving trends and that learning to use TikTok would mean a huge investment of their time and effort to 'stay up-to-date all the time'.

Growing Regionality

But by the time I conducted follow-up interviews in 2020, sentiments had changed. It became clear to this cohort of early adopters that TikTok had 'broken out' of the Chinese market, expanded beyond just a user base of Chinese diaspora, and had become regional. In an August 2019 interview with Martin Hong, the then Head of Social & Digital at Magnum & Co in Sydney, he asserted that the 'channel [platform] is always secondary to the audience we're trying to tap into'. After observing TikTok for some time, it was the *rapid expansion of its user base* and the increasing diversity of it that signalled that it was quickly gaining the potential for Influencer marketing. Alongside Instagram, Snapchat, TikTok, and YouTube, Martin indicated that the Australian brands were displaying more interest in East Asian platforms at large, under the perception of the 'new growing China market'. With a chuckle, he candidly reveals that he has been trying to educate clients that the Chinese market has been 'growing for years', but it was not until this global interest in TikTok that some local brands found the Chinese consumer 'difficult to ignore'.

Momentum in Asia

Among my informants is the CEO of a Singapore-based social media company who incubates creator talents and produces a variety of social media content including social media ads, Influencer campaigns, and memes. For the CEO, TikTok's widespread use indicated that momentum was fast building in Asia, which was a different 'turning point', so to speak. The company owns a creator network that operates in four Southeast Asian countries and was one of the first in Southeast Asia to focus on scouting and grooming talent specifically for TikTok. In the April 2020 iteration of our annual interviews, the CEO remembers taking the leap to invest in TikTok when its *global momentum filtered across Asia*. In his early market research, the CEO observed that the 'turning point' for Tik-Tok in the Global North was when 'big Hollywood stars' began to start their own accounts. He tells me that the Asian market still seemed to be lagging behind, with perceptions that the platform was not yet up to par: 'At that time, people were thinking, "oh, it's a creepy app, for creepy dancers, it's lousy, don't bother"', he recalls. But when young users in the Southeast Asian countries began to amass a huge following overnight from instantaneous virality, the CEO saw the opportunity to monetise this traffic. For him, the key 'turning point' was the growth of young TikTokers 'gaining traction' in Singapore, especially those who had only recently surfaced on social media and 'become famous in the last 6 months or so'.

In other words, these were fresh faces, a potentially new crop of would-be Influencers, who had as many as 'tens of thousands, hundreds of thousands' of followers, but with little to no knowledge of how to manage their visibility and how to monetise their fame. This very new market was especially exciting for the company, considering that the Influencer industry in Singapore, where the company is headquartered, first emerged around 2005, and was already quickly saturating across other platforms. To this end, Influencer talent agencies were also quick to respond.

Trend-Setting From the United States

One of the informants in my study is the CEO of an international multi-hyphenate company, focusing on Influencer marketing, talent acquisition, and entertainment and founded in Singapore in 2011. At the time of writing, the company has expanded into 10 country markets across the Asia–Pacific and in the United States. By June 2020, the Group CEO tells me that she was already planning to acquire and groom talent to set up a 'blog squad on TikTok'. Unlike the years her company has assisted Influencer talents in the Southeast Asia region to on-board new apps – e.g. training bloggers for YouTube, training YouTubers for Instagram, and training Instagrammers for livestreaming – they aimed to build a 'new community' of fresh talent and Influencers who were 'not yet thriving' elsewhere.

This impetus came from her observation of a *new cohort of trend-setters* in the US market, where young people were dictating niche contents and shaping new genres on TikTok. She tells me: 'TikTok is like... the new Vine... that's how the Americans who are "culture setters" have set it out to be'. The Group CEO had likened TikTok to Vine for its ability to have eyes focused on even the most mundane of everyday contents; this was where the absurdity of humour, the creativity of music, and the entertainment of dance seemed to afford users a demotic potential to gain traction, in an otherwise Influencer-saturated market already too engrossed with picture perfect Instagram.

Inspiration Across Regions

What were the Influencers making of this? Some of the early adopter Influencers in my initial wave of interviews revealed that while TikTok was not yet mainstream within their genre, it was precisely its sense of distance, novelty, and foreign-ness that made it a good well of *cross-cultural inspiration for fresh ideas*. 17-year-old Happy Rogers, who while being a minor spoke to me with parental permission, is an Influencer managed by Gushcloud Singapore. Alongside her family YouTube channel 'Bee Happy with the Rogers', she and her sister are also popular *laowai wanghong* – expat or foreigner internet celebrities, who are usually fluent in Chinese and Chinese culture – on the Chinese video platform Bilibili. It is thus no surprise that her fluency with Chinese social media platforms, and the distinctive preferences of her Chinese followers, has honed her interest in TikTok. In our July 2020 interview, she talks me through her process of content ideation and filming production with her sister, including routines such as surveying content that performs well with audiences in the Global North and in Southeast Asia, and taking inspiration to adapt that into a version that would perform well for her Chinese followers.

(In)compatibility of Regional Norms

Where the Group CEO of the international Influencer company took TikTok's success in the Global North as an indication that it was ripe for the Asian market, the CEO of the Singapore-based social media company was waiting to observe its early performance in Southeast Asia. There is a sense of inter-regionality at play, where agencies observed thresholds for TikTok's success across a group of geo-located countries with similar cultures, before embarking on their investments. Regionality is also observed in Happy's awareness of how content that appeals to her followers in the Global North and Southeast Asia might require adaptation for the

Chinese market. But market calculations aside, the regionality of TikTok also pertains to the *compatibility (or lack thereof) of norms across regions*.

South Korea-based Billy Kong is an established YouTube Influencer, better known as 'Korean Billy', who has gone viral for his spot-on impressions of various British accents and dialects. He is also a prominent inter-cultural Influencer for educating Korean audiences about British culture and enriching international audiences with knowledge on Korean cultures. In June 2020, as the COVID-19 pandemic was waging on across Asia, Billy tells me that he had earlier 'played around with TikTok' by splicing his YouTube contents into more digestible snippets for the app; his TikTok biography included a link to his YouTube for interested viewers. In the Asia region, Billy's TikTok contents continued to perform well, as inter-cultural knowledge sharing and 'a day in the life' diaries were an especially popular genre.

However, when the same videos were viewed by TikTokers in the United Kingdom, Billy was met with anti-Asian xenophobia: 'Because of COVID-19, because some people still think it is an "Asian disease", some [British commenters] would say things like "all Asians are bad" and express hatred with more mean words'. A brief takeaway from this is that while producers and creators may calculate risks and study content strategies across regions as they embark on TikTok, the performance and success of creators and posts on the platform are still beholden to the cultural specificities of a viewer's situated context.

TIKTOK'S EARLY MARKET ENTRIES

As TikTok began to break into the Asia–Pacific market through various strategies – including aggressive promotions, the on-boarding of seed cohorts of users, and even setting up numerous local country offices – digital marketing firms, Influencer agencies, and Influencers themselves began sizing up the platform's local presence in their assessment of whether the app was worth their time and investment.

Infrastructure Issues

In Seoul, Digital Marketing expert Katelyn Lee of M&K PR ventures that TikTok's initial entry into South Korea was fraught due to the lack of infrastructural support in the country. In our December 2019 interview, she explains that TikTok arrived when the country was transiting from 3G to 4G and 5G, and as such, there were often issues like 'problems with loading videos and images'. This was something she had to communicate to clients who were keen to consider the 'new app on the block' but who were puzzled over TikTok's slow uptake among the general public. Katelyn explained that as 5G technology became more affordable and reliable in the country, the 'data-draining' endless feed style of short videos on TikTok became less of an issue and the popularity of the app was 'shifting'.

Corporate Distrust

Many of the marketing firms that I had interviewed also explicitly underscored a lack of confidence in the corporate partnerships and support offered by ByteDance. Specifically, industry insiders express that while the base of users and viewers on TikTok was growing by the day, the platform was slow to capitalise on the momentum to partner with domestic collaborators – many of whom had 'reached out' to broker connections to their local Influencer industries. On the condition of anonymity in April 2020, one CEO of an Influencer incubator company tells me 'Where it's really scary is... TikTok as a platform, as a company in Southeast Asia, feels like it is not established enough. It doesn't feel like it's ready for all this momentum from the creator side... We, and many others also, have reached out to them, but they seem to lack trust in potential partners and we cannot access the analytics'.

Influencer (Mis)seeding

While some marketing firms were bewildered, so too were Influencers. In Bangkok, I spoke to a Country Director of an Influencer talent management agency in June 2020, who tells me that TikTok's aggressive seeding – or rather, mis-seeding – of Influencers in the Thai market had gotten it off to a bad start: 'One of the problems with TikTok in Thailand is that when they started off... they just... spend money on Influencers on Instagram to create TikTok content [and crosspost] on TikTok'. However, the first wave of Influencers that TikTok had engaged to populate their platform in Thailand were mainly users who were well known for pranks, slapstick jokes, or even provocative dances – content genres that the country director explains were considered 'low brow' – and that thus detracted value for brands and investors.

This was a similar issue when TikTok first entered the South Korea market in 2018. However, by June 2020, TikTok Influencers like Billy reported that the app was seeing an influx of traditional entertainment celebrities and swiftly growing in reputation: 'They are really trying to bring on celebrities to attract people [to use the app]. I can see more and more Korean celebrities who are [probably] getting paid for posting on TikTok. And there are official Korean adverts [on billboards and television] about TikTok. It's all just about idols and celebrities'. What was the counterpoint for the South Korean market? How did TikTok recoup from its initial missteps? The next section presents an ethnographic case study of the 'TikTok Stage' series of events in South Korea.

CASE STUDY: TIKTOK'S ENTRY INTO SOUTH KOREA

In 2019, just before the onset of the pandemic, I made consecutive trips to Hong Kong, Shanghai, Seoul, Singapore, and Tokyo to conduct ethnographic fieldwork on the Influencer industry. This included the study of TikTok's development in the region. In Hong Kong, I shadowed several Influencer managers at events and learnt that many local Influencers were managing both TikTok and Douyin accounts to maintain revenue and advertising possibilities in both the Hong Kong and Mainland Chinese markets.

Of the various Influencer tours I had attended in Shanghai, one gave me the opportunity to witness first-hand how agencies were recruiting Kuaishou *wanghong* for Douyin; *haiwai wanghong* – Chinese diaspora Influencers based outside of Mainland or Chinese expat Influencers dispatched abroad – were also being recruited from Douyin to start TikTok accounts that KOL firms were offering to manage. In Tokyo, I learnt from Influencer scouts that TikTok was 'harvesting' teen talents mostly from the then-defunct Vine, compromising mainly high school students who had first honed their craft and grown their following by producing prank and humour videos. In Seoul, most industry insiders I spoke to seemed ambivalent about TikTok altogether.

In both Tokyo and Seoul, I spotted TikTok ads splashed across digital billboards, screens on the subway and on buses, and even in print magazines. And competitor apps took notice too. Where rival ads in Tokyo featured the livestreaming app Bigo, in Seoul TikTok seemed up against Instagram. Every city appeared to have a distinctive backstory for TikTok's foray into its market even where Douyin already had a stronghold. This section looks especially at TikTok in the South Korean market based on collaborative work I led with media studies scholar Jin Lee during 2019 to 2023.

TikTok was first launched in South Korea in November 2017 but not to much fanfare. In our mixed method approach – comprising press archival research, industry document analysis, content analysis of TikTok trends and posts, and digital ethnography of South Korean TikTok cultures – Lee and I surmise the three main stages of TikTok's entry into the South Korean market,[81] each typified by the South Korean public's initial reactions to the app: an *aversion* to TikTok as a 'Chinese app', an *annoyance* at TikTok as a 'vulgar app', and an emergent *acceptance* to TikTok as a 'K-pop (challenge) app'.

An Aversion to a 'Chinese App'

TikTok's first attempt to enter the South Korean media market was fraught with anti-Chinese sentiments. This took place against the backdrop of the Chinese-owned platform being embroiled in geopolitical controversies, specifically as it was widely considered to be a threat to Anglo-American society nominally due to concerns about data security and user privacy but actually because of the rise of Chinese hegemony.[82] In South Korea, these feelings were especially prevalent among Gen Z users who criticised the Chinese government's authoritarian regime, including the violent crackdown on the democratic movements in Hong Kong.[83] During this period, tensions between South Korean and Chinese users became especially volatile on social media, as a war of words broke out on several issues including China's copyright violations of South Korean media content[84] and the Chinese government's ban on South Korean media content as a retaliative move against the South Korea–US alliance.[85] Against this background, the platform-isation of TikTok in the Korean media market was unsuccessful as TikTok became a centre of political debates, yielding diplomatic tensions particularly concerning the discourse around emerging Chinese media surveillance.

An Annoyance at a 'Vulgar App'

Another route taken by TikTok to promote its uptake in South Korea was through coordinated advertising on traditional and social media platforms. Throughout 2019, the ads often included video footage of young people dancing to addictive and repetitive music, as a way to demonstrate the visual culture of TikTok to prospective users. However, these often featured young women in skin-tight clothes showing off their body curves while repeating a simple, short dance to catchy music. While the 'dance' snippet undertaken in the campaign encapsulated TikTok's most distinctive brand as a 'short video platform', the contents of the ad per se roused displeasure among the Korean public for being vulgar. Combined with the onslaught of digital billboard and print advertising, the public cringe towards TikTok curtailed its footing in the South Korean market.

An Acceptance as a 'K-Pop (Challenge) App'

Perhaps the most successful of TikTok's forays into South Korea were its partnerships with the traditional entertainment industry. Since 2018, the platform has sponsored bespoke prizes at major music award ceremonies, including Mnet's MAMA (December 2018) and the Golden Disc Awards (January 2020). To promote their platform and expand their user base, TikTok had structured the outcome of these awards to be contingent upon fan voting on the app, thus leveraging on the popularity of K-pop stars and the loyalty of fans to give their platform a boost. By 2019, TikTok was partnering with a string of K-pop stars to advertise their platform in commercials, and by 2020, the first K-pop stars began to on-board TikTok en masse to engage with their fans. In our digital ethnography, we witnessed how the rise of 'K-pop challenges' on TikTok was critical for mainstreaming the platform in South Korea.

In brief, a 'challenge' on TikTok is a 'genre that involves completing a goal, inviting other users to participate, and sharing the content'.[86,87] In the case of K-pop TikTok challenges, this usually involves replicating a dance move accompanying a specific snippet of a K-pop song, usually after the star or idol themselves have publicised a 'dance tutorial' as a guide (see Fig. 1). Early successes include solo rapper and singer Zico's #AnySongChallenge, idol group WINNER's #DDeumChallengeOnTikTok, and solo rapper and singer Jessi's #NunuNanaChallenge.

PLATFORM WARS: INSTAGRAM VS TIKTOK

As TikTok's features and vernacular continued to grow increasingly popular among young audiences worldwide, Silicon Valley platforms took notice and began to conspicuously imitate the visual template of vertical short video that had already long been popular in the Chinese market.

Fig. 1. Artist Impression of K-Pop Dance Tutorials on TikTok. Image Commissioned by and Copyrighted to Crystal Abidin. Art Provided by Ardine Keyla.

Instagram's Reels was launched in August 2020[88] and described as 'a *new* way to create and discover short, entertaining videos' on the platform (emphasis mine). Yet despite touting its feature as being 'new', strings of news reports pointed out the obvious, calling Reels out as Instagram's 'attempt to keep you off TikTok',[89] 'a direct competitor to TikTok'[90] or simply 'a copycat of TikTok'. In the early publicity, Instagram focused its efforts on the taglines 'Creating Reels', 'Sharing Reels', and 'Watching Reels'.[88]

A month later, YouTube announced that it was developing Shorts in September 2020[91] and rolling out a beta test version in one of its largest markets – India. YouTube's early messaging leaned into its long history in the video market, asserting that 'user-generated short videos were born on YouTube' as the first uploads on the platform ever were merely seconds long.[91] Its three taglines were 'Create', 'Get Discovered', and 'Watch'.[91] As Shorts commenced its roll-out to more than a 100 countries throughout 2021, tech reporters continued to underscore its imitation of not just TikTok's format but also its constantly updated innovative features. In one *Variety* article, with a headline calling Shorts a 'TikTok copycat',[92] it was noted that '[l]ike TikTok, YouTube Shorts provides features like a multi-segment camera to string multiple video clips together, the ability to record with music, and control speed settings' and that YouTube 'also launched the ability to swipe vertically from one video to the next (like TikTok)'.

Following in this trajectory, this section considers some of the cross-platform wars between TikTok and its competition, specifically reviewing the efforts by Instagram to siphon off viewers and creators via a string of ads on TikTok.

Just prior to Instagram's and YouTube's launches of Reels and Shorts, respectively, my longitudinal digital ethnography of TikTok picked up advertising by competitor platforms on TikTok. This was quite literally the case of Instagram disseminating paid ads on the TikTok app to promote its own products. Between May to September 2020, I curated a corpus of over a 100 examples of these instances during the period of Reels and Shorts launching, and below we will review a few of these.

A few months shy of launching Reels, Instagram appeared to concentrate on luring TikTok users (back) to Instagram by way of promoting its Stories feature – a transient, disappearing vertical format post of an image or video[93] that was a rather successful clone of the multimedia messaging app Snapchat.[94]

One particular in-app ad on TikTok's FYP, titled 'Tell your Story with Stories' (see Fig. 2), used a succession of quick video snippets to walk users through how to 'Watch Instagram Stories' by reviewing the different features on the Instagram app.

In another example, Instagram leaned into the 'instructional manual' template by walking users through how to install the app (see Fig. 3). The ad titled 'It starts with an install' quite literally demonstrates the options for TikTok users to visit the Apple App Store or Google Play Store locate and download Instagram.

In yet another example, Instagram focused on very specific content creation and editing features on its platform – such as the 'Superzoom' (see Fig. 4) – to promote its suite of tools, during a time when TikTok's user-friendly interface and attractive features were being touted for its success.[95]

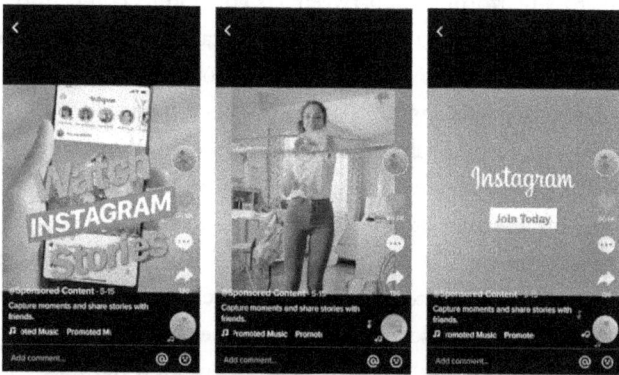

Fig. 2. 'Tell Your Story With Stories'.
@sponsoredcontent13151, 15 May 2020. https://
www.tiktok.com/sponsoredcontent13151/video/
6826738493566225669. Screengrab by Author.

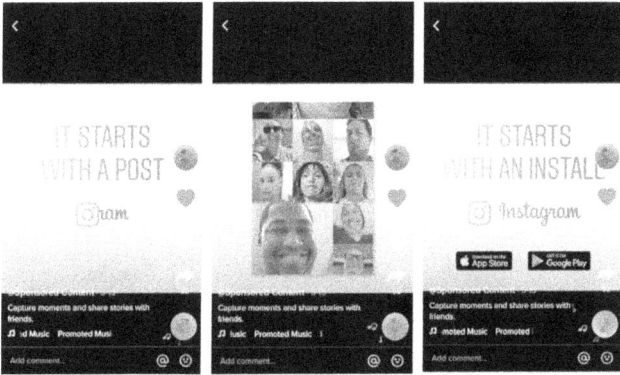

Fig. 3. 'It Starts With an Install'. @sponsoredcontent13151, 15 May 2020. https://www.tiktok.com/ sponsoredcontent13151/video/6826741171528666374. Screengrab by Author.

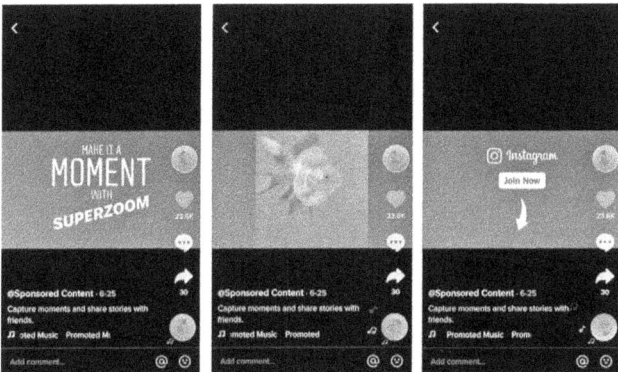

Fig. 4. 'Make It a Moment With Superzoom'. @sponsoredcontent13151, 25 June 2020. https:// www.tiktok.com/sponsoredcontent13151/video/ 6841968087491710214. Screengrab by Author.

Scholars have studied the uncanny ability of TikTok's proprietary algorithm to identify and bound users together via shared interests, in groupings variously described as an 'online

Fig. 5. 'Discover the World From all Angles (Skating)'.
@sponsoredcontent13151, 15 May 2020. https://
www.tiktok.com/sponsoredcontent13151/video/
6826740198273977605. Screengrab by Author.

community',[96] a 'content community',[97] a 'genre',[98] a 'side',[99]
and a 'silo'.[100] This observation was underscored in several of
Instagram's ad campaigns on TikTok that focused heavily on
'discovering' content subcultures, ranging from skating outdoors
(see Fig. 5) to amateur yoga that was popular during the season of
self-isolation in homes during the pandemic (see Fig. 6).

CONCLUSION

As Reels began to flourish alongside TikTok's momentous
growth, pundits of digital marketing commenced assessments
of each platform's strengths. Across the hundreds of news
articles and industry summaries, it was noted that TikTok
continued to lead the market for its much more extensive
library of licenced songs and the ability for creators to produce their own audio[101] and for its successful launch of live
shopping features.[102]

Fig. 6. 'Discover the World From all Angles (Yoga, as Post)'. @sponsoredcontent13151, 15 May 2020. https:// www.tiktok.com/sponsoredcontent13151/video/ 6826739329461652741. Screengrab by Author.

Instagram's press release announcing Reels noted: 'Reels in Explore offers anyone *the chance to become a creator* on Instagram and reach new audiences on a global stage' (emphasis mine).[88] Similarly, the following was included in the YouTube's press release: 'Shorts is a new short-form video experience for *creators and artists* who want to shoot short, catchy videos using nothing but their mobile phones'.[91]

Four years on, evaluations of TikTok vs Reels continue to point to the promise of creator culture for users. For instance, pundits have suggested that Instagram Reels' is a 'less saturated marketplace' for creators who were aspiring to 'expand [their] presence' and establish themselves in the market.[103] How have TikTokers taken root on this 'saturated marketplace'? This call back to engagements, content cultures, and creator communities will be the subject of Chapters 1 to 4, respectively. A list of TikTok's interface and features – accurate as at the time of writing – is available in the Appendix.

2

VISIBILITY AND ENGAGEMENT*

VISIBILITY LABOURS ON TIKTOK

In my early ethnography of internet celebrity cultures on TikTok,[1] I offered a framework for how TikTokers were generating and engaging in visibility labours. Recalling that internet celebrity is contingent upon high visibility on the internet, the following sections review some of the key strategies in which TikTokers engage to solicit the attention of followers. Visibility labour is the work that social media users perform to be noticed by their intended audiences, comprising self-posturing and the curation of self-presentations to be 'noticeable and positively prominent' among viewers.[2] Given that TikTok's propriety algorithmic is a well-guarded black box,[3] TikTokers have had to rely on repeated attempts, observed patterns, and gut feelings to figure out how the algorithm works, how to please the platform to facilitate their visibility, and how to have their popularity grow.

---

* This chapter features text from Abidin, Crystal. 2021. 'Mapping Internet Celebrity on TikTok: Exploring Attention Economies and Visibility Labours'. *Cultural Science Journal* 12(1): 77–103. https://sciendo.com/article/10.5334/csci.140

This sort of 'guestimation' and envisioning has been studied by media studies scholar Taina Bucher[4] as an 'algorithmic imaginary' ('ways of thinking about what algorithms are, what they should be, and how they function') and by digital humanities scholar Sophie Bishop as 'algorithmic gossip'[5] ('communally and socially informed theories and strategies pertaining to recommender algorithms, shared and implemented to engender financial consistency and visibility on algorithmically structured social media platforms') and 'algorithmic lore'[6] ('how the subjective decision-making practices of human intermediaries continues to play a significant role in even ostensibly algorithmic symbolic production').

In the next sections, we consider four types of visibility labours popular on TikTok: Ownership practices, Algorithmic practices, Interactive practices, and Legacy practices.

OWNERSHIP PRACTICES

Ownership practices are users' engagements in assertive behaviour to stake their authorship and attribution claims, or desires for acknowledgement and credit, when others borrow, reuse, adapt from or remix a piece of content that they originated.

'Please Credit'

One of the most common types of ownership claims is the use of 'Please Credit' videos where TikTokers seek attribution, acknowledgement or authorship over specific videos, trends, dance moves or dialogues. For instance in Fig. 7a, @_owenz issues a plea to followers to credit him on his own videos when they copy, download or reshare them on various outlets. He tells followers that he has witnessed his username 'marked out' or erased from reposts of his videos and emphasises that while he does not earn an income from TikTok, he 'work[s] hard on every video' and wants to at least 'get some followers' from proper attribution.

In Fig. 7b and 7c, @palmparadisee and @immarksmith use the same audio meme 'Bulletproof – La Roux' to point out that they have started trends that have gone viral on TikTok but have not been credited for their creativity and labour. The lyrics in this audio template state: 'This time maybe I'll be bulletproof', and in the audio meme stream, it is variously used by TikTokers to talk about how their feelings have been hurt, as a display of resilience, as a reply to haters and harsh comments on TikTok, and to facilitate the disclosure of difficult issues like child abuse and intimate partner violence. @palmparadisee states in his overlay text: 'you think you can hurt my feelings? I started a trend on this app that helped ppl get millions of videos and only got hate when I asked for credit:/', referring to the 'You have entered' TikTok trend that will be discussed later.

Similarly @immarksmith claims to have started a popular TikTok trend, 'You must be the person that my son/daughter is dating', where TikTokers act out a skit where their significant other's parents mistake them for another person, thus inevitably revealing that their partner has been cheating on them. @immarksmith states in his overlay text he 'started one of the biggest trends of summer 2020', citing as 'proof' a screengrab of his first post dating back to 1 July 2020 but did not get credit for it.

In Fig. 7d, @thatgirlbishop laments that even though an original song of hers was 'trending' on TikTok, no one knows that she wrote it. She employs the audio meme 'stop complaining – <3', which is sampled from singer Ariana Grande's song 'Successful'. The template of this audio meme comprises three segments. In segment one, TikTokers act out a skit in which they are revelling in an apparent success to the tune of

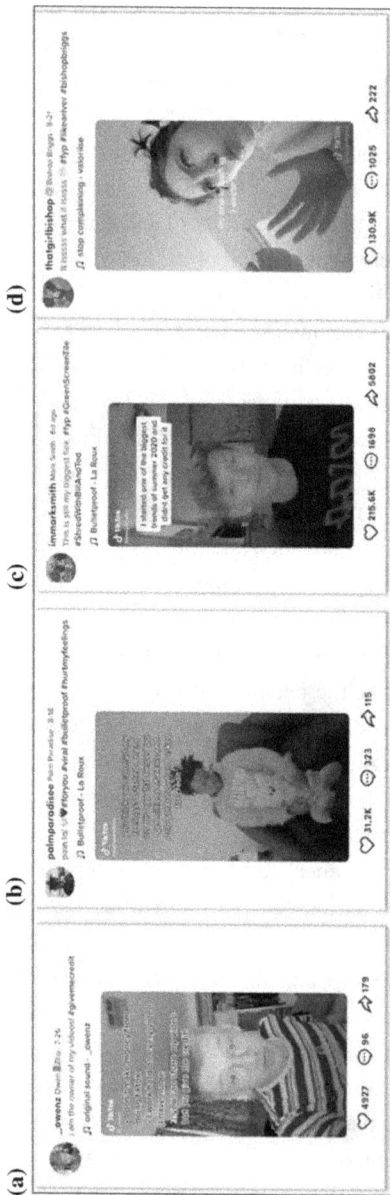

Fig. 7.   (L–R): (a) 'I Am the Owner…' (@_owenz 2020); (b) 'Pain Lol…' (@_owenz 2020); (c) 'This Is Still My…' (@immarksmith 2020); (d) 'It Isssss What It…' (@thatgirlbishop 2020). Screengrab by Author.

the lyrics 'Yeah, it feels so good to be so young/ And have this fun and be successful, yeah'. In segment two, the TikToker is abruptly interrupted by a dialogue overlay that probes 'But, what about…', usually accompanied by overlay text on the video pointing out a contradiction, dark secret or glaring issue that is swept under the carpet, and the TikToker displaying a concerned face. In the last segment, the TikToker quickly brushes off the interjection and swiftly returns to their celebratory moment, as the audio clip and lyrics see them living in denial with 'I'm so successful, yeah'.

For @thatbishopgirl, segment one sees her celebrating in a dance, with overlay text that reads 'my song river trending on TikTok'. The interjection from segment two shows her interrupting herself, with the overlay text 'no one knowing I wrote it', and segment three returns to her celebratory moment. This audio meme is often used by TikTokers to exhibit a sense of resignation, especially in the 'Please Credit' trend of videos, where their pleas for public acknowledgement are usually unheeded.

'Unwanted Reuse'

Another type of ownership claim is when the originators of audio memes, dialogue memes or other TikTok trends call out other TikTokers for the 'Unwanted Reuse' of their videos. One of the most prolific of such instances in when musician @absofacto's song 'Dissolve' was uploaded by another user as an audio meme under 'original sound – SunriseMusic'. The audio meme sampled the chorus with the lyrics 'I just wanted you to watch me dissolve/ Slowly/ In a pool full of your love', which @absofacto points out has been 'taken over by a gross daddy pov trend'

(Fig. 8a). In his caption, he asks for TikTokers to 'please rescue it, use it for something else', and in his overlay text, he calls for TikTokers to 'save it from being associated with this daddy playacting thing' and to 'take the song back over'.

Following this, many TikTokers immediately responded by creating various videos to 'take back' the audio from those who have misused it. Two days later, @absofacto posted an update using the same audio meme and thanks several groups of TikTok users – such as 'alt tik tok', 'lgbtq tiktok', 'kpop stans', and 'everyone who doesn't fit in any group' (Fig. 8b) – for working to 'rescue the song'. In a subsequent update 2 days later (Fig. 8c), @absofacto issues another teary plea to TikTokers to take down their 'Daddy/daughter pov [point of view] videos' and also calls out the TikTok Safety Team for not removing the offending contents. He states in the caption that such videos 'naturally lead to grooming and hurt child-hood sexual abuse (CSA) survivors' and emphasises in his dialogue that such videos harm people.

After a coordinated effort by several groups of TikTokers over weeks, @absofacto continues posting updates featuring reactions and replies to TikTokers who have removed their 'Daddy/daughter POV' videos and issued public apologies. Subsequent posts have also featured young women coming out to share their experiences of CSA and offering resources to helplines and help organisations. Other instances of 'Unwanted Reuse' on TikTok can be more political. For instance, when @mxmtoon's original audio meme 'prom dress – mxmtoon' was used by TikToker @americanblondie to make a pro-Trump video, the creator responded with a reaction video (Fig. 8d) explicitly stating 'Please don't ever f-cking use my song for this'

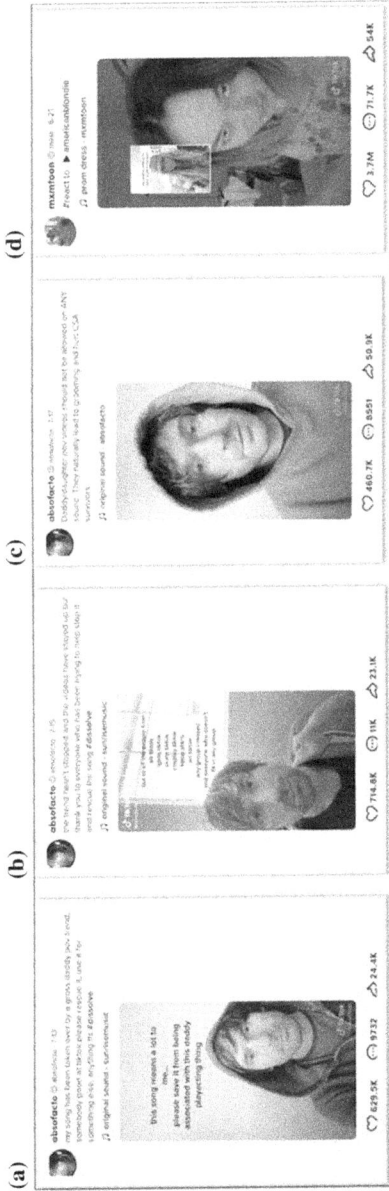

Fig. 8. (L–R): (a) 'My Song Has Been…' (@absofacto 2020a); (b) 'The Trend Hasn't Stopped…' (@absofacto 2020b); (c) 'Daddy/Daughter pov Videos…' (@absofacto 2020c); (d) '#react to @americanblondie…' (@mxmtoon 2020). Screengrab by Author.

ALGORITHMIC PRACTICES

Algorithmic practices are users' engagements in patterned and routine behaviour in the belief that their repeated actions will persuade and trigger the platform's algorithm to work in their favour and is informed by a collective 'algorithmic imaginary'.[4]

'You've Now Entered'

A popular algorithmic practice is the 'You've Now Entered' trend where TikTokers welcome each other into what they believe to be a specific and obscure 'rabbit hole' on TikTok that is otherwise difficult to discover. This video meme comprises TikTokers doing a little dance with a background and holding props that are meant to be stereotypical elements of their TikTok silo, with overlay text that formally names the 'rabbit hole' or silo that they believe they occupy.

Examples include @_whorelando's 'mcdonalds tiktok' symbolised by kitchen props and dancing in a kitchen (Fig. 9a); @t.h.e.ooooo's 'Scandinavian alt tik tok' comprising dancing in what is presumably a stereotypical Scandinavian balcony (Fig. 9b); @mycosymbiote's 'Hood Agriculture ALT Tik Tok' symbolised by a rake, baby chick, and khaki vest while dancing in an open grass patch (Fig. 9c) and @vintagechocolate's 'Black Australian Tiktok' presumably connoted by the TikToker's appearance himself as a black Australian (Fig. 9d). Users are then invited to 'stay while' or 'hang out' if they like, which in 'TikTok algorithmic speak' translates to an invitation to rewatch and loop the video for a longer period of time or to discover more of such similar content by engaging with the TikToker's other posts or hashtags.

The underlying intention is for the viewer's engagements with the post to teach the TikTok algorithmic recommendation system to serve them more of such similar posts. However,

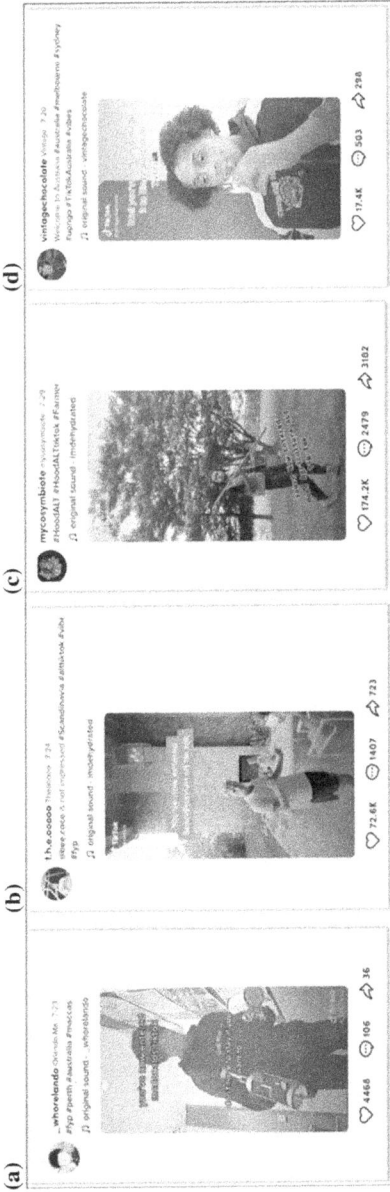

Fig. 9. (L–R): (a) '#fyp #perth #australia #maccas…' (@_whorelando 2020); (b) '@bee.coco Is Not Impressed…' (@t.h.e.ooooo 2020); (c) '#HoodALT #HoodALTtiktok #Farmer…' (@mycosymbiote 2020); (d) 'Welcome to Australia #australia…' (@vintagechocolate 2020). Screengrab by Author.

these rabbit roles and silos may be actual subcultures on TikTok, like 'Black Australian TikTok' (Fig. 9d), or comically esoteric ones, like 'mcdonalds tiktok' (Fig. 9a). The audio meme which houses this trend is 'original sound – Dirt' and samples of Kero Kero Bonito's 'I'd Rather Sleep'. The lyrics 'Now I know what's real, what's fake/ Rather sleep than stay awake' connote that entering these rabbit holes or TikTok silos is akin to discovering a new dreamlike corner of TikTok that one has yet to uncover and is usually paired with the use of a visual filter that displays a 'faded out' and dreamy effect.

'If You See This'

'If You See This' is an algorithmic trend that emphasises the magic of happenstance and chance encounters on TikTok. Given the TikTok algorithm's unpredictability, some users have taken up the challenge to create a gamified and fun experience for random users who may chance upon their videos on their FYP. A prominent content creator in this genre is @supah_jp. In Fig. 10a, he narrates in his textual overlay that 'the tiktok algorithm is weird/ I made three versions of this audio/ if you found this video first.../ you are the NON-PLAYBALE CHARACTER'. Clicking into his TikTok profile, users will see two other-related videos posted before and after the one in Fig. 10a, one assigning the viewer as a 'PLAYABLE CHARACTER' and another as the 'FINAL BOSS'. @supah_jp regularly posts such 'lucky dip' or POV videos, assigning viewers a position or standpoint at the whim of the FYP's offering, with interesting clusters of videos including whether one is assigned the starter Pokémon Bulbasaur/Squirtle/Charmander or the Harry Potter houses Hufflepuff/Ravenclaw/Gryffindor/Slytherine.

Another 'If You See This' trend came in the form of a mid-2020 viral 'hoax' that circulated on TikTok and claimed that 27 August marked a 'doomsday scenario'. Satirical conspiracy theories were even floating between TikTok and Twitter.[7] Although it was later revealed to be 'just a meme' and intended as a 'weird video',[7] TikTokers had spent weeks leading up to the date posting 'cryptic messages' and 'counting down' to the date.[8] This network of videos, including one from @the-august27thshow (Fig. 10b), generally indicated that viewers were 'selected' to access this content and that viewers were 'meant to see this' (Fig. 10c) given that in most cases no captions or hashtags are used.

This viral trend was housed in the audio meme 'Original Sound – Unknown', which samples 'The Time Song' from the cartoon 'Don't Hug Me I'm Scared' with equally enigmatic lyrics about time: 'Time is a tool you can put on the wall/ Or wear it on your wrist/ The past is far behind us/ The future doesn't exist (oh)/ What's the time?/ Its a quarter to nine, time to have a bath'. Variants of this trend include TikTokers pointing to arbitrary dates in the future, informing viewers that chancing upon the video in their FYP on the very date listed is akin to winning the 'TikTok lottery'. Comments under such videos often revealed viewers arriving 'too early' or 'too late' and have evolved into an algorithmic game on TikTok.

Another 'If You See This' trend is housed in the audio meme 'SH 996 – Von', which samples Von's electronica song 'SH 996'. Such videos (Fig. 10d) emphasise the chance encounters facilitated by the TikTok algorithm, by alluding to how 'rare' or 'elite' it is to 'stumble upon' this trend or audio meme. Overlay text also tends to mention that no hashtags or captions were used to increase discoverability, underscoring the happenstance nature of the encounter. Notably, these memes also tend to highlight that only a few videos have used this sound – 'only 50 videos', 'only 131 videos' and 'only 1720 videos', as indicated in various posts in this audio meme stream – thus ascribing the audio meme a degree of exclusivity.

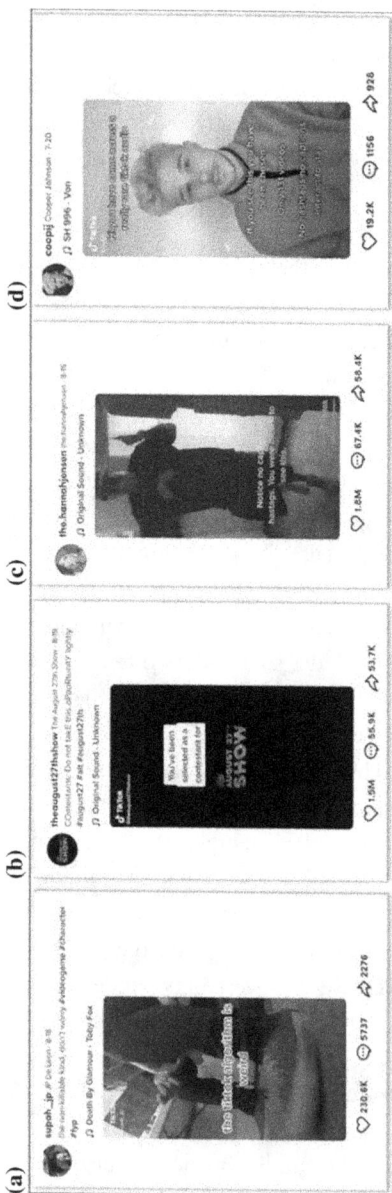

Fig. 10. (L–R): (a) 'The Non-Killable Kind, Don't…' (@supah_jp 2020); (b) 'Contestants: Do Not Take…' (@theaugust27thshow 2020); (c) '[Untitled]…' (@the.hannahjensen 2020); (d) '[Untitled]…' (@coopij 2020). Screengrab by Author.

Such renarrativising and repackaging of what is ultimately an 'unpopular' audio meme that did not or has not yet gone viral inverts the prestige markers of TikTok and assigns value and privilege to 'rare', 'elite', and yet-to-be discovered sounds over those that have already become mainstream and viral. It is a strategy to offer an alternative attention economy on TikTok that caters to the longtail of users who can only ever aspire to virality on the app.

'Please Interact'

'Please Interact' types of videos overtly call upon TikTokers to engage with one's posts – through follows, likes, comments, and shares – to drive up engagement. The purpose and intention of this engagement can be varied, including @arsenkujo's call for TikTokers to demonstrate solidarity and support towards 'fellow asians [who] are tired of being discriminated' (Fig. 11a), and @earthophia rallying TikTokers to subscribe to his account which advocates for the eco community, zero waste, and climate conservation (Fig. 11b). Apart from signal boosting, pleas for such engagements posit TikTokers' actions as endorsements for specific causes, and viewers respond by taking engagement button options (follows, likes, comments and shares) as a proxy to signpost one's support and political stance on an issue.

In some instances, TikTokers may call upon others to engage with their posts for affirmation. This was the case with @carli.mochi calling for viewers to 'press random buttons' so that she will 'wake up' to some activity on her account (Fig. 12a). Other times, TikTokers request for engagements from specific users of a specific demographic and silo in the belief that this will alter the algorithmic recommendations served to them. In Fig. 12b, @sushibtch announces that her TikTok

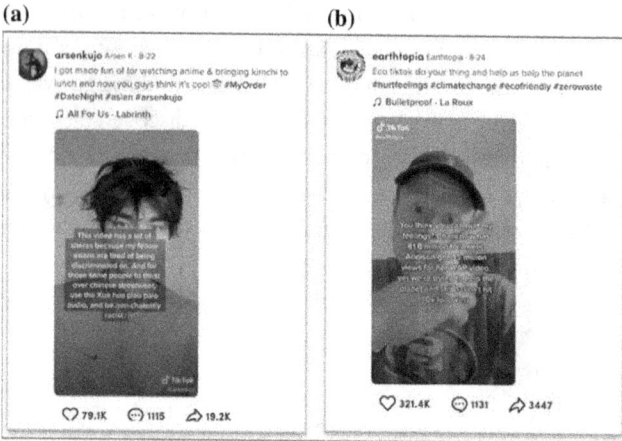

Fig. 11. (L–R): (a) 'I Got Made Fun…' (@arsenkujo 2020); (b) 'Eco TikTok Do Your…' (@earthtopia 2020). Screengrab by Author.

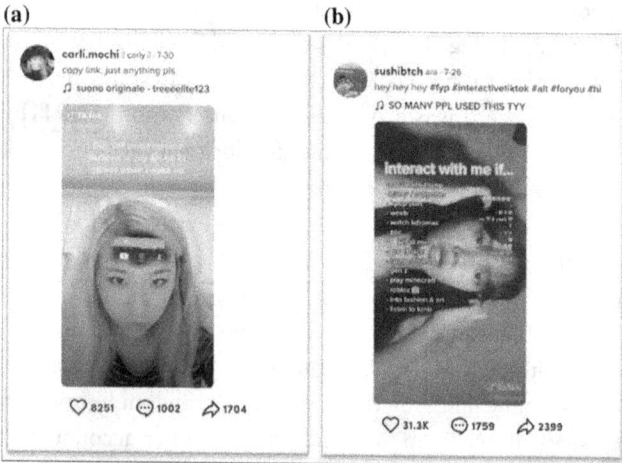

Fig. 12. (L–R): (a) 'Copy Link, Just Anything…' (@carli.mochi 2020); (b) 'Hey Hey Hey #fyp…' (@sushibtch 2020). Screengrab by Author.

'glitched' and that she is now on the 'str8 [straight] side'. To break out of this loop, she lists 14 interests and interest groups, such as 'lgbtq+/supporter' and 'kpop stan', and appeals to these TikTokers to 'interact' with her.

INTERACTIVE PRACTICES

Interactive practices are users' engagements in parasocial behaviour to appeal to others, manifest displays of support or disavowal towards specific users and issues, foster and maintain allegiances within trends and silos, and maintain feelings of connection and enjoyment among each other.

'Rally Support'

In August 2020, @bellapoarch rapidly ascended into virality when her 18 August 'Face Zoom' TikTok went viral. Set to the audio meme 'M to the B – Millie B', which samples from UK artist Soph Aspin Send's 'M to the B', the video is the most liked and viewed video on TikTok at the time of writing and facilitated @bellapoarch's swift attainment of internet celebrity through similar 'Face Zoom' TikToks. She was also soon verified by TikTok. However, this overnight explosion into internet fame provoked disgruntled haters and trolls to bully @bellapoarch through very harsh comments flooding her posts and reactions and duets criticising her. In the wake of this, many TikTokers posted videos to 'Rally support' for @bellapoarch to push back on and counter some of the aggression piled on her. For instance, @beazknees and @cindylovesbbt demonstrated support towards @bellapoarch, by 'disabling the comments' on their duets with her to kerb the onslaught of bullying and call out the 'negativity' (Fig. 13a)

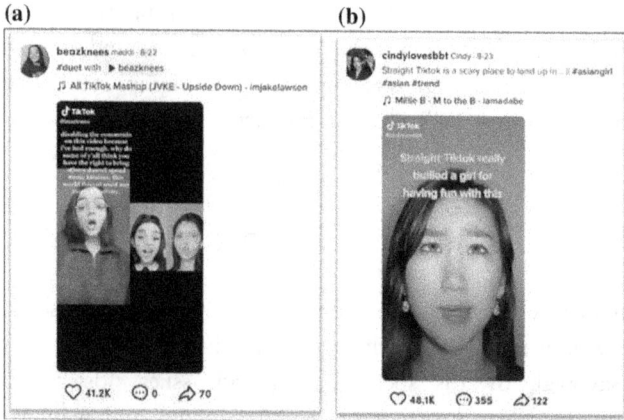

Fig. 13.   (L–R): (a) '#Duet With @beazknees...' (@beazknees 2020); (b) 'Straight TikTok Is a...' (@cindylovesbbt 2020). Screengrab by Author.

and by replicating her 'Face Zoom' TikTok with added commentary in the overlay text bringing awareness to the bullying and calling out bullies for being 'mean' (Fig. 13b). Such a response strategy allows TikTokers to indicate their stance and show their support towards fellow TikTokers, but the format of such replies as standalone TikTok posts themselves also enables responders to attain visibility and virality in their own right, accumulating internet celebrity while bandwagoning or piggybacking on other TikTokers' controversies.

'Chain Mail'

Another interactive strategy is 'Chain Mail' TikToks, which invite users to duet and respond to a video and pass it on to others who can in turn add to the thread with their own responses in a sequential fashion. 'Chain Mail' TikToks invite users to 'keep a trend going', as is very popular among minority culture and

**Fig. 14. (L–R): (a) '#Duet With @notoriouscree Keep...'
(@katyjean_91 2020); (b) 'This Has to Be...' (@ joelnilssonnn
2020). Screengrab by Author.**

Indigenous TikToks that showcase the beautiful varieties of
material cultures around the world (Fig. 14a). In other instances,
'Chain Mail' TikToks take on the tone of absurdist humour,
when users respond to and extend a theme in a thread in unexpected ways. Fig. 14b demonstrates one such chain, in which
over 13 TikTokers attempt to piece together a collage of a
chaotic group of friends linked together by a haphazard
connection of body parts and random objects.

LEGACY PRACTICES

Legacy practices are users' engagements in established
microcelebrity and Influencer behaviours that originated and
flourished outside of TikTok, by extrapolating, contextualis-
ing, and updating these visibility practices and Influencer
logics, in order that they may maintain some brand coherence

and sustain some attention outflow to their existing digital media estates.

There are dozens of subcultures that have been imported onto TikTok In this section, I will highlight just two.

'K-Pop TikTok'

Many prominent K-pop singers and groups have started dedicated TikTok accounts to use them as a launchpad for the further distribution, globalisation, and mainstreaming of their music. Their TikToks come in several forms, but prominent ones include tutorials of their dances to encourage remix and spreadability on TikTok (as in the case of @official_sunmi in Fig. 15a), lip-syncing to catchy snippets of their new releases to introduce different sound clips that can be used as audio memes on TikTok, behind-the-scenes scenes of their work, and challenges inviting TikToker to duet with them. Publicising their new work on TikTok in these creative and participatory manners essentially allows K-pop singers to accumulate free publicity for their songs, through the voluntary labour of fans and the unwittingly labour of other TikTok users who may casually use the audio meme but not be aware of the celebrity.

'TikTok News'

Mainstream media outlets have also taken to TikTok to promote their stories and attract outflow traffic to their sites. To do so on TikTok requires the mainstream media outlets to play with various elements of social media pop cultures in order to appeal to the young and trendy prospective audiences on the app. For instance, @washingtonpost has socialised and popularised newsworthy issues by posting a TikTok featuring

(a)   **(b)**

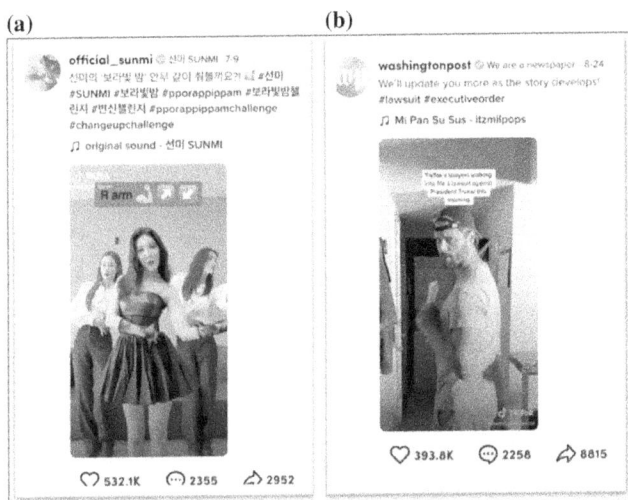

official_sunmi ⊙ 선미 SUNMI · 7-9
선미의 '보라빛 밤' 안무 같이 춰볼까요? ♫ #선미
#SUNMI #보라빛밤 #pporappippam #보라빛밤놀
린지 #빈신챌린지 #pporappippamchallenge
#changeupchallenge

♫ original sound · 선미 SUNMI

🅰 am 🎵 ⭐ 🌙

♡ 532.1K   ⊙ 2355   ⌁ 2952

washingtonpost ⊙ We are a newspaper · 8-24
We'll update you more as the story develops!
#lawsuit #executiveorder

♫ Mi Pan Su Sus · itzmilpops

♡ 393.8K   ⊙ 2258   ⌁ 8815

Fig. 15. (L–R) (a) '선미의…' (@official_sunmi 2020); (b) 'We'll Update You More…' (@washingtonpost 2020). Screengrab by Author.

a man acting out a POV of 'TikTok's lawyers walking [in to] file a lawsuit against President Trump' in light of the US's potential TikTok ban in August–September 2020 (Fig. 15b). This news snippet is made more palatable to young audiences through the use of the 'Mi Pan Su Sus –' audio meme, adapted from a Russian commercial for cereal featuring a dancing llama. This, perhaps, is the frontier of communicating the news to young people: Attention-baiting entertainment and education, all wrapped up in a 6-second clip.

ENGAGEMENT STRATEGIES

The growing scholarship on TikTok has focused on the notion of 'engagement', a mode of assessing how audiences interact with and respond towards content. A large body of scholarship has focused on the interface and architecture of TikTok's platform and how it is designed to maximise engagement activities from all users. This includes the use of natural language processing, computer vision, and hashtag analysis to identify user preferences and make recommendations,[9] including assessments of users' engagement as measured by 'viewing', 'liking', 'commenting', 'sharing', and 'following',[10] and recommendations of viral filters, sounds, and hashtags for creators to consider.[11]

In the vein of scholarship on microcelebrities and Influencers, various studies qualify engagement by TikTok creators through the content of their posts. A study on athletes on TikTok[12] qualified creator engagement as sharing 'the personal side' of their lives outside of their profession, partaking in TikTok challenges that revealed some of their 'training routines', and posting 'game highlights'. Another study on plastic surgeons on TikTok[13] offered that creators engage with viewers by 'rectify[ing] misinformation', 'offer[ing] educational content', and 'supporting the quality and safety of [their] practice'. In still another study I conducted with a collaborator assessing how teachers on TikTok construct their authority,[14] we found the creator engagement involved a matrix of 11 themes, including being 'humourous' by 'sharing jokes, memes and funny situation relate to school life'; being 'intimate' by 'sharing stories from the teacher's personal life outside the classroom' and being 'emotional' by 'sharing feelings and emotions about what their profession entails'.

Another body of work assesses engagement by TikTok creators through their deployment of the platform's specific features. For example, the study on teachers on TikTok undertaken by my collaborator and I[14] focused on 'reacts', 'duets', 'greenscreens', and 'stiches' as the features most commonly used to solicit interactions from students. In another example, a study on legacy news media's use of

TikTok to disseminate news[15] offers that posts that use 'visual features' like filters and stickers, employ 'second-person view' to speak directly to audiences, and present 'negative sentiment' tended to solicit more interactions from viewers.

This growing body of knowledge on how engagement on TikTok works has also groomed a parallel economy of marketing professionals, pseudo-experts, and peer educators whom we can think of as a collective of 'engagement gurus'. An 'engagement guru' on TikTok is a leader, whether self-proclaimed or professional, who identifies as an authority on enhancing viewer interaction and experience with creators, brands or the platform itself. They usually provide timely explainers, tutorials, and advice on the newest strategies that creators can consider, based on their assessment of the current landscape of trends on TikTok (see Fig. 16). In the sections below, I briefly outline some of the engagement generation strategies that have become mainstream and widely used during my longitudinal digital ethnography on TikTok.

Reloops

In a graphic conceptual glossary that I had produced for teaching,[16] I focused on the new ways that attention is being 'baited, generated, and played with online'. Turning to Tik-Tok, I offer that as the short video app format only allows posts that are between 5 seconds and 3 minutes long – with an average post usually measuring between 15 to 60 seconds – there is but a very short runway to get viewers 'hooked' onto content. To retain viewer interest and increase watch-time, 'reloops' have become an important strategy.

'Reloops' are short videos designed to encourage consecutive replays on auto-repeat. The auto-repeat is more likely to occur subconsciously, when the end and start of a clip blend

Fig. 16. Artist's Impression of an 'Engagement Guru' on TikTok. Image Commissioned by and Copyrighted to Crystal Abidin. Art Provided by River Juno.

so seamlessly that viewers are less likely to observe the loop. The auto-repeat also occurs more easily with shorter videos. As such, effective relooping requires a combination of excellent editing and short catchy content. While there are many ways to encourage relooping, three of the most common ones are faux pas reloops, easter egg reloops, and omission reloops.

In 'faux pas' reloops, creators intentionally introduce typos, mispronunciations, wrong facts, and other rather obvious errors into their post. This entices viewers to replay the video on a double take, leave the video on loop while they correct the TikToker in the comments section, and stimulate engagements by relying on the faith that 'angered' or 'triggered' commenters will 'correct' their errors in the comments section.

In 'easter egg' reloops, creators strategically sneak in hidden messages, signs or symbols into their videos to encourage users to replay the videos in order to decode what has been veiled. The most common strategy thus far involves planting ghastly hints of the supernatural (e.g. ghosts, spirits, unexplained shadows inanimate objects moving, UFOs, voiced whispers) in the background (see Fig. 17).

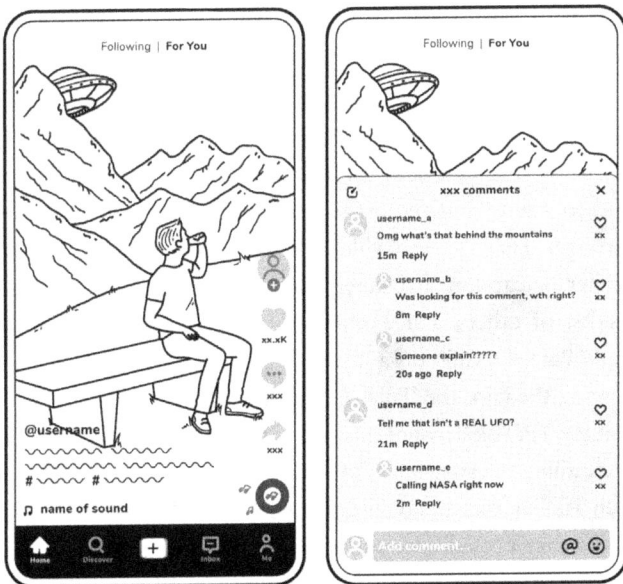

Fig. 17. Artist's Impression of a TikTok Deploying the Engagement Strategy of an 'Easter Egg Reloop'. Image Commissioned by and Copyrighted to Crystal Abidin. Art Provided by River Juno.

In 'omission' reloops, creators deliberately produce a Tik-Tok video that is indecipherable without context, leaving users baffled. This usually takes the form of cryptic captions or overlay text insinuating a situation that is not readily understood by the viewer given the lack of visual cues in the video post, which then draws viewers to click into and scroll through comments section in search of clues or answers to decode the post.

Cliff-Hangers

'Cliff-hangers' are videos that appear prematurely truncated or unresolved to generate suspense and a sense of anticipation for more content. The sense of anticipation is more likely to spur viewer action if there are cues pointing them to pathways to further their participation. Two popular cliff-hanger devices on TikTok are 'Part X' and 'Follow for part two'.

The 'Part X' cliff-hanger is commonly used by creators who tend to curate and re-post movies or TV shows in multiple parts on TikTok. The videos often include a text overlay banner or caption that labels the clip as just one video in a playlist of others. For example, a text overlay banner may read 'Part 47/160' or a caption may read 'Part 4'. Upon viewing the clip, the 'Part X' signpost encourages viewers to visit the TikTok account in search of a playlist or other videos to continue the storyline. However, the reality is that many of such TikTok creators intentionally mislabel their posts and do not in fact provide the full playlist of 'parts' for viewers to access. This leads frustrated viewers to spend more time on their account page and on their contents by the trial-and-error of scrolling and clicking to locate the next video, thus registering more engagement for the account.

'Follow for part two' is a similar strategy where creators share the first half of an enthralling story – usually gossip or a currently unfolding scandal – and invite viewers to follow their account to stay tuned for a follow up. This cliff-hanger usually sees creators withholding part two for some time to generate more suspense and anticipation, as evidenced in comments sections where viewers ask to be tagged or notified when there is an update. It is also not uncommon for creators to simply not follow through with 'part two', as they would have successfully increased their follower count through the first cliff-hanger.

Extended Preambles

'Extended preambles' are videos designed with a longer than necessary introduction that meanders before delivering the signposted content, plot or punchline. The intention is to draw out the interest of viewers and extend their watch-time in a video that is otherwise short on content. This engagement generation strategy became popular when TikTok launched its 'Creativity Program Beta' in 2023[17] and its subsequent Creator Rewards launched in 2024,[18] which allow creators to monetise videos that are longer than a minute.

While 'extended preambles' are popular among many creators who now include disclaimers, cautions, backstories, and similar to prolong their introductions, this strategy is perhaps most prominent among K-pop fans on TikTok. On TikTok, K-pop fans have been known to curate fancams and edits of their favourite idols. These may include highlights of their recent activities, listicles of achievements or snippets of their performances. To qualify their videos for monetisation, many K-pop TikTokers begin their videos with introductions featuring clips of dances, performances or idols that are

currently viral, even if the introductory content is unrelated to
their fandom or the main content of the post. It is also common courtesy to include a text overlay in the preamble clip to
indicate the 'runway' to the content by stating the duration of
the introduction and signposting the actual content to come.
Examples include:

Main title: 'It Girl of Each Generation'

Subtitle: '(Intro 16s pls watch tks)'

Interpretation: 'The introduction is 16-seconds, please watch,
thanks'

Main title: 'Best rappers in Kpop'

Subtitle: '(13s cr BM fans)'

Interpretation: 'This is a 13-second introduction, the clip
featured is credited to Babymonster fans'

Main title: 'Chaotic idols'

Subtitle: '(cr illit magnetic wait 12s)'

Interpretation: 'The introductory clip is credited to the idol
group Illit, featuring the song Magnetic, please wait 12-
seconds for the compilation'

No Context

'No context' posts are designed to be intentionally obscure,
illegible or unintelligible. They serve to bewilder and confuse
viewers enough such that they will engage with the content by
clicking to expand the captions, locate understanding in the
comments section or search for similar content on TikTok to
corroborate meaning. Two popular 'no context' examples on
TikTok are the 'IYKYK' parlance and the 'normalise context'
audio meme.

'IYKYK' is an abbreviation of 'If You Know, You Know', a Gen Z slang that loosely means that only people with inside knowledge or relevant information will be privy to this otherwise gatekept knowledge. In the scholarship, this parlance has been studied as the lived experience of interpersonal relationality that only people in a subculture understand, such as Asian migrants in Australia[19] and Black queer women in spaces of religiosity.[20] 'IYKYK' is also used to demarcate and close off shared spaces for subcultural groups and can even create the potential for 'subversive space'.[21] On TikTok, 'IYKYK' is often used in text overlays, captions, or hashtags as commentary that the post is only legible to other users with 'firsthand experience'.[22] In its sincere uses, 'IYKYK' was often deployed to hint at emerging gossip in creator networks, to point to inside jokes within TikTok communities or convey to an intense experience of emotion (e.g. love for an idol, depression) that only specific groups of people (e.g. a fan, a person experiencing grief) will understand.

However, as an engagement generation strategy, creators deliberately post perplexing or disorienting TikToks intended to confuse and include the 'IYKYK' tag to falsely convey the impression that there is more to the post than meets the eye. A popular skit on TikTok features person A asking person B what 'IYKYK' means, with the latter simply responding with 'IYKYK' repeatedly to further confuse the interlocutor. A typical script is as follows:

Person A: 'What is IYKYK?'

Person B: 'If You Know, You Know'.

Person A: 'I don't know. What is it?'

Person B: 'If You Know, You Know'.

Person A: 'As I said, I don't know! What does IYKYK mean?'

Person B: 'If You Know, You Know'.

Person A: 'I don't know! Just tell me!'
Person B: 'If You Know, You Know'.

In response to the rise of 'IYKYK' spam on TikTok, new audio memes have emerged. Creators are observed stitching 'IYKYK' posts out of annoyance, with captions and comments sections calling for users to 'normalise giving context' to their posts rather than 'wasting time', sending others on 'a rabbit hunt' or 'pretending to be niche'. Creators are also calling out 'IYKYK' posts for being exclusive and discriminatory to neurodiverse users who may require contextual cues to decode meaning in everyday life. However, 'no context' appears to hold its place as an engagement generation strategy as creators tend to extend the engagement on their posts by responding to these call outs with flippant shutdowns such as 'trust me you don't wanna know'; 'normalise no context'; and 'actually idk' [actually I don't know].

Greenscreen Voldemorting

On the flip side of engagement generation strategies are engagement circumvention strategies, where users work to hinder Search Engine Optimization (SEO) or suppress the visibility of sources by restricting backlinks. On TikTok, this practice is usually enacted when users create duets or reacts to call out a specific account or post but also want to ensure that the source account or post does not receive augmented traffic (Fig. 18) – either due to the controversial nature of the post or to prevent the account from profiting off the increased traffic and visibility.

Digital media scholar Emily van der Nagel[23] describes such practices as a key tactic to 'avoid connections' and presents in

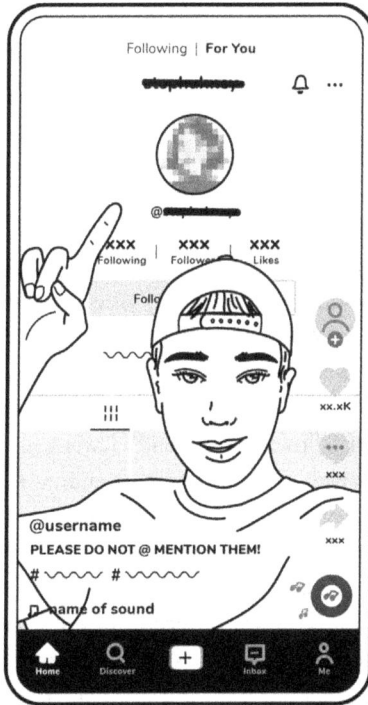

Fig. 18. Artist's Impression of a TikToker Engaging in 'Greenscreen Voldemorting'. Image Commissioned by and Copyrighted to Crystal Abidin. Art Provided by River Juno.

her work the tactics of 'Voldermorting' or 'not mentioning words or names in order to avoid a forced connection' and 'screenshotting' or 'making content visible without sending its website traffic'.[23] 'Greenscreen voldemorting' has emerged on TikTok as a pastiche of these two strategies, where creators use the greenscreen feature to display a screenshot of the piece of content that they wish to discuss, while including in their narration, captions or text overlay a plea to viewers to not overtly mention the original content, original poster or key terms pertaining to the topic in order to break the algorithmic connection to the source.

CONCLUSION

This chapter has delved into empirical case studies to consider the plethora of strategies undertaken by TikTok creators to generate (or in some cases, restrict) visibility and engagement for their content. We focused on the practice of TikTok creators as situated across their changing understanding of TikTok's interface and its proprietary algorithm, their standpoint in a network of fellow creators and viewers, and some novel tactics to enhance or circumvent attention norms on the platform. Many of these tactics have grown so established and mainstream to the point of becoming platform-specific memes[24,25] particular to TikTok. Thus, the next chapter reviews some of the memetic practices that are unique to, or that have originated on, TikTok and the implications on the types of capital that generate and circulate among users.

3

MEMES AND CAPITAL

In an interview with the *ABC*, I once described TikTok as comprising 'the performativity of YouTube, the scrolling interface of Instagram, and the deeply weird humour usually reserved for platforms like Vine and Tumblr'.[1] In later work, Kaye et al.[2] dipped into similar metaphors, describing a set of international short-video platforms that have 'paved the way' for TikTok via their most notable features, namely:

- Vine's template: Short duration; scrolling feed including trending content and ability to follow other users.

- Snapchat's stories: Short video or photo compilations; video-centric status updates.

- Flipagram's music: Mashups and remixes; audio-centric posts.

- Musical.ly's community: User collaborations; user monetisation.

Indeed, the swift uptake of TikTok is in part due to social media users' familiarity with an assortment of features and content norms from other platforms. Alongside this, the myriad of TikTok features have also contributed to a thriving ecology of content, many of which facilitate its highly vibrant meme cultures. This chapter begins with a quick review of the interface and key features of TikTok, considers some of the memetic practices popular among TikTok users and then offers five forms of capital that circulate among TikTok meme communities: Niche, Subcultural, Cross-cultural, Discursive, and Cross-platform.

MEMETIC PRACTICES

There are many routes to discovering the burgeoning meme cultures on TikTok. Users who are unfamiliar with TikTok are likely to learn about these meme cultures when the press puts out another primer on the latest viral trend or when they encounter versions of memetic practices on other platforms like Instagram's Reels, YouTube's Shorts or Facebook videos after the phenomenon has become mainstream. But for avid TikTok users, a sensitivity to meme literacies on TikTok can generally be honed through an understanding of some of the key memetic practices on the platform.

Memetic practices are an exemplar of 'emergent platform practices', which Kaye et al.[3] define as 'user-driven practices, which have emerged with or without encouragement from the platform'. For example, on TikTok it is has been long established that male creators who wish to depict female characters in their skits or 'POV' videos can simply wear the neck ring of a t-shirt over the crown of their heads and have the fabric swing to the back of their necks to resemble a wig. It is also not uncommon for creators to post videos of animals who produce melodic sounds as 'starter dough' content for musically talented TikTokers to layer in vocal or instrument accompaniments to create a collaborative song. Creators with an eye for humour and editing skills are also often on the look-out for curious depictions of the human body, to stitch in composites of extended limbs and other appendages and co-create a hybrid humanoid for laughs. Kaye et al.[4] have offered five emergent platform practices – Lip-synching, Challenges, Calls for participation, Attribution, and Appropriation – that contribute to the memetic practices of users. In the list below, I adapt from their list and offer a concise definition for these practices:

1. Lip-sync: To select an existing audio and mime it in your own new video (see also Zeng & Abidin[5]).

2. Challenge: To participate in a networked activity by completing an objective, sharing your completed content with other users, and calling upon other users to participate (see also Vizcaíno-Verdú & Abidin[6]).

3. Call for participation: To appeal to fellow users to respond to the post through active engagement.

4. Attribute: To acknowledge the originator of the content by naming them or creating hyperlinks to the original user or source.

5. Appropriate: To adapt without permission or without attribution the practices or beliefs from a different user of social group in ways that are unethical or not respectful.

In particular, the memetic practices of attribution and appropriation point to an ongoing tension among creators on TikTok, where there is friction between 'meme logics' and 'influencer logics'. For instance, meme logics measure the success of a meme by its spreadability, and the extent of its remix and reuse by a myriad others, through expanding and layered networks. However, influencer logics dictate that all contents should have their ownership stamped, and inspired off-shoots should clearly indicate credits, as such back-traces are important for assigning proprietorship and potential monetary value. On TikTok, both logics converge when the memes that spark viral trends and challenges are the primary instigators of visibility and viewership, which can in turn be ultimately 'cashed out' via handsome creator and reward funds. And while it may appear trivial or sound silly to the uninitiated that creators are wrestling over the ownership and credit of contents – including dance moves, catchphrases, discursive scripts, audio, and the like – bear in mind that on TikTok views of viral contents can quickly amass tens of millions of views within days. When the stakes are high and the tangible conversions are real, creators expend energy and effort to study and make prominent the minutiae of content creation. In this section, I briefly discuss four further memetic practices arising from TikTok's key features and how they are popular devices that encourage participation, play, and possession among creators.

Duet Chains

As introduced earlier, the 'duet' feature on TikTok allows users to select an existing video to embed beside their own new video in a split screen format. It is usually used to respond, react or relate to existing content. While the most common format of duet is a 1:1, comprising the original video on the right-hand side and the new video on the left-hand side, 'duet chains' are a popular memetic practice where creators sequentially extend previously dueted posts by appending their own duets. The result is a succession of newer and newer duets, each connected to an existing one like links on a chain. With a bit of creative flare, duet chains present opportunities for TikTok users to co-create a pastiche of independent videos that when read together, constitute collaborative comedy. In the case of the 'hybrid human' duet chain (see Fig. 19), an original video featuring a talking head of a TikToker was dueted to include an innocent waving arm in the first instance, before TikTok jesters came together to append a beer belly, a hairy arm, dog legs, and other body parts in the collaborative meme.

Green Screens

Among the many effects offered on TikTok is the option to upload an image as a 'green screen' for a video. A green screen is a faux visual layer that digitally replaces the actual background in a video, such that creators can craft and simulate any backdrop as a bespoke environment for their content. This memetic practice is especially popular among 'POV actors' and 'role-play characters' (see Chapter 4) that may use dedicated green screen backdrops for the different characters that they play. It is not uncommon for creators to use screenshots of social media posts, text messages, and other correspondence as a green screen to be presented as evidence or reference material in their post. However, there are times when a green screen video does not record as planned. One such viral instance is the 'green screen fail' (see Fig. 20): A young man had uploaded a green screen video of a group of nondescript people dancing and positioned himself front and centre to give the impression that he was dancing with a crowd. However mid-way through the video, it appears that his phone slipped off its stand and fell to the ground, and the man in the frame quite literally 'flew' off screen. Despite this

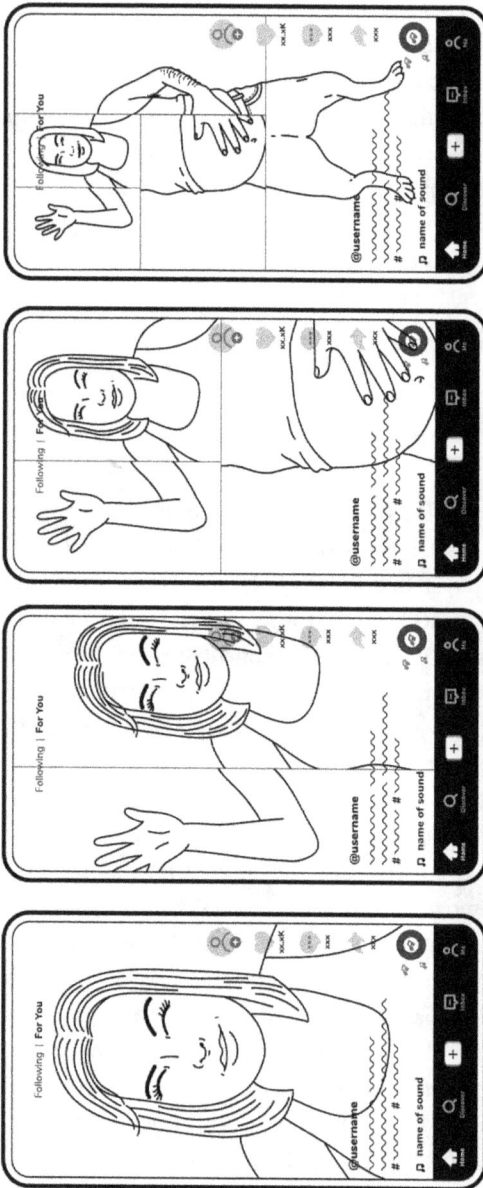

Fig. 19. Artist's Impression of a 'Hybrid Human' Duet Chain Meme on TikTok. Image Commissioned by and Copyrighted to Crystal Abidin. Art Provided by River Juno.

Fig. 20. Artist's Impression of the Original 'Green Screen Fail' Meme on TikTok. Image Commissioned by and Copyrighted to Crystal Abidin. Art Provided by River Juno.

mishap, the video made for good comedy, and once posted on TikTok, it swiftly became a viral meme. Soon, other creators were replicating the green screen fail meme by intentionally dropping their phones mid-video to simulate flight out of different green screen backdrops.

Filters

Visual filters are pre-set layers that creators can superimpose on their own videos to augment their image. On TikTok, among the most popular of these are selfie filters, which alter a creator's facial features. Selfie filters may be used in earnest, such as 'beauty filters' that enhance one's appearance to fit various beauty standards, or used ironically, such as 'clown filters' which radically distort one's appearance for amusement. There are also 'prophetic filters' which read a creator's face before assigning them a specific distortion, such as editing them to be younger or older, fair skin or tanned skin, and happy or angry. Prophetic filters have evolved into a memetic game on TikTok, where users would test how different filters would read them, whether the results are consistent with each attempt, and whether there are patterns in the results among groups of users. Implicit to the game is the whimsy of how machine vision would interpret each face differently and what the boundaries of each category might be. A popular memetic game on TikTok is the 'boy/girl filter' meme (see Fig. 21), which reads a face before augmenting it to be a male- or

Fig. 21. Artist's Impression of the 'Boy/Girl Filter' Meme on TikTok. Image Commissioned by and Copyrighted to Crystal Abidin. Art Provided by Ardine Keyla.

female-animated character. Where the male interpretation has a longer face, darker brows, stronger nose, and other stereotypical masculine features, the female interpretation bears a rounder face, lighter browns, softer nose, and gentler stereotypical feminine features. However, the memetic game is not the transformation of a person into an animated character per se but whether the filter reads a face as male or female, masculine or feminine. In particular, some 'boy/girl filter' meme posts have gone viral specifically because the filter has read the creator's face as an opposing gender. In other instances, the filter has perceived the creator's face as androgynous, toggling between the male and female animation repeatedly, thus generating discourse about the permissibility of gender stereotypes and play when filters are encoded.

Follow/Unfollow

On TikTok, the metrics for an account's following, followers, and likes are rounded down to one decimal point once the number is past 1,000. It is not uncommon for creators whose number of followers are at the cusp of the next milestone to plead for more followers, in anticipation that 9.9K would grow to 10K, 99.9K to 100K, 999.9K to 1M, and so on. It is also common for creators who own merchandise or small businesses to conduct giveaways to celebrate such momentous achievements. Yet, this pursuit for the glorious 'round number' has incidentally created a vernacular game among followers known as the 'follow/unfollow' meme. In this memetic practice, followers go on a hunt for accounts whose follower counts are on the threshold of 'rounding up' to the next 1,000 and post a green screen video of themselves following and unfollowing the account to demonstrate that they were in the critical position to help the account 'level up' (see Fig. 22). The discourse in the

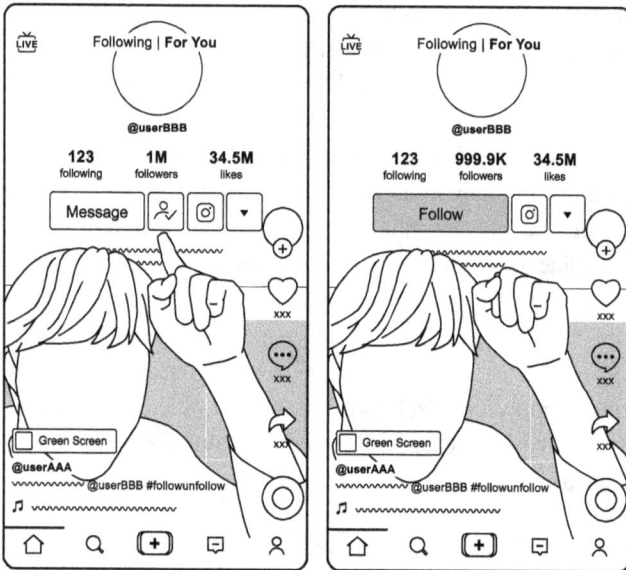

Fig. 22. Artist's Impression of the 'Follow/Unfollow' Meme on TikTok. Image Commissioned by and Copyrighted to Crystal Abidin. Art Provided by Phoebe Tan.

text overlay, captions or comment sections of such posts often indicate that this creator 'holds the power', is 'the gatekeeper', and can 'shift the tides' for the account. Similar games occur for other significant numbers, such as following an account to take it from 776 to 777 followers ('I saw that you're on the cusp of the lucky 7s and followed you to help. Good luck!') or unfollowing account to take it from 667 to 666 followers ('Sorry mate, I unfollowed to bring you back to the land of the unholy!')

Having reviewed some of the key memetic practices that are unique to TikTok, the rest of the chapter introduces five types of capital that are generated and circulated among meme cultures on TikTok (see Table 3). Through a series of brief

Table 3. A Summary of the Types of Capital Generated and Circulated Among Meme Cultures on TikTok. Table by Author.

Capital and Definition	Memetic Genre and Examples
Niche capital: The set of privileges, resources and status markers accorded to a user when they are able to aptly demonstrate that they can integrate into the specific environment, demonstrate the same characteristics and adopt the same preferences of a specialised segment of a community.	Duet chain relays • Polyphony chains • Remixed addendums • Pastiche commentaries • Corroborative perspectives • Patchwork communities
Subcultural capital: The visual performance of aesthetics and practices, insider knowledge of beliefs and ideologies and alternative valuation of status bestowed upon a user as a recognised or self-proclaimed member of a relatively stable alternative community that is segmented off from the mainstream.	Tech skills and talents • Beauty filters • Transition tutorials • Inside jokes • Cottagecore
Cross-cultural capital: The experiential knowledge and specialised skillset gleaned from an intercultural positionality and vantage point, a situated understanding of local markets rooted in cultural relativism and an ability to flexibly adapt to the communicative norms and nuances of different audience segments.	Blended cultures • Asian parenting • Mixed race families • Foreigner vlogs
Discursive capital: The oratory and literary ability to manufacture persuasive argumentation through the	Social movements and social justice • Disquisition

(Continued)

Table 3. *(Continued)*

Capital and Definition	Memetic Genre and Examples
mobilisation of moral hierarchies, the mapping of lateral relevance across communities of difference and the messaging of minority relationality to invoke empathy, reflection and resonance among interlocutors.	• Diversion • Deflection • Decoy
Cross-platform capital: The mastery of platform-specific affordances and its resulting communicative norms, a keen understanding of vernacular vocabularies and registers of platform-specific communities, and the intermediary leadership of mitigating the gaps between two or more platforms to proficiently communicate phenomena originating from one platform on another.	'Syndicated' content and plagiarism • 'Chinese TikTok' • Movie grabs • Sludge content

case studies to illustrate each concept, we will consider: Niche capital, Subcultural capital, Cross-cultural capital, Discursive capital, and Cross-platform capital.

NICHE CAPITAL: DUET CHAIN RELAYS

In their study of the sociology of 'the niche',[7] Popielarz and Neal offer that 'the niche of a species is a set of environmental states in which it thrives'. Drawing on biology, the authors offer that 'characteristics' of the species that successfully thrive in the niche environment are 'produced in future generations through genetic transmission and come to define a new species'.[8]

However, this process involves a 'dynamic negotiation' through 'competition for resources'.[8] As such, a 'niche' refers to 'the physiological capacities of the members of the population'.[9]

Mapped onto meme cultures on TikTok, niche capital is the set of privileges, resources, and status markers accorded to a user when they are able to aptly demonstrate that they can integrate into the specific environment, demonstrate the same characteristics, and adopt the same preferences of a specialised segment of a community. As mentioned above, 'duet chains' are a popular memetic practice where creators sequentially extend previously dueted posts by appending their own duets. To create a new 'duet post' or 'link', the creator first needs to thoroughly understand the niche content, format, tone, and register of the pre-existing chain. Like the metaphor of a 4 × 100 race, duet chains are on the lookout for the next 'runner' to pass the 'baton' to and assess prospective new candidates by how well they fit into the already existing niche of the memetic chain. Duet creators who possess niche capital are thus able to offer duet posts or links that best cohere into the existing memetic chain and extend the meme into a continuous duet chain relay.

Polyphony Chains

A very popular genre of duet chain relays are polyphony chains, where videos of melodic sounds by an assortment of animals are used as the baseline for musically talented TikTokers to layer in vocal or instrument accompaniments, ultimately culminating in a wondrous animal-human hybrid of a collaborative song. My most favourite example of this is Shy Little Frog, which begins with the baseline of a frog croaking in a relatively stable tempo, with TikTok musicians subsequently layering in beats from a drum kit, piano chords, and a dance accompaniment (see Fig. 23). This song is particularly

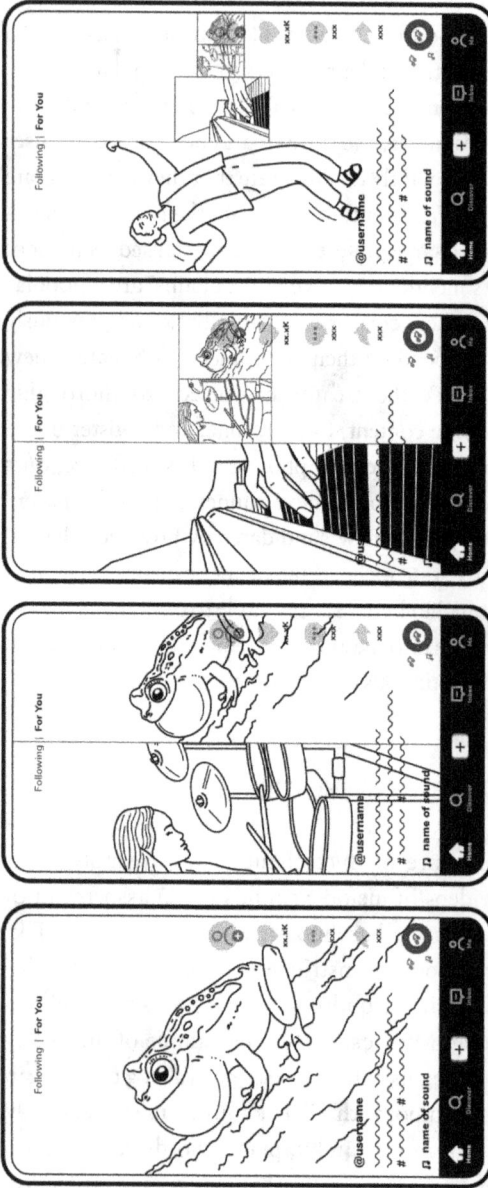

Fig. 23. Artist's Impression of the 'Shy Little Frog' Meme Chain on TikTok. Image Commissioned by and Copyrighted to Crystal Abidin. Art Provided by River Juno.

hypnotic, with the first layer of lyrics layered in being: 'Shy little frog, singing along to this fun tune'.

Simpler versions of polyphonic chains have been described as 'duet jams' or 'music collaborations using the duet function'.[10] They have been studied as being 'built on a foundation of remixing and bricolage'[11] and have proven successful for TikTok musicians to attract new prospective fans to discover their original music by way of these creative viral remixes. In 2021, Shy Little Frog was released on Spotify by the TikTok remix musician Sushisingz with a full prose of lyrics collaboratively authored by multiple TikTokers.

Remixed Addendums

Remixed addendums are duet chain relays where a creator has compiled a selection of TikToks that already layer well together into a grid and superimpose their vocal or audio contributions as a duet at the end to close out the video with an outro. A popular example of this is TikTokers who curate the many versions of harmony of a song offered by various creators, layered and blended together to form 4-, 6- or even 8-part harmonic frameworks, giving some time for the video to run for viewers to enjoy the curation and then appending an outro to conclude their creation. Popular addendums include outros like 'And this has been the TikTok choir, singing [name of song]' and simply 'The end...'.

A comedic version of such remixed addendums is when the curator adds a voiceover of little to no value or that is unexpected and catches viewers off guard. Known in the vernacular as the 'no value add' meme chain, this may include curators imitating the voiceover of a Spotify voice actor interrupting the song to promote the platform or insert an advertisement or curators suddenly taking on the persona of an over-excited DJ by screaming or yelling to 'hype' viewers up (see Fig. 24). When done well, such unexpected duet chains demonstrate niche capital in their understanding of how a memetic community might embrace their comedy. However, there are also many instances where remixed addendums are perceived as a nuisance as they sully the work of otherwise sincere musicians offering their craft for collaborative duets.

Fig. 24. Artist's Impression of the 'No Value Add' Meme Chain on TikTok. Image Commissioned by and Copyrighted to Crystal Abidin. Art Provided by Phoebe Tan.

Pastiche Commentaries

Pastiche commentaries are a sequence of videos stitched together consecutively that act as commentary on the first video in the chain relay. Rather than talking heads or any form of dialogue, they are usually quiet, voiceless reenactments of the original video in different scenarios to point out the absurdity or humour of the source material.

A popular pastiche commentary on TikTok is the 'hairless shave' meme, which begins with a male TikToker with shaving cream lathered all over his face, taking a razor to his cheek. As he begins to 'shave' one side of his jaw, it is evident that the man is already hairless – in fact, he does not even reveal a stubble beneath the very thick coat of shaving cream slobbered on. In response, various TikTokers have stitched this video with their own takes of 'useless chores', such as a man with a bandaged ankle intentionally holding a broom upside down to use as an inefficient crutch, a hijabi simulating the intricate actions of hair straightening with no hair in sight or a chef rubbing already shredded pieces of cheese against a steel grater (see Fig. 25). While pastiche commentaries initially started out as a lighthearted way to poke fun at some of the whimsical posts by TikTokers, they are such a popular duet chain that TikTokers have begun to strategise over ridiculous source posts for others to append their video commentaries too, as an inside joke within the niche community.

Corroborative Perspectives

Corroborative perspectives are when TikToks by different creators posted around the same time offer various points of view or framings of the very same event. These discrete posts are not usually hyperlinked in any way nor do they reference

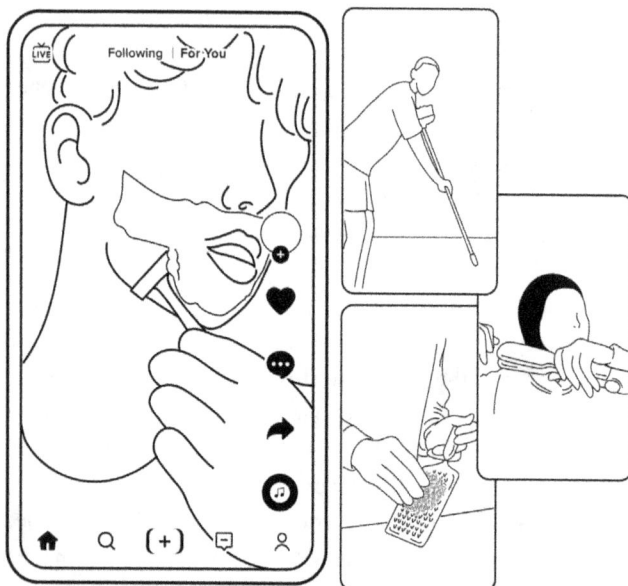

Fig. 25. Artist's Impression of the 'Hairless Shave' Meme Chain on TikTok. Image Commissioned by and Copyrighted to Crystal Abidin. Art Provided by Ardine Keyla.

each other. However, users often chance upon the various perspectives due to the sensitivity and attentiveness of their FYPs that would offer different corroborative posts sandwiched between dozens of posts in a single scrolling experience.

Innocuous corroborative perspectives may include chain relays of TikTokers living in the same vicinity sharing videos of fireworks as observed from different vantage points, like the various floors of neighbouring apartment blocks (see Fig. 26). However, there have been many instances where corroborative perspectives have also been incidentally deployed as important records and evidence of calamity: Many TikTokers captured on video the developments of the Astroworld crowd crush in

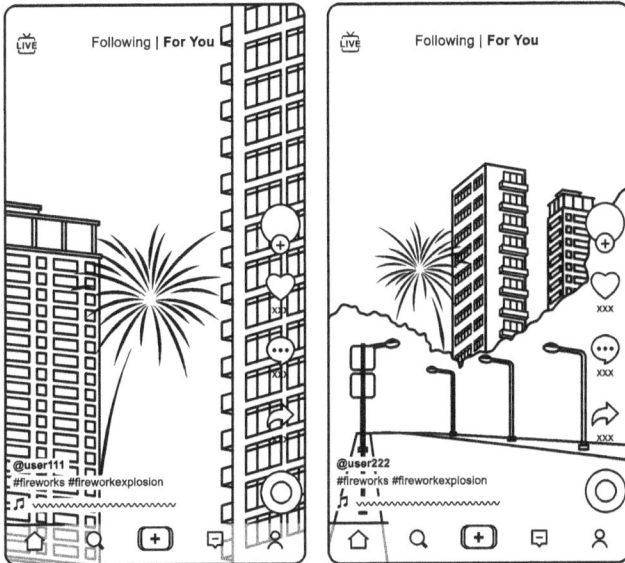

Fig. 26. Artist's Impression of Two TikTok Posts Showing Different POVs of the Same Event. Image Commissioned by and Copyrighted to Crystal Abidin. Art Provided by Phoebe Tan.

Texas in November 2021 and the Seoul Halloween crowd crush in the Itaewon neighbourhood in Seoul in October 2022. Both incidents saw fatal injuries, and TikTok posts of the various vantage points were widely re-broadcast by the mainstream media as citizen journalism.

Patchwork Communities

Patchwork communities are groups of TikTokers who come to see themselves as a community when duet chains that piece together their disparate posts demonstrate the coherence of their shared visual identity. In other words, like the needlework

of textile patchwork, the affordances of TikTok knit together
these otherwise disconnected TikTokers and enable them to
perceive each other as parts of a whole.

One of the more lighthearted examples of patchwork
communities are cosplayers of specific interests who come to
discover each other through meme chains, like 'fairy alters'
(Fig. 27). The TikTok videos shows compilations of Tik-
Tokers who first appear in normal everyday attire, before the
'group' transitions to reveal their costumes and outfits as a
collective. In other instances, the same meme chain template
has been adapted by First Nations peoples from around the
world, who similarly reveal themselves in beautiful traditional
regalia to represent their heritage and start conversations

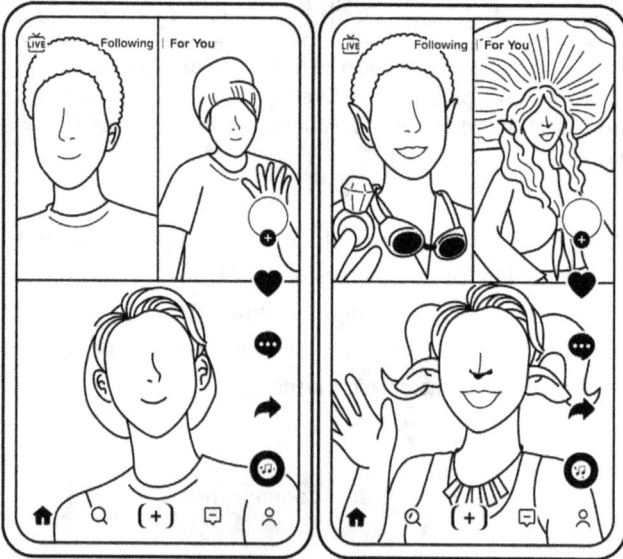

**Fig. 27. Artist's Impression of the 'Fairy Alters' Meme
Chain on TikTok. Image Commissioned by and Copyrighted
to Crystal Abidin. Art Provided by Ardine Keyla.**

about their various roots and legacies. Still, more comedic versions abound, such as instances where TikTokers discover their doppelgangers who are so strikingly similar in their appearance, down to fashion choices, facial accessories, and make-up preferences.

SUBCULTURAL CAPITAL: TECH SKILLS AND TALENTS

Sociologists generally conceive of subcultures as a deviation stream of cultures that are in opposition to mainstream popular culture. A notable piece of work by sociologist Sarah Thornton[12] focused on youth in clubs who would use their musical preferences and bodily endorsement to gauge each other's expertise and level of belonging to the subculture and who would elevate their own status within the subculture by way of accumulating more knowledge and commodities as forms of distinction. Some subcultures may prefer to identify themselves as holding 'underground cultural capital' to further deviate and sequester away from the mainstream, in the belief that what is 'truly underground' is 'credible', 'real', and 'cool'.[13] In brief, subcultures primarily aim to create 'new market relations' that in turn structure new 'value hierarchies based on knowledge, taste, and authenticity'.[13]

Scholars who have studied subcultures on TikTok offer that they are usually watered down to become mere commodified, romanticised, and digitised aesthetics on the platform[14] given the highly visual nature of this social media. They also argue that subcultures as portrayed on TikTok are generally more simplistic that the actual 'values, deeper meanings, and origins' of the original because TikTok users are simply 'curating a selective representation of what is palatable or marketable to the public'.[15]

To me as an ethnographer of TikTok, subcultural capital is the visual performance of aesthetics and practices, insider knowledge of beliefs and ideologies, and alternative valuation of status bestowed upon a user as a recognised or self-proclaimed member of a relatively stable alternative community that is segmented off from the mainstream. On TikTok, subcultures are generally identified as silos by users when they find themselves immersed in algorithmically-recommended streams of coherently curated contents that share the same aesthetics, qualities, and norms (see 'algorithmic practices' in Chapter 2). Yet, from an etic, outsider perspective, subcultures on TikTok really only 'come into being' when news articles publish headlines declaring a set of TikToks as coherently known as X-Tok (e.g. BookTok, KidTok), X-core (e.g. Cottagecore, Hopecore) or unique names like 'dark academia' or 'baddies'; the reality is that a new TikTok subculture 'debuts' in such headlines every single day.

Many journalists who spotlight established TikTok subcultures are usually encountering them in ways where the culture is not legible or literate to them. As such, their primers tend to adopt ethnocentric language that paints the community out to be 'exotic', 'exceptional' or 'exclusive' (see Abidin[16]) when they may in fact self-identify to be simply 'everyday'. This is often the case when journalists of White, English-speaking, upper middle-class, heteronormative backgrounds 'discover' subcultures among people of colour, non-English speakers, lower middle-class groups, and queer and gender diverse peoples. It is thus important for sincere interlocutors to understand TikTok subcultures from their vantage points to peel back on the packaging of their mere aesthetics and uncover their sociopolitical intentions. This section briefly introduces four TikTok subcultures anchored on tech skills and talents.

Beauty Filters

As noted earlier, TikTok is known for its expansive range of filters. Beauty filters are particularly popular and their use on TikTok is widely acceptable. However, a popular subculture on TikTok sees creators revealing the backstage processes of applying multiple beauty filters to their likeness, demonstrating how each layer augments a specific feature on their face. An example of this is a woman with a beautifully made up face who removes one filter from her live video at a time, with one stage transiting from flawless smooth skin to her actual uneven skin texture, another stage transiting from full plump lips and white teeth to her actual thin lips and yellowed teeth, another stage transiting from widened eyes and enlarged pupils to her actual eye shape and small pupil size, and still another stage transiting from a narrow v-shaped jaw line to a more rounded and heavy jaw line (see Fig. 28).

While seemingly innocuous, the origins of this trend draw from the phenomenon of *xiezhuang* (卸妆) videos that are popular on Douyin, where Chinese women would shed layers of make-up in sequence to reveal the work that has gone into their 'public face' and demonstrate their cosmetic prowess. Some of the more laborious cosmetic enhancements include wearing temporary silicon layers on their noses to give the appearance of a sharper bridge, using pins to tuck their ears back, and using face tape to stretch some skin on the jaw line back for a slimmer, sharper face. The general rule of thumb is that the greater the discrepancy between the 'after' and 'before' face, the more viral the video will become as users will come together to compliment and celebrate the Douyin creator on their expert skills. However, as these videos become widely cross-posted by others onto TikTok, the comments section often sees TikTok users heap criticism upon these women, calling them vain and frauds. The original spirit

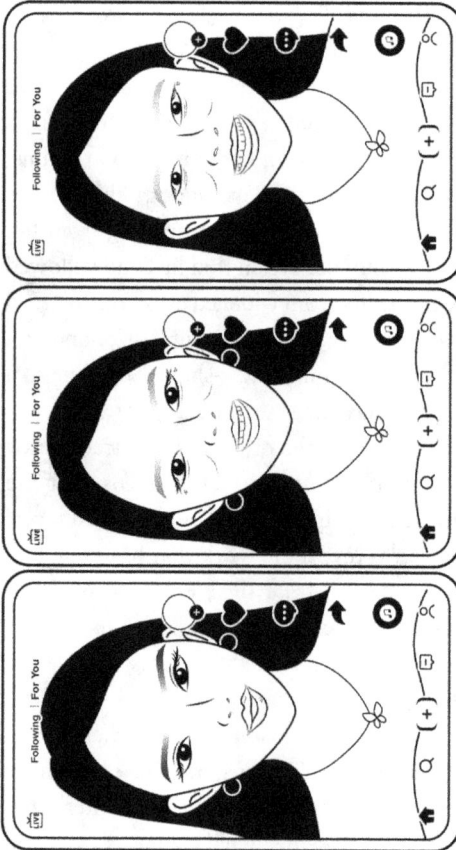

Fig. 28. Artist's Impression of the 'Make-up Off' Filter Meme on TikTok. Image Commissioned by and Copyrighted to Crystal Abidin. Art Provided by Ardine Keyla.

in which these *xiezhuang* videos were intended – to demonstrate the 'in real life' filter work of expert cosmetic skills and to celebrate that women literally come in all forms and faces – is usurped by spiralling and often misogynist chatter that police women's bodies and hold them to unrealistic beauty standards. As such, in the beauty subculture on TikTok, the 'make-up off' filter meme seeks to reenact the original intentions of *xiezhuang* videos, calling upon women to reveal themselves in their 'raw' forms and unabashedly reclaim their 'bare face' confidence.

Transition Tutorials

There is a subculture of users on TikTok whom commenters like to say are 'doing God's work'. Their subcultural capital lies in their technical knowledge and provision of accessible, user-friendly, step-by-step tutorials to demystify the video editing work and prop management behind the latest TikTok trends. Known as 'transition tutorials', these creators are perceived as trend disseminators, as their craft affords more users with the ability to replicate and participate in viral challenges. An example of this is the hoodie swap trend. The original video sees a TikTok user wearing a hoodie, pulling the hood up to cover their head and then slamming their face downwards, only to reveal in the subsequent upwards motion that they are now wearing a differently coloured or patterned hoodie.

The 'hoodie swap' transition tutorial offered by one such TikTok user sees them issuing explainers on where aspirant trend participants should pause their video recording, how they can use pieces of tape to mark the position of their bodies in the frame, how to quickly change into another hoodie, and subsequently, how to edit the video to seamlessly stitch the various snippets together (see Fig. 29).

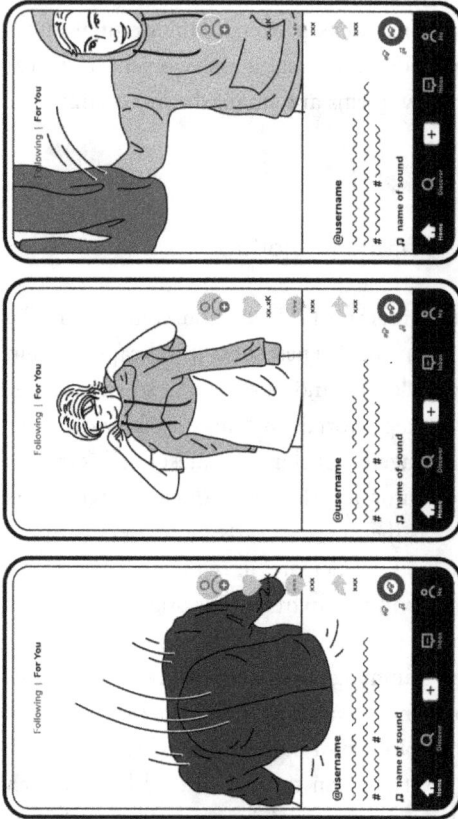

Fig. 29. Artist's Impression of the 'Hoodie Swap' Transition Tutorial on TikTok. Image Commissioned by and Copyrighted to Crystal Abidin. Art Provided by River Juno.

Inside Jokes

Inside jokes are difficult to spot on TikTok, as they can appear
as discrete, isolated instances of humour unless a coherent set
of posts referring to the same register of humour is surfaced by
algorithmic visibility (see Chapter 2). And even when users do
recognise an instance of an inside joke, they may not necessarily be let in on it. The subcultural capital attached to inside
jokes is thus bestowed upon those who have been 'let in' on
the joke or those who are savvy enough to decipher its origins
and backstory, decode the terms of reference to adequately
participate in the joke, and be recognised and acknowledged
by insiders for their participation. One of the most prominent
inside jokes on TikTok to have made news headlines is the
'chair in comments section' that first went viral in mid-2021. It
was during this time when TikTokers would see waves of
posts featuring a string of 'chair emoji' flooding every comments section. Users who were in the know would add to the
string of chair emoji or simply break the chain with a laughing
emoji, but there were also thousands of comments from
bewildered TikTokers querying the phenomenon or even
sincerely pondering if the platform had glitched. Later on, a
handful of news stories investigated the inside joke to explain
its origins as traced to viral joke instigator @blank.antho,[17]
who rallied his over 1.1 million followers to flood fellow
creator KSI's TikTok comments section with chair emoji,
stating that 'if you're watching this, you're part of the inside
joke'.[18] This caught on outside of the follower base of both
creators and became installed as part of TikTok's wider subculture of proliferating inside jokes, but the real politic is in
assessing the savvy of TikTok creators who could create
moments of instant virality and their persuasive impact over
even pedestrian TikTokers outside of their usual user base.

Cottagecore

The cottagecore subculture was first sighted on TikTok in late-2018 and sees young women who often have feminine-styled long hair living in oversized floral-printed and lacy dresses, frolicking in gardens and forests, engaging in traditional crafts like sewing and flower arrangement, and romanticising everyday chores like baking and gardening (see Fig. 30). Cottagecore has often been watered down as a mere

Fig. 30. Artist's Impression of a Typical 'Cottage Core' Post on TikTok. Image Commissioned by and Copyrighted to Crystal Abidin. Art Provided by Phoebe Tan.

'fashion trend' where TikTokers live in 'a permanent Instagram filter where everything is softly lit and slightly sepia-
toned'[19] and as a byproduct of pop singer Taylor Swift's
marketing efforts on her 2020 album Folklore, which
employed cottagecore symbolism.

However, its sociopolitical undertones became more
apparent when cottagecore became mainstream on TikTok
during the pandemic in 2020. The incarnation of a subculture
that previously debut on Tumblr, cottagecore TikTok of 2020
saw women reenacting these scenes as they yearned for
'another time or a fantasy world where things aren't as
complicated'[20] amid the tumultuous unfolding of mass
self-isolation worldwide due to COVID-19. The slow temporality and soothing nature of the sights and sounds were
intended to encourage TikTokers to consider how to 'slow
down' during the pandemic; to use the season to engage more
meaningfully with mindfulness and nature[21] and to provoke
introspection especially as the subculture was popular among
queer women.[22]

But there was also pushback against this intense romanti-
cisation of idyllic life as lifted from the early-1900s, as other
TikTokers called out the subculture for glossing over the
historical oppression faced by Indigenous peoples and the
ostracisation of LGBTQIA+ communities.[23] As such, cottagecore was assessed as several levels of 'escapism' at once:
From the enforced isolation of the pandemic, from the harsh
expectations of late-stage capitalism, from the fast-paced
tempo of modern society, and also from the politicised history of how such lifestyles were achieved at the expense of
oppression of marginal populations. This ultimately reflects
an upper-middle class privilege enjoyed by only a select few.

CROSS-CULTURAL CAPITAL: BLENDED CULTURES

There is a wealth of scholarship on cross-cultural capital from the discipline of the business school. The work usually focuses on 'international entrepreneurs',[24] 'expatriates',[25] 'international students' and 'migrants'[26] and even 'global virtual teams',[27] which collectively point to the value of workers who straddle between country markets. The scholarship offers that cross-cultural capital is the 'cross-cultural knowledge and experience, resulting from the entrepreneur's human capital and social capital gained largely in a foreign market'.[28] It asserts that these workers are able to engage in 'cross-cultural adjustment'[25] and 'cross-cultural adaptation'[26] and that their 'cross-cultural intelligence' is important for the 'global marketplace'.[29]

Mapped onto the international market and user base of TikTok, cross-cultural capital is the experiential knowledge and specialised skillset gleaned from an intercultural positionality and vantage point, a situated understanding of local markets rooted in cultural relativism, and an ability to flexibly adapt to the communicative norms and nuances of different audience segments. As cross-cultural capital usually arises from the lived experience of being betwixt and between, many experts come from migrant or diaspora backgrounds, are mixed race individuals or were raised in intercultural settings, like third culture kids.

Often the challenge of cross-cultural TikTokers is how to portray nuance in legible ways that are comprehensible by non-experts without sacrificing accuracy. Because this is particularly demanding, it is not uncommon for cross-cultural TikTokers to specialise in a specific cultural demographic or topic and grow their expertise and self-brand in that area. This section considers three examples of cross-cultural capital that demonstrates this.

Asian Parenting

In late-2020, I studied a trend on TikTok popular among East Asian locals and diaspora known as '*xuehua piaopiao*' (雪花飘飘). Named after the song popularised by Taiwanese singer Fei Yu-ching (费玉清), the first line of the chorus '*xuehua piaopiao, beifeng xiaoxiao*' (雪花飘飘 北风萧萧) references the melancholy of people in their hometowns watching the snow falling and the cold northern winds blowing in the depths of winter. It is often used to invoke longings of home, which is particularly apt for older migrants who would have to endure hardship to move their families to new countries and raise their children in foreign land. The *xuehua piaopiao* meme on TikTok saw second-generation diaspora young adults asking their parents to read out a list of five common sayings by Chinese parents, with a screengrab of the text usually used as a green screen for the backdrop of the video. The first four sayings were usually typical questions or chidings from Chinese parents, like 'What time are you coming home?', 'Why are you so late?', 'Why are you always on your phone?', 'Why don't you have straight As?', and 'Go and do your homework!'. However, the fifth line would list the opening line from the chorus of the *xuehua piaopiao* song, allowing Chinese parents around the world to demonstrate their singing talents.

The comments section of these viral TikToks were fascinated by the skills of these parents but also delved into commentary on how 'our parents' were also 'individuals' with their own talents and aspirations and were 'full human beings' beyond being 'just naggy Asian parents'. The deepening discourse pointed to the cross-cultural capital of migrant children who were now young adults; they were now able to reflect on their upbringing, recognise their common experiences and articulate the shared vocabulary and generational ordeal of being raised by overly strict Asian parents with very high expectations of academic achievement. Yet, in retrospect, they also acknowledged the 'tough love' conveyed by their parents are their love language, that the hardship undergone by their parents shaped them into the people they had become and that there must have been longings for home and self-actualisation goals that were sacrificed in the course of wanting to provide better futures for their family.

The trope of the Asian parent has become so common among cross-cultural TikTokers that role-players (see Chapter 4) who adopt the persona of Asian moms and dads often work to subvert the stereotype (e.g. Kubota[30]) and serve as a therapeutic congregational node for young diaspora TikTokers to convene and converse. One of the most popular Asian parent role-players on TikTok is Nick Cho, who goes by the moniker @yourkoreandad. Cho has been described by the media as a 'global parenting phenomenon', and many fans of his contents have offered that he 'eases the sense of loss' for those who have had 'absent, distant or deceased parents'.[31] His contents generally focus on taking TikTokers on journeys like grocery-shopping or going to the hardware store, providing company and insight on mundane chores like cooking and making coffee, and showering them with words of affirmation and advice.[32] Asian parent role-play TikTokers like Cho exemplify the phenomenon of 'parasocial parenting' or the 'internet parent', who use 'adoption rhetoric and engaging narrative structures' to audiences who seek 'parental figures'.[33] To do so successfully requires that TikTokers like Cho have an adept command of cross-cultural capital: They have to simultaneously understand and fulfil the desires of their target audiences (i.e. Asian diaspora children) while appealing to general audiences who may have previously only known of stereotypical Asian parenting via mass media portrayals.

Mixed Race Families

As a mixed race person myself, I have been curating a library of mixed race memes and challenges throughout the years. They variously invite TikTokers to demonstrate how they live 'between worlds' by showcasing a range of intercultural markers including phenotypic markers like skin tone and hair texture, skillsets like multilingualism and cultural competence, and heritage like family photos and home interior decor.

One of the earliest of such challenges is the '#WAsian check' challenge for White-Asian mixed race TikTokers – and its variants like '#Blasian check' for Black-Asian mixed race TikTokers – which invite users to showcase the two halves of their heritage. Sociologist Rebecca King-O'Riain,[34] who studied the #WAsian check meme on TikTok, argues that the trend allowed mixed race individuals to negotiate what being 'WAsian' actually means to them, with some communities preferring to use the term 'Hapa' that is more common in Hawaii, and others in the South East Asian region preferring the term 'Eurasian'. In so doing, mixed race White-Asians were coming to 'discover, test, confirm, and re-combine identities through playful cultural interactions'.

A similar audio meme includes 'Hold on, can we switch the language?', where mixed race TikTokers first introduce one aspect of their heritage through a series of image and video collages, before a record scratching sound indicates a pivot to the other aspect of their cultural background. Another one is 'What kind of Asian are you?', which invites mixed race TikTokers to showcase a juxtaposition of two or more cultures to demonstrate the diversity of their heritage. Yet another audio meme borrows a line from American hip hop group Das Racist's 2008 song 'Combination Pizza Hut and Taco Bell', with the catch phrase 'I'm at the Pizza Hut/ I'm at the Taco Bell/ I'm at the combination Pizza Hut and Taco Bell/

' inviting mixed race TikTokers to display old photographs of each parent individually, before revealing family photographs of their intercultural family comprising said parents and their mixed race children.

TikTokers who fare well in the trend demonstrate their ability to draw on their cross-cultural capital to succinctly communicate their unique vantage points, insights about their upbringing and home life, and topics about cultural hybridity that would be of interest to monocultural individuals.

Foreigner Vlogs

Given its mobile interface and its international user base, it is no surprise that TikTok is home to a melting point of cultures. One of the most prominent groups to contribute to the cross-cultural discourse on the platform are foreigners and expatriates. In the Asia Pacific region, foreigner or expat vlogs are very popular in China, Japan, and Korea, with tourists and workers curating snapshots of their impressions of local sights and sounds. Often, these posts are video montages of typical landmarks and activities in which visitors to the country might engage, like visiting Mount Fuji, enjoying neon signs and billboards, and eating sushi in conveyor belt restaurants in Japan (see Fig. 31). However, the discourse in the comments section also frequently evidence discussions of whether these snapshots are ethnocentric or simply exoticising these locales.

There are often negotiations among short-term tourists, frequent visitors, longer-term expats, life-long migrants, and locals as to whether these foreigner vlogs are doing portrayals of these destinations and their cultures justice. For example, comments often feature competitive discourse as to which TikTokers feel more proximity and affinity with the local cultures, with tourists variously claiming that their take is 'more authentic'

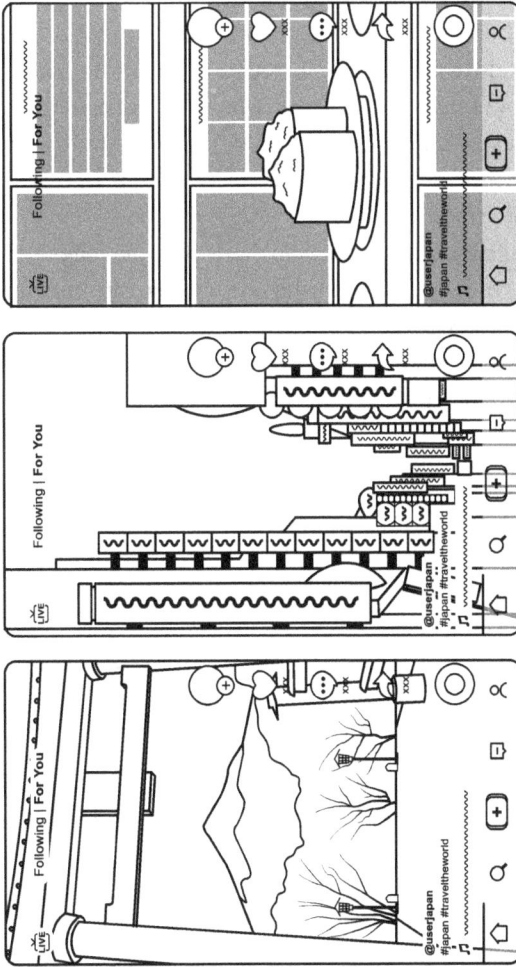

Fig. 31. Artist's Impression of 'Japan Snaps' Travel Vlogs on TikTok. Image Commissioned by and Copyrighted to Crystal Abidin. Art Provided by Phoebe Tan.

because they 'visit Japan every year', 'actually learnt to speak Korean in school' or 'have grown up with Chinese neighbours' – these claims to authenticity strive to articulate the relevance and experience of these visitors, as they compete over whose cross-cultural knowledge is more 'accurate' or 'valid'. In response, it is also common for ESL teachers – usually American, Australian, and British young people who work as English as a Second Language (ESL) teachers in China, Japan, and Korea – to deliver perspectives of local cities that provide more context than those from short-term tourists.

In turn, life-long migrants who have been in long-term partnerships with locals and who are raising intercultural children in these cities may offer a more nuanced vantage point as their personal and domestic lives are much more integrated into the local cultures. Finally, locals who are born and bred in these local cities may then offer an even more detailed and specific outlook, pointing out discrepancies or cultural blind spots in all of the recounts above. Collectively, this constant one-upmanship is an exercise in displays of cross-cultural capital, with TikTokers variously laying claim to expertise based on their unique standpoints.

DISCURSIVE CAPITAL: SOCIAL MOVEMENTS AND SOCIAL JUSTICE

Discursive capital has been studied as 'a practice of valuation through language' where 'subject positions become valuable by absorbing the time and energy of the members of the discourse community'.[35] These negotiations splinter the standing of moralities within communities, as there emerge 'social, political and economic hierarchies of more and less valued subject positions'.[36] However, discursive capital can also be deployed as a commodity and usurped by different communities. In their study of how atheists appropriate the metaphor of 'the closet' from queer folks, communication studies scholar Whitney Anspach and colleagues observed instances of 'lateral appropriation', where the 'means commonly associated with and/or perceived as belonging to one marginalized group are used by another marginalized group to further its own ends'.[37,38] This activation of 'a marginalized status' can serve to 'mobilize political action'.[39]

Mapped onto TikTok, discursive capital is the oratory and literary ability to manufacture persuasive argumentation through the mobilisation of moral hierarchies, the mapping of lateral relevance across communities of difference, and the messaging of minority relationality to invoke empathy, reflection, and resonance among interlocutors. Operationally, this sees the phenomenon of young people creatively deploying the features and function of TikTok to expand the potentials and possibilities of their participation in sociopolitical discussion, thanks to the lowered barriers of entry for public engagement and visibility. There are many discursive and aesthetic templates for participating in sociopolitical discussion on TikTok, such as performing one-person skits (see Fig. 32a), using a 'wall of text' (see Fig. 32b), appealing to the good conscience of viewers (see Fig. 32c) or simply hijacking trends and challenges on TikTok (see Fig. 32d) to compete for audience attention. This section offers four examples of how social justice messaging can be delivered on TikTok, through disquisition, diversion, deflection, and decoy tactics.

Disquisition

Disquisition tactics involve TikTokers presenting information that is often preachy and elaborate, serving to provide

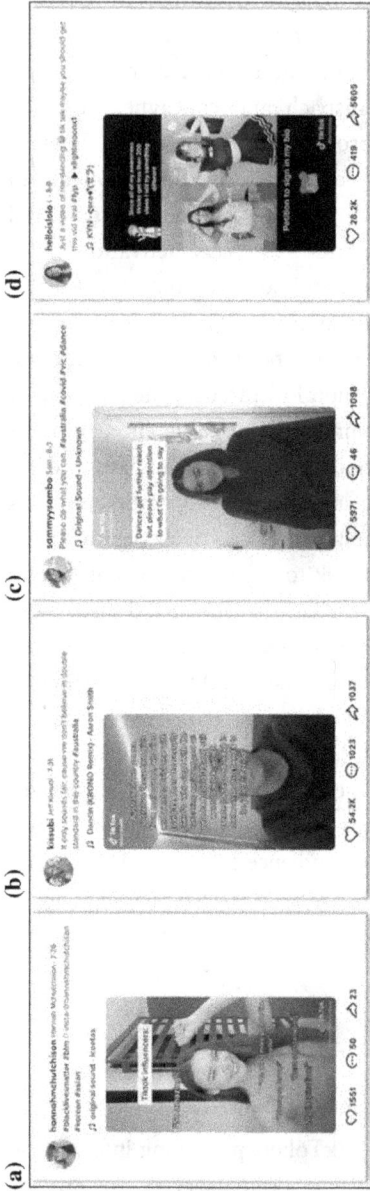

Fig. 32. (L–R): (a) '#blacklivesmatter #blm…' (@hannahmchutchison 2020); (b) 'It Only Sounds Fair…' (@kissubi 2020); (c) 'Please Do What You…' (@sammysambo 2020); (d) 'Just a Video of…' (@helloislolo 2020). Screengrab by Author.

sufficient evidence for discussion that an issue they have identified is worthy of conversation or debate. Aesthetically, this often takes the form of an extensive wall of text overlayed over a video post, or of TikTokers role-playing different positions to emphasise the discrepancies between the moral values of two different groups. One of the most popular disquisition tactics on TikTok are call-outs.

'Call-out cultures' are a mainstay on TikTok, with many users gaining visibility and virality for bringing TikTokers' attention to specific social justice issues or social causes. For example, many TikTokers rely on humour to lubricate the delivery of challenging messages and to disarm potentially aggressive rebuttals. In one such one-person skit, a young woman (see Fig. 32a) places herself in the position of a Tik-Toker who simply states the obvious – that 'racism is bad' – before being enveloped in overwhelming praise by a crowd of anonymous supporters. In doing so, she highlights how low the bar is for bestowing credit and reputation to TikTokers who languidly participate in the most basic of social justice discourse. In a similar vein, Fig. 32b features another Tik-Toker addressing his country (i.e. 'Australia if we gonna sentence...'), presenting the topic for discussion (i.e. people who have violated COVID-19 lockdown rules in Melbourne during the pandemic), offering a point of contention (i.e. the male rule-breakers did not receive punishments proportional to their crime), and furthering a social justice message (i.e. the uneven application of the law between the female and male violators points to issues of injustice, misogyny, and racism).

In another example, sociologist Xinyu (Andy) Zhao and I closely studied the 'Fox Eye' challenge that trended on social media in 2020 as a case study in anti-racism activism by (East) Asian users on TikTok. The 'Fox Eye' challenge was a trend in which both celebrities and ordinary users – often predominantly White women – posted photos and short videos on how to wear specific styles of make-up to achieve almond-shaped eyes or 'fox eyes'. This was often accompanied with a 'migraine pose' where a user pushes their index and middle fingers up against the temples on both sides of their head to 'lift' the corners of their upper eyelids (see Fig. 33) and was colloquially referred to as a 'Chinese' or 'oriental' look.[40]

In response, (East) Asian users on TikTok called out the historically racist undertones of this seemingly superficial trend, using the features and affordances of the platform to

Fig. 33. Artist's Impression of a Post Depicting the 'Fox Eye Trend' on TikTok. Image Commissioned by and Copyrighted to Crystal Abidin. Art Provided by Phoebe Tan.

produce everyday, non-heroic forms of digital activism, as an act of civic engagement and activist campaigning. Building on the scholarship on digital activism, we considered how Tik-Tok emerged as an alternative activist space for young people, specifically as it served users as a video production and sharing app. We specifically focused on the audiovisual aesthetics of the TikTok narratives in the counter-Fox Eye trend campaign, wherein the strategic and templatable deployments of vernacular TikTok aesthetics – curated image selections, creative uses of sound and audio memes, specific renders of visual filters and effects – play a central role in giving meaning to the online activist narratives created.[40]

As a disquisition tactic, trends like the 'Fox Eye' challenge have given rise to platformed activism in the TikTok vernacular that we term 'gesticular activism', which focuses on the generation of visibility and virality as awareness-building and consciousness-raising tactics,[40] rather than more engaged and involved forms of activist work.[41] 'Gesticular activism' describes the dramatisation of networked activism work that is contingent upon curating hyper-visible, at times even self-indulgent, performances to adapt to the algorithmic logics of platforms, and thus enhance the funnelling of attention and awareness to a discourse.[42]

Gesticular activists often utilise a 'competitive onedown-manship'[43] approach to signal their membership in a(n oppressed) community, where the mere encounter with an infraction of social norms or group mores bestows upon them an experiential authority to contribute to the discourse. The value of such activism work is often limited due to low awareness-to-action conversion rates, as users focus on using their personal biographies and lived experiences to gesture towards their everyday 'small p' politics. These serve as identity markers or in-group membership statements, rather than encouraging others to respond via more involved engagements. In fact, the didactic tone might even be off-putting to internet pedestrians who suddenly find themselves in the position of being 'lectured to' or who feel excluded from a social movement by virtue of not having experienced the oppression themselves.

While it may be tempting to dismiss such forms of activism work as mere clickativism or slacktivism, there is value in their work for accommodating different degrees of political participation.[44,45] Further, the reality is that these TikTok activists are activating platform-specific knowledge and savvy as they shape their dramatised discursive tactics to compete for both algorithmic and analogue visibility[46,47] and to maximise the networked spreadability of their activist discourse. Thus, while it may appear self-indulgent, gesticular activism can be a useful initial tactic for competitively funnelling attention and awareness towards a discourse. However, once said attention has been secured and awareness has been raised, continued gesticular activism may well deprecate into mere lip service. It is at this counterpoint that some activists on TikTok are called out for misdirected tonalities in their contents or for bandwagoning on a trend altogether.[48]

Diversion

Diversion tactics involve TikTokers first using one mode of performance or content to capture audience attention – usually something provocative like sexy content as bait, or something familiar and unsuspecting like TikTok dances – then rerouting this attention to focus on a more important conversation. TikTokers who have accumulated discursive capital are usually attuned to the most timely trends to use as bait and cultivate segues that are so subtle or so shocking that audiences cannot help but stay on as their attention is diverted.

For example, a TikToker opens her COVID-19 post with a text overlay that reads 'Dances get further reach but please pay attention to what I'm going to say' (see Fig. 32c). In another example, another TikToker experiments with over-laying her message to demolish the 'ICE' [Immigration and Customs Enforcement] in the United States over a viral Tik-Tok dance, citing that 'all of [her] awareness tiktoks get less than 200 views' and she was therefore trying 'something different' (see Fig. 32d). She also diverts viewer attention to her bio, where she has linked a petition inviting signees.

Deflection

Deflection tactics involve TikTokers adapting from pre-existing discursive and aesthetic templates to integrate social justice messaging, crucially relying on both the plat-form's and audience's (over-)familiarity with the templates to bypass automated censorship or analogue censure. This strategy displays discursive capital as TikTokers must be careful to ensure that they maintain sufficient fidelity to the source templates to remain recognisable to both the machine and the human eye yet deviate sufficiently from the usual deployments and original intentions of the templates so as to capture audience attention and convey their message.

One of the earliest examples of this is human rights activist Feroza Aziz's use of a 'makeup tutorial' post to deliver a mini lecture on the plight of Uighur Muslims in Xinjiang, China in 2019. The visual emblems of the video demonstrate Aziz partaking in a routine 'makeup tutorial' on TikTok, instructing users on the correct application of eye shadow, eyeliner, and the like. However, the oratory elements reveal Aziz calling upon her audience to please pay attention, to not use any contentious words in the comments section, and to listen to what she has to say about the Chinese government's alleged mistreatment of the Muslim minority in Xinjiang. Hundreds of thousands of TikTokers flocked to the comments, and in agreement with Aziz, deployed code-switching and innuendos in their conversation. While Aziz's post was swiftly taken down from the platform, after some international media furore and campaigns by several communities of TikTokers, TikTok reinstated the post citing an automated error. The alleged 'technical glitch' served to further publicise Aziz's creative deflection tactics on an international scale, and it soon became a staple on TikTok for young people to hone their discursive capital by experimenting with similar deflection tactics to avoid platform takedowns.

Decoy

Decoy tactics involve TikTokers imitating a discursive template to distract or sidetrack unwanted viewers who would usually not be interested in the topic while retaining their target audience who are able to decode the nuance and context of the situation. This intentional trickery is meant to filter out disinterested interlocutors to focus efforts on cultivating a shared ethos on specific social values rather than expend efforts on defending their stance. More often than not, decoy tactics are also a way to temporarily cultivate safe spaces for conversations intended for specific groups of people, by luring away other parties who might disrupt the conversational space due to opposing values or different standpoints.

Popular decoy templates on TikTok are often stereotypically gendered: Female TikTokers are seen beginning their TikToks discussing menstruation, breastfeeding or an assortment of ailments specific to the female body in the first few seconds, before pivoting with statements to the effect of 'Okay, now that all the men have left...', then diving into more serious topics like dealing with intimate abuse, financial abuse, and similar. Male TikTokers are seen beginning their TikToks discussing car engine models, tyre makes, and an assortment of machine and gear-related topics, before pivoting with statements to the effect of 'So now that it's all boys...', then diving into somewhat embarrassing topics like how to please their female partners in bed, how to manage emotional breakdowns, and the like.

CROSS-PLATFORM CAPITAL: 'SYNDICATED' CONTENT AND PLAGIARISM

In the field of platform studies and digital labour studies, several scholars have dedicated efforts towards understanding the production and circulation of capital. For instance, in their study of digital labour by food delivery workers who work for Deliveroo, sociologist Karen Gregory and political economist Jathan Sadowski offer the notion of 'platform capital' to describe how workers are objectified to become 'merely (extensions of) machines, treating them as nodes in the network, forcing them to work in concert with various machines, while also becoming mechanical in how they work and live'.[49] Their study demonstrates how food delivery workers strive to cultivate 'flexibility, vitality, and legibility' as forms of 'biopolitical governance' to accumulate human and data capital on such platforms[50] in order to best capitalise on the opportunities of gig work.

In another instance, geographer Giulia Dal Maso and colleagues studied the RealTech company Juwai, which aims to connect international estate agents and Chinese buyers.[51]

They found that the platform relies on 'mediating cultural asymmetries [as] a process of extraction that is a central component of their business model'[52] and 'seeks to foment an idea of the "other culture as risky" to fuel wary attitudes between buyers and developers, and to subsequently develop its mediating role therein'.[53] For Maso et al.,[54] platforms like Juwai 'agitat[e] the cultural borders between the two sides' and then 'rus[h] in to rescue its Chinese clients from the risks associated with misunderstanding Western legal and market systems'.[55] They offer the notion of 'cultural platform capital' to describe how platforms 'can reveal how cultural difference and cultural risk are commodified through platform technologies to drive more users to access platform content, thus generating more user data and sustaining the digital circulation of this cultural economy'.[54]

Extending from these understandings of 'platform capital' and 'cultural platform capital', my study of TikTok offers 'cross-platform capital' as the mastery of platform-specific affordances and its resulting communicative norms, a keen understanding of vernacular vocabularies and registers of platform-specific communities, and the intermediary leadership of mitigating the gaps between two or more platforms to proficiently communicate phenomena originating from one platform on another.

'Chinese TikTok'

Having studied both Silicon Valley and Chinese platforms for several years, I often feel a mild exasperation at the latter being sized up as 'the Chinese version of something else' when surmised for an international audience. By now, those of us who are familiar with media studies or with international platforms would be familiar with quips like micro-blogging site Weibo being touted as the 'Chinese Twitter' or video platform Bilibili being touted as the 'Chinese YouTube'. In a similar vein, Douyin is regularly referred to as the 'Chinese TikTok' despite predating the latter and offering distinctive features and affordances, distinctive marketplace and vernacular cultures, and distinctive user experiences. In any case, among TikTokers who are proficient in cross-platform discourse, 'Chinese TikTok' has emerged as a shorthand for a repertoire of contents, genres, and trends that originate on Douyin and have been ported over to TikTok via cross-platform intermediaries (see Chapter 4 on 'cross-platform curators'). Given that Douyin dominantly features Chinese language speakers and contents with Chinese cultural and sociopolitical nuance, cross-platform TikTokers who mediate the flow of contents from Douyin to TikTok are usually intercultural individuals themselves – migrants, diaspora, expats, mixed-race folks, ESL teachers, and the like.

One of the first 'Chinese TikTok' trends to go viral on TikTok was compilations of Chinese street style. The posts usually involve TikTokers curating Douyin posts of Chinese young people strutting down the streets while showcasing their impeccable fashion sense (see Fig. 34). It is not uncommon for these videos to have been augmented by appearance and beauty filters that are popularly used on Douyin, such as skin whitening, chin sharpening, eye widening, and leg lengthening, to name a few usual suspects. The popularity of Chinese street style on TikTok has been attributed to 'quarantine scrolling',[56] and many America-based TikTokers have attempted to replicate the trend.[57]

Despite performing very well on TikTok, such compilations of Chinese street style videos native to Douyin are often stripped of context. While on Douyin it is common for the clothes worn by these creators to be tagged as advertising contents, for fashion brands to be introduced and featured in

Fig. 34. Artist's Impression of a Typical 'Chinese Street Fashion' Post on TikTok. Image Commissioned by and Copyrighted to Crystal Abidin. Art Provided by Ardine Keyla.

the captions, and for creators to be acknowledged by their user handles, these promotional threads are often deleted when cross-posted onto TikTok.[56] Worst still, when these micro-fashion trends go viral, retailers outside of the Chinese market often scramble to produce replicas for sale, outrightly copying and siphoning sales away from the original brands. Small businesses and Douyin users have called out these omissions, as brands are not acknowledged for their creative work and Douyin creators are plagiarised.

In other situations, the decontextualisation has resulted in inaccurate backstories of Douyin creators. For instance, the TikTok account @loora888 features a pair of sisters who often go viral for their Chinese street style videos. Their visual brand is prominent and instantly recognisable as the older woman appears more masculine and has been described as 'cool and collected' while the younger woman appears more feminine and is thought to be 'lively and bubbly'. My digital ethnography studying reposts and compilations of @loora888 found little to no attribution to their original posts or accounts even though the Douyin creators also curate their own TikTok account. My study also found thousands of reposts and comments on TikTok misperceiving the sisters as a 'lesbian couple', romanticising their 'WLW' or 'women who love women' relationship, speculating the power dynamics between the couple through an over-scrutiny of their micro-gestures and body language, and off-track discussions about how 'forward' China is to embrace such 'public displays of homosexual relationships'. At least one popular media article has also pointed to this discrepancy.[58] Despite users familiar with Douyin clarifying in TikTok comments sections that the pair are sisters, and despite the sisters themselves responding to comments on TikTok to clarify their relationship, their fan lore on TikTok has spiralled so quickly that small fandoms have be founded around their imagined lesbian relationship. During my last foray into digital ethnography on this topic, there was even dedicated WLW fan fiction based on the pair circulating on TikTok.

There are glimpses of optimism despite the rampant unau-thorised syndication, pilfering, and plagiarism of content from Douyin onto TikTok, as many TikTokers with cross-platform capital have emerged as cross-platform curators (see Chapter 4) to adequately contextualise and sincerely showcase Chinese cultures to an international audience. But what remains worrying is the mainstream press coverage by (usually) American and British media, who often deploy orientalising language in their description of such trend reports such as 'unorthodox',[59] 'quirky',[60] 'unusual'[61] or 'hilarious'.[62]

Movie Grabs

Movie grabs are another form of unauthorised syndication as many TikTok accounts tend to compile and repost longform films or television shows in a series of multi-parted clips. The accounts are usually anonymous, with little known about their creators. However, they are widely popular among TikTokers who are enticed to fall down a rabbit hole of sequential clips[63] I have offered in media interviews (e.g. Nyce[63]) that such movie grab TikTok accounts use innovative engagement strategies (see Chapter 2) to retain audiences, such as labelling specific clips 'Part 3' without offering Parts 1 and 2 or inviting audiences to 'follow for the next scene/episode' without ever posting the update, thus inciting audiences to 'rac[k] up engagement as they desperately search'.[63] While many of such clips and accounts are removed due to successful copyright strikes,[64] their popularity is persistent as movie grab curators exhibit an uncanny ability to mobilise their cross-platform capital and constantly innovate to evade the automated censorship by TikTok. During my last stint of digital ethnography, popular strategies include flipping scenes left-to-right or upside down, superimposing filters to change the colour or introduce a floating gif layer onto the screen, or augmenting the pitch of the actors' voices, all to avoid detection by the platform's automated screening. As such, movie grabs continue to be viewed as a 'potential threat' to the subscription business of on-demand platforms like Netflix.[65] In 2023, Paramount Pictures released the popular movie Mean Girls on TikTok in 23 parts,[66] in response to fan demand given that bootleg versions of the film have already been widely circulated by movie grab accounts.

Sludge Content

Perhaps the pinnacle of cross-platform capital on TikTok are the masters of sludge content – the genre of TikToks that combine and pastiche several unrelated videos playing at once for the sole purpose of extending viewing time. Visually, the most basic of sludge contents usually sees a TikTok post dividing a screen into half, where the top half may be screening a movie grab snippet (see above) and the bottom half may be screening an unrelated video, usually Autonomous Sensory Meridian Response (ASMR) contents like slime-making or paint-mixing. The genre has been described as comforting 'overstimulation',[67] a form of 'escapism',[68] 'stim-tok', 'cocktail content', and 'second screening'.[69] News reports indicate that sludge content TikToks are 'viewed for eight times longer than the average TikTok video'[70] and are adept at evading platform censorship[71] even though the pieces are almost always plagiarised from other creators or lifted from other platforms.

CONCLUSION

This Chapter has taken readers on a deep dive into memes as capital on TikTok through an anthropological lens. It offers a framework of five forms of capital – niche, subcultural, cross-cultural, discursive, and cross-platform – that while emblematic of the way value is produced and circulated via meme cultures on TikTok can be mapped onto other platforms and phenomena. The next chapter focuses more squarely on capital in the literal sense, as we pivot our focus to small businesses and marketplace cultures on TikTok.

4

CREATORS AND GENRES

THE EVOLUTION OF SOCIOCULTURAL NORMS IN INFLUENCER CULTURE

In a prior body of work, I traced the connections between internet celebrity and Influencer cultures, focusing specifically on some shifts that were occurring in the latter during the 2010s.[1] Here, I recap five of these shifts and explicate how they have shaped change in the content strategies by Influencers and subsequently how they enacted change in the sociocultural norms experienced by followers (see Table 4).

Curation to Co-Presence

Influencer culture in the 2010s was shifting from 'archive culture' to 'streaming culture'. Livestreaming platforms like Twitch (launched 2011)[2] and Discord (launched 2015)[3] became mainstream outside of video game and e-sports subcultures, Bilibili (launched 2009)[4] and BIGO LIVE (launched 2016)[5] rapidly became major players in livestream shopping, and major Silicon Valley platforms released in-app live video stream features too: YouTube Live was launched in 2011,[6]

Table 4. A Summary of How Shifts in Influencer Industry in 2010s Correspond to Changes in Influencer Content Strategies and Changes in Follower Experiences of Sociocultural Norms. Table by Author.

2010s Shifts in the Influencer Industry[1]	Change in Content Strategies	Change in Sociocultural Norms
Archive culture to Streaming culture	Repository format to Transient format	Curation to Co-presence
Tasteful consumption to Amateur aesthetic	Luxury content to Everyday content	Aspiration to Relatability
Platformed fame to Cross-platform influence	Coherent narrative to Cohesive narrative	Master status to Persona play
Attention economy to Affection economy	Corporate branding to Personal branding	Endorsement to Testimonial
Quantitative metrics to Qualitative impact	Pedestrian access to Subscriber access	Engagement to Reputation

Facebook Live was launched in 2015, Twitter acquired and integrated Periscope in 2015[8] and Instagram Live launched in 2016.[9]

Correspondingly, Influencers expanded their content strategies from the 'repository format' of neatly archived image grids and chronological posts to embrace 'transient format' contents such as live-chatting and ephemeral short video posts. Several of the Influencers I had interviewed throughout my longitudinal fieldwork in the Asia Pacific region expressed discomfort with this shift, especially the early generation of bloggers and Instagrammers who were long conditioned to preserve and make searchable all their contents, as a living portfolio to showcase to potential clients and as a growing catalogue of lifestyle content to maintain their personal brand. However, newer Influencers appreciated the new playing field as they did not feel pressured to curate a library of personal lore to establish themselves with new followers.

For followers, the sociocultural norms focused less on browsing through curated content libraries to pursuing co-presence: Scheduling their participation in synchronous dialogue with Influencers in livestreams; witnessing content delivery in situ with highly contextualised nuance linked to a shared albeit transient temporality; feeling the pressure of 'FOMO' (Fear Of Missing Out) as streams were not always recorded for later viewing and desiring to show up every time as Influencer lore and personal backstories were being co-created live with viewers and knowledge was fast accumulating through chronological feeds.

Aspiration to Relatability

Influencer culture in the 2010s was shifting from 'tasteful consumption' to an 'amateur aesthetic',[10] where the Instagram bubble of picture perfection and 'luxury content' was making a return to 'everyday content'. For followers, the popularity of two new live photo apps in the market signals this shift. The premise involves apps like minutiae (released in 2017) and BeReal (released in 2020) sending a simultaneous notification to users worldwide at a random time once a day, instructing them to use the in-app camera to take a photo at that very moment and to share it on the platform. BeReal allows users a 2-minute window[11] to make their upload while minutiae accommodates a 1-minute window to view a notification and a mere 5-second buffer to upload a photograph.[12] The practice is meant to compel users to be more spontaneous and

truthful with their photo documentary, unlike the highly
curated and edited feeds *a la* Instagram.

minutiae brands itself as an 'anti-social media app' that
encourages uses to photograph and post the 'normally
undocumented moments of life', the 'daily experiences' that are
mundane.[12] It cites in its FAQ examples such as the 'daily
commute to work', 'starting blankly at your laptop screen',
and 'waiting in line' at the grocery store.[12] The app also limits
users' scrolling to just 1 minute a day[13] and of content that is
anonymous at that, resulting in connections that are 'singular
and random'.[14] BeReal's tagline is 'Your daily dose of real life'
for 'meaningful connections', 'spontaneous moments', and
'authentic real life' from 'the people you care most about'.[15]
For followers, the sociocultural norms now focus less on
aspiration and more on relatability, desiring connection with
peers, equals, and other users on a more level-status playing
field.

However, this optimism needs to be approached with
caution as such platforms graduate from being start-ups and
begin to monetise. minutiae earns revenue through sub-
scriptions to the iOS version of the app[16] and a personalised
photobook featuring 1 year of the users' minutiae posts.[17]
Since its inception, BeReal has introduced new features such
as RealPeople and RealBrands, which are BeReal accounts run
by celebrities and brands, respectively.[18] Users can also sub-
scribe to RealPeople and RealBrands as RealFans to access
locked content.[19] As monthly active users began to decline, in
2023 BeReal launched the Bonus BeReal feature allowing
users who post on time to share two more additional posts.[20]
The app was subsequently acquired by videogame developer
VooDoo in 2024.[21]

More crucially, digital media scholars have observed that
the relatability and authenticity afforded by such apps that
promise 'in-the-moment temporality'[22] or 'sporadic

authenticity'[23] – where authenticity is equated with an uncurated and unfiltered liveness captured through the demand to post instantaneously – are merely 'repackaged version[s] of authenticity'.[24] In reality, they 'accelerate' the pressures of social media use on users, demanding that they be 'interesting all the time, always ready to create content' for the app.[25] In recent years, new live photo apps have joined the market – including Locket[26] and Daylyy[27] – which perhaps underscores users' desires for spontaneous and instantaneous posts of mundane, everyday, and relatable content.

Master Status to Persona Play

Influencer culture in the 2010s was shifting from 'platformed fame' to a 'cross-platform influence' where Influencers were branching out from establishing a singular identity on their debut platform to managing different voicing and branding strategies across multiple platforms. Operationally, this saw early-generation Influencers who may have established themselves in one genre on text-based blog platforms branch out to simultaneously explore other genres on image-based platforms like Instagram or short-video platforms like TikTok. Consequently, Influencers were accorded more freedom to stray away from a previously singular and 'coherent narrative' to indulge in a variety of content directions so long as they were largely still a 'cohesive narrative'.

For example, Vietnamese–Canadian Leenda Dong first went viral on TikTok in 2020 for her character @yoleenda-dong: A young woman without makeup, who wears glasses in a large frame, is usually clad in comfortable but mismatched loungewear, with her signature unkempt hair in a topknot, and who speaks in an exaggerated pan-Asian accent, all to paint the impression of being an 'uncool nerd'. Her TikTok character is wildly popular, boasting over 17 million followers and over 940 million likes at the time of writing.

Followers who are familiar with Leenda's trajectory will remember her as one of the pioneering Asian–American/Canadian YouTubers from the 2010s. Her YouTube channel @LeendaDProductions was launched in 2011 and focused on short emotional or comedic skits about dating and romance, usually featuring other pioneers like Phillip Wang from the American YouTube channel Wong Fu Productions. Leenda was also a frequent cast member or guest in the skits produced by other YouTube pioneers in the United States. In 2013, she launched her vlog channel @LeendaVlogs to feature updates about her personal life and share blooper reels and behind-the-scenes content from her main channel. @LeendaDProductions was last updated in 2018 and recorded over 1.1 million subscribers. Given her experience as producer, writer, and actress and her track record of playing several recurring roles across these channels, it would be no surprise to long-term followers that @yoleendadong's nerdy character on TikTok is another persona in her repertoire.

However, a year into @yoleendadong's growing popularity on TikTok, followers who were new to her began to discover Leenda's illustrious history as a pioneering YouTuber. In the comment threads of her TikTok posts and on forums like Reddit, followers shared their shock that unlike the character @yoleendadong, the actress Leenda Dong was beautiful and spoke with an anglicised Canadian accent. There was some initial outrage at this discovery, even sparking op-eds that @yoleendadong's TikTok caricature and its exaggerated pan-Asian accent was comedy at the expense of 'internalised racism'.[28] However, other commentators also pointed out that comedy and parody was Leenda's expertise given her heyday on YouTube and that she was 'defying Asian stereotypes' through satire.[29] In 2024, Leenda returned to posting her self-written and directed skits on YouTube as her TikTok character. The YouTube channel @YoLeendaDong also features other popular TikTok creators like @haleyybaylee.

Alongside the YouTube channels @LeendaDProductions, @LeendaVlogs, and @YoLeendaDong, Leenda also manages several Instagram accounts with different personas: @yoleendadong contains memes featuring her TikTok character; @leendaphotodumps is her travel photo diary in the vein of a lifestyle Influencer; @feelgoodlittlenotes is her content account featuring positive quotes about mental health; and @leendadong is an amalgamation of all of the above *a la* a diary. For followers, Leenda's narrative as an Influencer is not coherent and singular, but they are cohesive and compatible as each feed ultimately focuses on uplifting content, whether through comedy, lifestyle role-modelling or mental health encouragement.

For followers, the expansion of Influencer practice across personas and platforms means that they are no longer focused on the 'master status' of Influencers but rather open to 'persona play' and the myriad of personalities that they have to offer. However, this only appears to be sustainable as long as the personas are cohesive. To give a very brief counter example, an Influencer whom I have been interviewing consistently over the last 11 years revealed to me that she was struggling to 'port over' or 'encourage' followers from one platform to take interest in her other accounts. While she posts beauty advice and tutorials on TikTok, her Instagram feed focuses on fashion, and her blog focuses on lifestyle content including travel. However, the platform on which she has the most followers and which she is most known for is OnlyFans, where she posts borderline adult content. While this Influencer has embraced a cross-platform strategy, her persona and branding across platforms is not cohesive to followers, and she finds herself unable to leverage on the popularity from any of her platforms or persona to grow her OnlyFans presence.

Endorsement to Testimonial

Influencer culture in the 2010s was shifting from an 'attention economy' to an 'affection economy' where it has become more crucial to pivot attention from 'corporate branding' to 'personal branding' via strategic practices of creator labour (see 'Creator labour' below). In a very saturated social media climate with a cacophony of ads vying for consumer attention, followers are becoming less interested in the formal corporate branding of a product and more attached to the personal stories that are told about the consumer experience. For early-cohorts of Influencers who had previously transited from long-form, text-heavy advertorials on blogs to the pithy quick caption and stock-like image of Instagram ads, reverting to diary writing as their mainstay was a welcome change. For followers, this shift from photographic 'endorsements' via the likes of product placement selfies[30] to full-fledged 'testimonials' was embraced as Influencer content felt personalised and intimate once again.

Engagement to Reputation

Influencer culture in the 2010s was shifting from being measured by 'quantitative metrics' to impressions of 'qualitative impact'. This was largely driven by attempts by early cohorts of Influencers to push back on and resist some of the automation by platform culture that tended to group Influencers into tiers and belts based on their number of followers, views or likes alone. During this period, the pioneer cohorts of Influencers whom I had interviewed would lament that the writing discipline and parasocial practice that they had honed over many years was no longer as valued, as newer generations of Influencers focused entirely on generating 'visibility for engagement numbers'. However, as a natural consequence of reverting from 'endorsements' to 'testimonials' (see above), these early-generation Influencers warmly welcomed the return to a sense of online community where followers took a personal interest in their lives. Influencers reshaped their contents from broadly targeting 'pedestrian access' to exclusively catering to 'subscriber access', and followers subsequently pivoted their evaluation of Influencers from mere 'engagement' to personal appraisals of 'reputation'.

FROM INFLUENCER CULTURE TO CREATOR CULTURE

Internet infrastructure has been progressively advancing from Web 1.0 to Web 4.0.[31] The key elements of each succession include:

- Web 1.0: read-only web

  - 'Web of *information* connections'.[32]

  - Commencing approx. 1969.

  - Introduction of ARPANET, HTMLs and URLs.

  - Users can *move* between static web pages.

- Web 2.0: read/write web

  - 'Web of *people* connections'.[32]

  - Commencing approx. early-2000s.

  - Introduction of user-generated content, websites and social media.

- Users can *create* content, comment on content, and communicate using content.

• Web 3.0: read/write/own web

  - 'Web of *knowledge* connections'.[32]

  - Commencing approx. 1991, flourishing approx. 2009.

  - Introduction of blockchain technology made popular via the launch of Bitcoin during the financial crisis.

  - Users can *apply* blockchain technology outside of cryptocurrency for other decentralised initiatives.

• Web 4.0: read/write/own/govern web

  - 'Web of *intelligent* connections'.[32]

  - Commencing approx. early-2010s, flourishing approx. early-2020s.

  - Introduction of artificial intelligence technology mainstreamed by augmented reality and virtual reality.

  - Users can *automate* infrastructure and processing with the assistance of autonomous machine learning.

Where Web 1.0 saw the rise of microcelebrities and Influencers as *hosts* of content, Web 2.0 saw a proliferation of internet celebrities and creators as *creators* of content. Where Web 3.0 saw influential users as *owners* of fediverses who could design the environment to host their content, Web 4.0 is presently seeing expert users as *trainers* of software to autonomously create content. The shift from 'Influencer culture' to 'Creator culture' has unfolded between Web 1.0 and Web 2.0 where the structures previously intertwining followers in affective online communities have been reshaped to lure them in via algorithmically-driven attention schemes.

A brief side-track: I note that the shift from Web 2.0 to Web 3.0 has mainstreamed the growth of virtual Influencers in augmented milieus and proliferated new forms of creator leadership in the tech and finance industries and that the shift from Web 3.0 to Web 4.0 has challenged dispensability of creator labour. However, these are discussions for another time.

Having reviewed the evolution of sociocultural norms in Influencer culture above, this section considers some of the key distinctions between 'Influencer culture' and 'Creator culture' in light of the progression from Web 1.0 to Web 2.0. Drawing on comparative ethnographic analysis from longitudinal traditional and digital ethnography in Asia Pacific markets between 2008 and 2024, below I offer a framework of elements to guide the appraisal of both social media cultures. We will briefly survey 10 key elements: Definition, anchor, primary dependant, visibility, relationality, production, value, monetisation model, maintenance, and tension (see Table 5).

Where Influencers can be defined as everyday individuals who publicise their 'privacy' to commodify their lifestyles,[33] Creators are platform users who create 'content' to relate to the lifestyles of their audience. As such, Influencers are anchored on cultivating a persona who is primarily dependent on the interest from their online community, while Creators are anchored on producing content that is primarily dependent on the interface of platforms. For Influencers, visibility is primarily affective, and they strive to maintain relationality with followers primarily through analogue forms of para-sociality; for Creators, visibility is primarily algorithmic and they strive to maintain relationality with viewers primarily through automated forms of engagement. The production by

Table 5. Key Distinctions Between 'Influencer Culture' and 'Creator Culture'. Table by Author.

Element	Influencer	Creator
Definition	Everyday individuals + Publicise 'privacy' + Commodify lifestyles	Platform users + Create 'content' + Relatable lifestyles
Anchor	Persona	Content
Primary dependant	Online community	Platform
Visibility	Affective	Algorithmic
Relationality	Parasociality + Analogue	Engagement + Automation
Production	Coherence + Self-branding	Transience + Responsiveness
Value	Reputation + Trust	Visibility + Entertainment
Monetisation model	Advertorials + Sponsorship	Platform payouts + Affiliation
Vulnerability	Call-out/cancel cultures	(De)influencing

Influencers has thus far focused on coherence and an innate self-branding, whereas for Creators this has focused on transience based on ever-changing trends and an innate responsiveness to norms and the market. The resulting implications are that Influencers become valuable for their reputation and pedal in trust among their followers; their monetisation model focuses on personal advertorials and sponsorship marketing. However, Creators become valuable for their visibility and peddle in entertainment among their viewers; their monetisation model focuses on systemic platform payouts and affiliate marketing. Finally, in the age of late-stage capitalism and a climate of justice awareness, Influencers are most vulnerable to call-out and cancel cultures as they are sought for their leadership and authenticity, whereas Creators are most vulnerable to accusations of becoming overly-elevated and no longer relatable if they appear to veer to close into self-branded commercial territory.

CREATOR CULTURE IN THE AGE OF TIKTOK

Although the term 'creator' predates TikTok and was most prominently used among YouTubers,[34] TikTok has invigorated pedestrian understandings of creator culture, mainstreamed knowledge of the tools for content creation, and broadened access to the promises and potentials of creator culture in unprecedented ways. Whereas we have reviewed the evolution of sociocultural norms in Influencer culture in the 2010s (see above), here we briefly consider whether creator cultures on TikTok have followed these pathways or disrupted them in the 2020s.

Where Influencer culture was progressing from curation to co-presence, Creator culture on TikTok saw the twin rise of both elements through different features. The algorithmically curated delivery of content on TikTok's For You Page does not usually follow chronology, and posts that are decontextualised from temporality can be constantly circulated across the FYPs of users. While curation work is still occurring, on TikTok it is less guided by the creator and almost entirely led by the platform. TikTok Live has facilitated the mainstreaming of livestreaming on mobile, which enhanced co-presence especially through interactive role-playing via Non-Player

Characters (NPC) streamers,[35] virtual gifting[36] and live shopping[37] (see also 'Digital begging' below).

Where Influencer culture was progressing from aspiration to relatability, and from master status to persona play, Creator culture on TikTok boosted these shifts in its embrace of 'demotic'[38] content, visibility, and celebrity, and focused on the vernacular, the colloquial, and the ordinary. Among my interviewees, luxury Influencers from the high fashion genre on blogs and Instagram tell me that their early pivot to TikTok necessitated a brand new parsing of class. While they were once able to unabashedly flaunt their designer wares in aesthetically framed Instagram photoshoots at iconic landmarks and in exotic locations around the world, the community norms on TikTok dictated that they needed to 'come down to earth' and cultivate interest through more intimate modes of communication.

To illustrate this, I share a snippet from my fieldwork: One high fashion Influencer recounts that their first foray into TikTok was in early-2019 where they would post short videos of themselves getting dressed and conspicuously flash their designer wears in 'get ready with me' posts. They report that while there was initial growth in their follower base, this quickly stalled and comments sections of their posts often called them out for being 'a show-off', 'too atas' (a Malay colloquial term; lit. trans. 'too high'; connotation 'too high class or high maintenance'), or 'out of touch'. This was during the era of TikTok where Gen Zs were the strongest user base and used the platform to advocate for forms of social justice (see Chapter 3). Shortly after, pandemic culture on TikTok saw the proliferation of memes in 2020,[39] and they found success in creating skits that caricatured their 'first-world problems' of not being able to physically shop in luxury stores, nor flaunt their new wares in public during periods of self-isolation, nor 'grab breakfast in Paris and dinner in Japan'.

The plethora of meme templates that was burgeoning in vernacular TikTok culture also facilitated their participation on the platform, and they became prominent for using their designer goods as props. In the post-pandemic period from 2022 onwards, luxury content appeared to have found its footing and niche in vernacular TikTok culture. A casual scroll through this Influencer's TikTok feeds reveals that they have returned to their staple 'Get Ready With Me videos' that are now more personal as the dress-up is accompanied by personal life updates in dialogue with their viewers. They have also delved into TikTok vlogs where they talk viewers through how to acquire exclusive luxury goods around the world, how to spot imitations or how to hunt down specific vintage models. In other words, like many other luxury Influencers who have expanded their repertoire to include TikTok, these Influencers parse aspirational consumption as accessible by demystifying viewer curiosity about their lifestyle and spending habits but do not actually democratise the process.

Finally, where Influencer culture was progressing from endorsements to testimonials, and from engagement to reputation, Creator culture on TikTok seemed to focus on the reverse. Rather than rely on testimonial content, many TikTok creators tended to produce entertainment content to keep viewers watching, in the hopes that they might be curious enough to query the products displayed throughout their videos, whether explicitly or implicitly. The most popular of these are creators who film pantry or fridge restocks, or vlog home organisation and decoration tips, and who direct viewers to their TikTok bios that bear a link to their Amazon storefront or similar to earn revenue through affiliate marketing. In a very saturated TikTok economy, it is challenging for creators to stand out unless they have a strong visual and brand identity in their genre (see 'Creator genres' below). As such, most creators on TikTok tend to focus on generating engagements rather than the more arduous and lengthy pathway to solidifying a reputation, and the result is that creator culture on TikTok can sometimes depressingly focus on pure visibility (see 'Absurdist gimmicks' below).

CREATOR LABOUR

Before diving into the taxonomy of the creator genres on TikTok, it is important to note that the work undertaken by these creators are driven by varying motivations. Some creators aim to leverage on their TikTok fame for professional careers off-platform; some creators strive to grow their visibility in the hopes of cashing out via in-app rewards programmes; some creators work to foster a sense of community; and still some other users are merely accidental creators who have chanced into providing content for a willing audience. Across the variety of creator labour spans a variety of intentions. Academic scholarship has taken seriously the forms of labour undertaken by workers like TikTok creators and their predecessors, and this section takes a brief detour to review some of these key concepts.

The Nature of Creator Labour

The first group of concepts can be applied to the nature of creator labour on digital platforms. Creators are broadly engaged in *digital labour* as they are workers 'within the digital media industry' including unpaid 'user labour', 'platform-mediated workers' from the gig and creator economies, and 'formal workers' spanning a range of elite positions from content moderators to programmers.[40] Being simultaneously creators and consumers of social media content, they are involved in *co-creative labour,* as 'consumers increasingly participating in the process of making and circulating media content and experiences'.[41] The work they produce is based on *immaterial labour,* or 'labour [that] produces immaterial goods such as a service, a cultural product, knowledge or communication'.[42] Their work is also largely a form of *creative labour* as 'jobs [that are] centred on the activity of symbol-making, which are to be found in large numbers in the cultural industries'.[43] Creators also have a degree of autonomy with their *flexible labour,* which describes 'the arrangement of one's work that is not fixed, particularly regarding the work location and schedule'.[44]

The Condition of Creator Labour

The second group of concepts can be applied to the conditions of creator labour as they are beholden to the structure and organisation of social media platforms. Despite the allure of flexibility, the reality is that creators are a subset within the larger phenomenon of *precarious labour,* where employment is short-term and 'involving greater levels of outsourcing/ subcontracting'.[45] Their success is tied to their understanding, acceptance, and skilful management of platform logics, reiterating the pressure of *algorithmic labour,* where 'the automated implementation of company policies on the behaviors and practices' of gig workers.[46] As creators are subject to the governance by platforms, they are also entangled in *sticky labour* or 'an intensification of surveillance and labour discipline with a declining autonomy and an increasing attachment of the workers to the platform on a collective level'.[44] In other words, despite not being formal 'employees' of the social media platforms on which they work, creators are continually invited to volunteer their *venture labour,* which entails 'the investment of time, energy, human capital, and other personal resources that ordinary employees make in the companies where they work'.[47] Despite these conditions, creators continue to engage in self-improvement to enhance their chance at success, by engaging in *aesthetic labour,* which is 'the supply of embodied capacities and attributes possessed by workers at the point of entry into employment'.[48] Ultimately, they are also engaging in *entrepreneurial labour,* which while seemingly promising via the acculturation of 'cool, creativity, autonomy', actually demands 'self-investment, compulsory networking, portfolio evaluations, international competition, and foreshortened careers'.[49]

The Strategy of Creator Labour

The third group of concepts can be applied to the strategy of creator labour to describe the work they do to foster a strong self-brand and cultivate a community. In spite of the stark realities structuring the conditions of their work, creators are groomed by the structure and culture of the creator industry to perceive that their work is *affective labour,* which creates 'a feeling of ease, well-being, satisfaction, excitement, passion-even a sense of connected-ness or community'.[50] To grow their community of followers, creators must adopt *relational labour* or 'regular, ongoing communication with audiences over time to build social relationships that foster paid work'.[51] This constant communication underscores their *intimacy labour,* comprising the 'commercial, interactive, reciprocal and disclosure' work undertaken to maintain parasocial relations on social media.[33] Yet, as the creator industry is fast growing saturated, creators must maintain *glamour labour,* including 'both the body work to manage appearance in person and the online image work to create and maintain one's "cool" quotient', and a 'demand to be always "on" and seen everywhere'.[52] To avoid becoming targets of online hate or censorship by platforms, most creators end up practising a 'Goldilocks' model of *visibility labour*, which is the 'work enacted to flexibly demonstrate gradients of self-conspicuousness in digital or physical spaces depending on intention or circumstance for favourable ends'.[53]

The Anticipation of Creator Labour

Finally, the fourth group of concepts can be applied to the promise of possibility and potential in the creator industry, in light of the nature of their work, in spite of the condition of their work, as an anticipative outcome of the strategy of their work. Most creators commence working for free as a form of *prospective labour*, 'an established mode of unpaid work' where workers 'have to perform extensive free labour in order to even stand a chance of success'.[54] This points to the underlying rhetoric of *passionate labour*: 'the structural conditions of co-creative work, the subject positions of those doing free labour and the discourses and perspectives they make possible'.[55] In recognition that as the predecessor to the presently mainstream creator industry, the Influencer industry was largely dominated by women, *aspirational labour* describes the 'highly gendered, forward-looking and entrepreneurial enactment of creativity' where usually young women 'hold the promise of social and economic capital' despite a reward system that is 'highly uneven'.[56] This investment is *speculative labour* and unpaid work undertaken outside of formal employment to compete for paid opportunities and as an 'illustration of what future work might entail'.[57] Ultimately, creators buy into the optimism of continuous *hope labour*, 'un- or under-compensated work carried out in the present, often for experience or exposure, in the hope that future employment opportunities may follow'.[58]

CREATOR GENRES ON TIKTOK

In their book reviewing creativity and culture on TikTok, Kaye et al.[59] outline creators as being 'nomads' or 'natives'. Where 'nomads' are TikTok users who are able to draw from prior experience and participation in other short-video platforms, 'natives' have their initial experience and participation in short-video cultures rooted in TikTok. The authors then outline three main communities on TikTok:

1. TikTok-famous: 'individuals featured in viral content on TikTok', usually through 'accidental virality'.[60]

2. Hype houses: 'collaborative houses' from the YouTube and Vine era that are rebranded for TikTok.[61]

3. Niche communities: Networks that are 'partially constituted by familiar features, such as hashtags or specific challenges... [or] vague amalgamations or creators, content, and viewers'.[62]

In evaluating the success of a community of TikTok creators known as 'JazzTok', Kaye et al.[63] further outline three features of TikTok musicians:

1. The 'famous by accident' who become famous when their audio tracks become viral on TikTok.

2. 'Professional artists at an early stage in their career' who introduce music to TikTok audiences with the hopes of growing their career.

3. 'The well-established pop star[s]', who build and maintain their brand with fans on TikTok.

Drawing on longitudinal digital ethnography, this section
delves deeper into creator genres on TikTok to outline the
main categories that have emerged. The key qualities of their
practice are outlined below (see Table 6).

**Table 6. A Summary of TikTok Creator Genres and Their
Main Practice. Table by Author.**

Creator Genre	Practice
TikTok talents	Artists and performers who establish their reputation and fame through displaying their skill on TikTok
Creator collectives	Clusters of users who usually live and work together and self-brand as a closed pod of frequent collaborators
Reactors	Personas who ricochet off original content from other users by responding in a consistent but exaggerated demeanour to entertain
POV actors	Caricatures who imitate and exaggerate how stereotypical figures would respond in imaginary scenarios for comedic effect and/or social commentary
Role-players	Characters who assume a consistent repertoire of acting styles and qualities that are coherent to their online personality
Viral stars	Instantaneous (but potentially short-lived) internet celebrities who (unwittingly) become memorable for their appearance in viral contents
Absurdist gimmicks	Users who perform shocking, contrived or inappropriate stunts to attract (usually transient) attention and publicity
Cross-platform curators	Editors who archive, contextualise, and cross-post contents originating from other platforms for viewers who are otherwise unfamiliar with these trends

TikTok Talents

TikTok talents are artists and performers who establish their reputation and fame through displaying their skill on TikTok. Perhaps the most prominent example is Filipino-American singer Denarie Bautista Taylor, better known as @bella-poarch, who swiftly rose to fame via her infamous 'head bop' videos where she would lip-sync to music accompanied by exaggerated facial expressions in zoomed-in angles.[64] In Australia, then-teenager @sarahmagusara rose to fame in 2019 through her dance videos featuring her pregnant belly (see Fig. 35). Dancers, especially young Black American teens, are popular TikTok talents although they have often been denied attribution and credit for their choreography work.[65] Some dancers have even parlayed their TikTok fame into reality TV series or docuseries.[66] Some actors and musicians have leveraged on their TikTok fame to enter Broadway[67] while some musicians and singers have been scouted by recording companies[59] or have been able to sell their audio memes as soundtracks. A prominent example of the latter is the viral success of an audio meme 'I'm an account' by TikTok creator and actor Rocky Paterra aka @rockysroad,[68] who shortly after announced the sale of his soundtrack on iTunes (see Fig. 36).

Creator Collectives

Creator collectives are clusters of users who usually live and work together and self-brand as a closed pod of frequent collaborators. While there are now TikTok creator collectives around the world, the original is Hype House featuring a group of LA-based young adults. Their prominence as a group landed them a reality TV series,[69] which shed light on some of their struggles with fame and co-living. The overt Whiteness of the

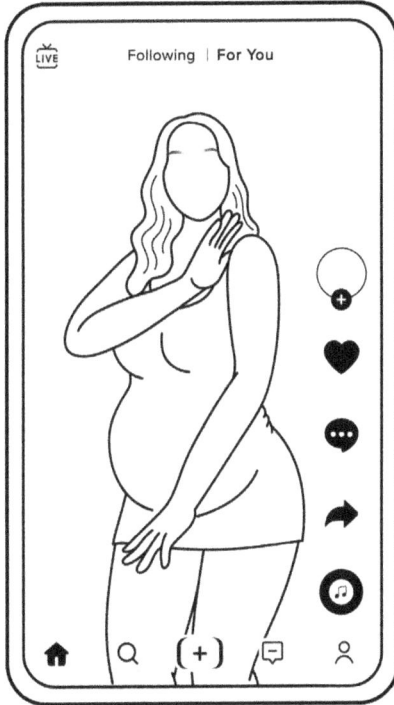

Fig. 35. Artist's Impression of a Typical TikTok by @sarahmagusara When She Was Pregnant With Her First Child. Image Commissioned by and Copyrighted to Crystal Abidin. Art Provided by Ardine Keyla.

first cohorts of TikTok creator collectives has been critiqued for tacitly reinforcing cultural appropriation, oppression, and racism.[65] Recently, a Netflix documentary 'Dancing For The Devil: The 7M TikTok Cult' investigated a TikTok creator collective of young Americans who were allegedly embroiled in a Christian cult and subject to exploitative working conditions.[70] Outside of the entertainment industry, academic scholarship has investigated the emergence of 'political Hype Houses' among Conservatives and Republicans in the United States.[71]

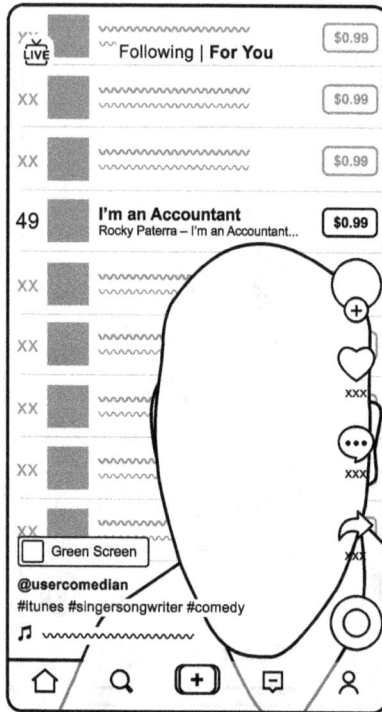

Fig. 36. Artist's Impression of the TikTok Post by @rockysroad Announcing the Sale of His Audio Soundtrack on iTunes. Image Commissioned by and Copyrighted to Crystal Abidin. Art Provided by Phoebe Tan.

Reactors

Reactors are personas who ricochet off original content from other users by responding in a consistent but exaggerated demeanour to entertain. There are many subgenres of reactors on TikTok who may focus on performing specific expressions (e.g. bewilderment, anger), representing a specific demographic (e.g. middle-aged women, Black men), representing a specific community or subculture (e.g. K-pop fans, goths) or speaking to a specific category of content (e.g. home décor, relationship management), among others. In the first subgenre of expression reactors, three of the most recognisable creators are @khaby.lame who stiches silly or pointless life hack videos with a deadpan face and hands pointing to his own solution (see Fig. 37); @why_guy_ who stitches confusing videos with a face of bewilderment marked by his signature curved eyebrows (see Fig. 38) and @angryreactions who stitches a variety of videos from uplifting to provocative content with his 'default' angry scrunched nose (see Fig. 39).

Fig. 37. Artist's Impression of @khaby.lame. Image Commissioned by and Copyrighted to Crystal Abidin. Art Provided by Ardine Keyla.

Fig. 38. Artist's Impression of @why_guy_. Image Commissioned by and Copyrighted to Crystal Abidin. Art Provided by Ardine Keyla.

POV Actors

POV actors are caricatures who imitate and exaggerate how stereotypical figures would respond in imaginary scenarios for comedic effect and/or social commentary. In Singapore, a popular POV actor on TikTok is @hibye.lovez also known as Amandy, who maintains several playlists of POVs of 'toxic' characters.[72] These include 'toxic guy' who resorts to sexist and misogynist behaviour to appeal to women; 'work povs'

Fig. 39. Artist's Impression of @angryreactions. Image Commissioned by and Copyrighted to Crystal Abidin. Art Provided by Ardine Keyla.

featuring bosses and colleagues who overstep their boundaries and who push for unhealthy work–life balance and 'toxic friend' featuring a variety of people who are manipulative and awful towards their peers. The success of @hibye.lovez's POV acting is evident across her collection of posts. Frequent sentiments from followers include 'this is not real' to remind themselves that despite her convincing acting, the infuriating character is merely acting out a skit; and 'it me' or 'seen' to indicate that the followers have experienced the exact toxic scenario that is being acted out.

Role-Play Characters

Role-play characters are users who assume a consistent repertoire of acting styles and qualities that are coherent to their online personality. These can include creators who are playing exaggerated versions of themselves (e.g. an elder exaggerating their clumsiness or detachment from social media trends); creators who are camping up the stereotypes usually associated with their appearance (e.g. a young blonde woman presenting as a clueless Barbie); creators who are parodying celebrities and public figures (e.g. a pair of siblings imitating the mannerisms of the Kardashian-Jenner sisters) or creators who are fully immersed in live action role-playing (LARP) games drawing from characters inspired by fantasy worlds or ones original to TikTok-native fantasy spaces (e.g. an inn-keeper serving travellers who are resting from a journey after fighting mythical creatures). A particularly wholesome example is @YourKoreanDad, who has been described as a 'global parenting phenomenon'.[73] His role-play character assumes the figure of a caring dad who checks in on your well-being, gives you pep talks, and provides a warm and assuring presence. The comments section across his videos always feature words of gratitude from followers who appreciate that his character helps fill the gap of their 'absent, distant, or deceased parents'.[73] It is also important to note that as a Korean–American man, @YourKoreanDad's content responds to a larger discourse of an older generation of Asian parents who have been very harsh on their children, demanding high expectations while withholding affection; this is best encapsulated by the vintage macros meme 'High Expectations Asian Father'.[74] As such, his warmth and wisdom has stood in as a surrogate for many millennial and Gen Z users on TikTok who find his character and his contents to be redemptive and healing.

Viral Stars

Viral stars are instantaneous (but potentially short lived) internet celebrities who (unwittingly) become memorable for their appearance in viral contents. In prior work,[75] I have noted that viral stars can be 'accidental and transient' forms of online celebrity, who while potentially able to 'cash in' on their instant fame at times can also be humiliated and exploited by viewers and the media at other times. Some viral stars can also progress to becoming the 'faces of memes', whose viral clip and likeness 'become memorialized solely for the comedic value of the meme'.[76] A recurring instance of viral stars on TikTok that is particularly fruitful is when users share a clip of an anonymous performance – usually singing, dancing, and similar performing arts – that they have found to be outstanding, and the post goes viral on TikTok as users collectively search for the original performer. These are usually networked efforts to locate the performer to acknowledge them by name, attribute the viral post to them, and garner fan support for their talents. The cherry on the cake is when users successfully track down the performer or if the performer reveals themselves after chancing upon the viral search (see Fig. 40). In my longitudinal digital ethnography, I also discovered several instances of viral stars who are likely to be unaware of their TikTok fame. One comedic example is a very short TikTok clip that features a zoomed-in snippet of an elderly man's face that then cuts to a shot of his feet and then abruptly ends (see Fig. 41). In this 'elderly glitch' clip, the scenario appears to be of an elderly man who was toggling between the front- and back-facing camera lens on his phone and who had most likely accidently uploaded a video of themselves trying to navigate the TikTok interface. In the comments section, users were complimenting his selfie video skills, admiring his footwear,

Fig. 40. Artist's Impression of a TikToker Stitching a Viral Post to Reveal That She is the Person of Interest. Image Commissioned by and Copyrighted to Crystal Abidin. Art Provided by Ardine Keyla.

self-declaring that they were his fans, and cracking jokes about 'trending him' so a young person in his milieu would learn of his viral mishap and teach him to use TikTok properly.

Absurdist Gimmicks

Absurdist gimmicks are users who perform shocking, contrived or inappropriate stunts to attract (usually transient) attention and publicity. Two of the most popular subgenres of absurdist gimmicks are 'time-wasters' and 'dangerous activities'. 'Time-wasters' are videos featuring a creator engaging in overly complicated actions or routines that are ultimately futile or

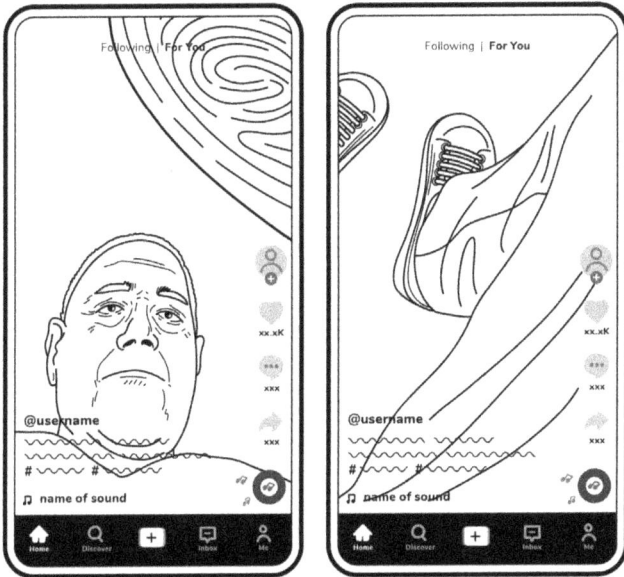

Fig. 41. Artist's Impression of the 'Elderly Glitch' Viral TikTok. Image Commissioned by and Copyrighted to Crystal Abidin. Art Provided by River Juno.

meaningless. Many accounts on TikTok are dedicated to such gimmicks. Examples include a creator in the setting of a professional-looking culinary tutorial who adds cups and cups of various ingredients into a mixing bowl only to discard it all into a bin or a creator who presents the appearance of struggling with a very simple task such as uncapping a pen. A cousin of 'time-wasters' is 'parody life hack videos' where 'creators perform a simple task in a ridiculous and impractical manner'.[77] 'Dangerous activities' are videos where creators appear to be engaging in hazardous or violent behaviour. Such stunts emerge as the newest viral trend every couple of weeks and often make news headlines as dangerous 'TikTok challenges'. Examples include users holding jellyfish with their bare hands, licking public toilets, and pranking strangers in public. In response to the uptick in absurdist gimmicks, TikTok has updated its Community Guidelines regarding content that will be removed, restricted, or made ineligible for the For You Feed[78]; regarding creator best practice for creating 'high-quality content'[79]; and regarding advertising policies on 'violence and dangerous activities'.[80]

Cross-Platform Curators

Cross-platform curators are editors who archive, con-textualise, and cross-post contents originating from other platforms for viewers who are otherwise unfamiliar with these trends. As I note in prior work,[81] the most common platform that is pilfered for cross-posting on TikTok appears to be Douyin. In July 2020, one of the milestone viral trends on TikTok was the popularity of 'Chinese TikTok', where users would collate and repost Douyin videos on their TikTok accounts, provide 'digital tours' of Douyin, sound out and replicate the latest trends from Douyin on TikTok, and even venture out to start their own Douyin accounts through the use of Virtual Private Network (VPN). One of the iconic trends during this period was TikTok's fascination over street fashion videos in China, also hashtagged as '#chinesestreetfashion', which comprised videos of locals strutting down boulevards and flaunting their outfits in slow motion. This trend was primarily housed in the audio meme 'Street Fashion Game – JVLES', which samples an instrumental segment from JVLA's 'Such a Whore (Stellular Remix)'. TikTokers like @eromei (Fig. 42a) and @christinazhuu (Fig. 42b) were among the most active of users to compile and repost Chinese street fashion videos and quickly accumulated new followers for their work as cultural mediators. In the next wave,

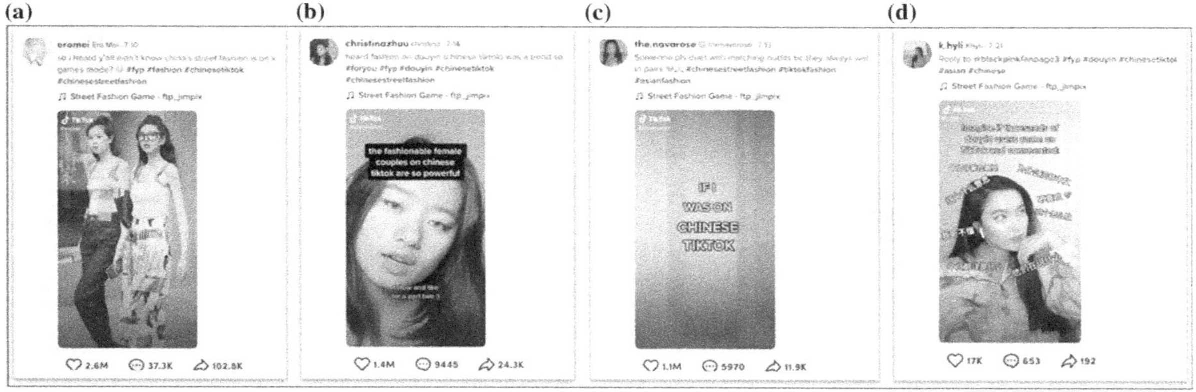

Fig. 42. (L–R): (a) 'So I Heard y'all…' (@eromei 2020); (b) 'Heard Fashion on Douyin…' (@christinazhuu 2020); (c) 'Someone pls Duet With…' (@the.navarose 2020); (d) 'Reply to @blackpinkfanpage3…' (@k. hyli 2020); Screengrab by the Author.

prominent fashion TikTokers like @the.navarose would replicate and produce their own Chinese street fashion (Fig. 42c) in 'If I was on Chinese TikTok' POV videos. At the peak of this trend, TikTokers were posting tutorials on how to use VPN to access Douyin, issuing brief translation guides for how to access Douyin, and offering to seek out prolific Douyin users that TikTokers could 'stalk'. However, within a week there was swift backlash over the alleged 'colonisation' of Douyin by TikTok users due to the influx of English-language comment spam on Douyin videos demanding sub-titles for non-Chinese speakers or complaining about how difficult it was for them to navigate the Douyin interface. Many TikTokers, especially those who were Chinese diaspora like @k.hyli (Fig. 42d), were quick to point out that the sud-den interest in and infiltration of Douyin by TikTokers was overwhelming, disrespectful, and at times even orientalising. One of the general sentiments among TikTokers who were pushing back against the 'colonisation' of Douyin called for each user group to keep to their own apps, and if really necessary, to quietly observe the other app within interfering with the cultural and user norms already established in either space.

CASE STUDY: DIGITAL BEGGING

'Creator business models' describe 'creator strategies for generating revenues from platform labour'.[82] Kaye et al.'s review[83] offers that TikTok creators can earn an income in three main ways: (1) Gifts, coins, and diamonds; (2) Influencer sponsorships and (3) The TikTok Creator Fund. At the time of writing, there are multiple opportunities for monetisation on TikTok. In an early mapping of internet celebrity on TikTok, I noted that in the first month since the initial launch of the TikTok Creator Fund in 2020, some creators were already 'pleading with fellow users for "interacts" in order that they may "cash out" with TikTok to support urgent financial needs, ranging from medical support to escaping instances of domestic violence'.[84] This type of practice was more eloquently parsed by Maris et al.[85] as 'algorithmic mutual aid', demonstrating 'efforts by platform communities to re(direct) value they create on-platform to care for one another'. At the tumultuous intersection of a plethora of monetisation opportunities on TikTok and war and conflict across several nations, an extreme instance of algorithmic mutual aid that has emerged on TikTok Live is digital begging. This section presents a brief case study on the phenomenon.

TikTok Live is a feature that allows users who are above 16-years-old and who have at least 1,000 followers to live-stream; viewers who are above 18-years-old are able to purchase virtual gifts that can be gifted to creators during livestreams. Streamers who accrue sufficient virtual gifts are able to 'cash out' and receive some revenue from their streams.[86] In late-2022, a string of news reports highlighted the use of the TikTok Live feature for 'digital begging'. These were livestreams featuring displaced families and asylum-seekers in Syrian camps, in postures of pleading such as kneeling with palms up or pressed together, literally calling upon viewers to make donations through the virtual gift feature on TikTok.[86,87]

A BBC news investigation found that while livestreams were earning up to GBP900 an hour, the TikTok platform took 'up to 70% of the proceeds'.[87] In some Syrian camps, digital begging was reportedly mediated by 'TikTok middlemen' who provided the equipment for families to livestream and who were working with 'agencies affiliated to TikTok'.[87] While the set-up may appear as a creative and viable form of content creation for these families to earn an income through charity and philanthropy, the comments section of such livestream were conflicting.

One stream of discourse encouraged fellow viewers to use the virtual gift feature generously, with some prominent Tik-Tok creators rallying their own followers to make donations. But the conversation also included accusations that these predominantly White TikTok creators were exercising a 'saviour complex' in wanting to 'save' the war-torn families.

Another stream of discourse saw viewers expressing great discomfort over the scenes, accusing TikTok for facilitating 'pity porn' by allowing the families to livestream themselves in humiliating and compromising circumstances without offering them tangible aid as a multi-billion corporation. Conversations in the comments section shared the stance of the BBC news report,[87] at once condemning TikTok for exploiting the families 'for engagement' and commanding the platform to ensure that all 'proceeds' from the virtual gifts were directed to the families in need.

Still another stream of discourse featured cynical viewers who would dissect every element of the stream – such as the backdrop, the attire worn by the beggars, their posture, and even the range of emotion allegedly conveyed through their facial expressions – and accuse the set-up of being staged. Users in the comments section would also point out that the digital beggars usually included vulnerable children who would stream for hours.[87]

The use of the TikTok to solicit charity is not new. Throughout 2017 to 2019, international news reports highlighted the rise of 'beg-packers'[88,89] or backpackers who were resorting to bagging on the streets to support their travels. Beg-packers tend to be White young people soliciting charity in Southeast Asian nations like Hong Kong, Thailand, and Singapore.[89] While it has been observed that beg-packers use crowdfunding sites like Indiegogo and Kickstarter to finance their travels,[89] beg-packers also turned to TikTok Live for crowdfunding when the feature was released in 2019. In our digital ethnography of uses of TikTok during the pandemic,[39] my collaborators and I observed groups of TikTok users who were selling homemade craft – such as jewellery, knitting, and small art pieces – as a means to 'survive' the lockdown.[84] TikTok viewers have also demonstrated generosity to creators who post vlogs about living out of a car while homeless, racking in revenue through viral views and donations.[90,91]

In each of these instances, fieldnotes from my longitudinal digital ethnography indicate that the beg-packers, pandemic crafters, and car-dwellers tended to be received by viewers as creators. Comment sections feature Q&As, requests for more insight into the personal lives of these creators, and even recommend specific ideas for their TikTok vlogs – for instance, many viewers were keen to know how car-dwellers showered, how pandemic crafters budgeted for groceries or which destinations beg-packers were aiming for next. While only some comments refer to their gifting as 'donations' or 'charity', the mainstream sentiment tended to frame the monetary contributions as 'crowd-sourcing', 'fundraising' or simply 'support'. Yet, the visceral response to Syrian families requesting for similar aid on TikTok Live has been framed in the discourse as mere 'begging', pointing to racist and orientalist overtones.

In 2023, the news reported on similar instances of TikTok Live begging undertaken by elderly women across Indonesia, who staged themselves in humiliating scenarios – such as taking 'mud baths' and 'pouring dirty river water' over their bodies – in exchange for virtual gifts.[93] The emerging scholarship on the topic by local scholars have pointed to both the possible 'exploitation of older adults',[94] their potential to 'attract empathy'[95] and to use TikTok as an 'online fundraising platform'.[95]

CONCLUSION

This chapter has focused on the conditions that have facilitated the rise of creator culture and genres on TikTok.
Commencing with a review of the evolution of sociocultural
norms in Influencer culture at large, we considered a framework for how Influencer culture was pivoting to Creator
culture and the resulting consequences on both producers and
consumers of social media content. The chapter assessed the
iteration of creator culture on TikTok and surmised some key
concepts in the scholarship that speak to the nature, condition, strategy, and anticipation of creator labour. Turning to
empirical data, I outlined some of the most prominent creator
genres on TikTok and considered a contentious case study on
digital begging that sits at the uncomfortable intersection of
philanthropy, monetisation, and exploitation. Following in
this vein of monetisation, the final chapter considers small
businesses and marketplace cultures on TikTok.

5

SMALL BUSINESSES AND MARKETPLACE CULTURES

In Chapter 3, we delved into the social and cultural capital generated by various TikTokers who extensively engage and experiment with the memes. In Chapter 4, we focused on a typology of TikTok creators and their content genres to understand how they engaged in various labours to produce the capital underscoring their practice. In this Chapter, we consider capital in the literal sense, looking into how small businesses and marketplace cultures on TikTok generate income.

PLATFORMED COMMERCE

In prior work, I studied how Influencers on the (then) photo-app Instagram were among the first users to adapt the platform for commercial uses, such as posting sponsored contents and advertorials, even ahead of the platform's formal introduction of creator partnerships and brand advertising features. I had also studied instances of vernacular commerce on the blog platform Tumblr, where users would curate photographs and links from small businesses to promote them to networks of users for a small fee, overtly post links to their online shop fronts or use creative methods to redirect followers to other subscription-only platforms where exclusive contents could be unlocked for a fee. These also took place outside of the formal modes of platform-directed advertising by Tumblr. However, TikTok presents a departure from these models as commercial opportunities and potentials for users have been built into the platform from its very onset through various features and campaigns.

TikTok has been identified as a suitable platform for businesses with 'low visibility and budget', given that its algorithmically-driven visibility 'allows creators to reach an audience beyond their followers'.[1] For brands, advertising strategy on TikTok departs from traditional modes of publicity on websites or older social media platforms like Facebook as the TikTok users seek branded contents that are entertaining and that allow them to feel a degree of closeness and proximity with the brand.[1] It is for this reason that many brand accounts on TikTok usually adopt the tone of 'a young intern', who is up-to-date and aligned with the frontiers of social media pop cultures and able to articulate timely trends in creative ways that bring attention to the brand's account rather than outrightly promoting their products and services per se. This points to the importance of prioritising a 'gratification of connection with their audience, entertainment and information provision needs' and a 'gratification of creativity and spontaneity needs',[2] where special attention is paid to fostering and maintaining brand–customer relationships. However, TikTok is also a popular avenue for small businesses.

Since its inception, each major update of TikTok's interface has brought its features in closer alignment to the offerings from sister platform Douyin, which boasts a thriving e-commerce ecology. The most important of these features is the seamlessly integrated payment system that allows users to complete the advertising to purchase cycle entirely within the app itself. In 2022, TikTok introduced features integrated with major e-commerce platform Shopify and launched its TikTok Live features[3] to facilitate this streamlined in-app consumer experience, fostering consumer awareness, boosting traffic, and enhancing sales for small businesses on TikTok through its iconic 'the creation and sharing of low-cost videos'.[4]

Another important commercial feature on TikTok is the TikTok Shop, which is especially popular in local markets. Scholars have identified how markets that still rely on word-of-mouth marketing, low-fi technologies or community-based advertising like WhatsApp group chats have taken up the TikTok Shop feature especially well; while this is an occurrence through Southeast Asia, the scholarship has identified instances where TikTok Shop is an especially important lifeline for small businesses in countries like Indonesia, where home-based businesses rely almost entirely on online sales while based in villages or the more rural areas.[5] As these are also populations of users who largely depend on mobile phones as their primary device, as opposed to the more sophisticated set-ups comprising laptops and desktops, the mobile-friendly, and indeed the mobile-only, interface of TikTok Shop has been embraced by small businesses and consumers alike.

So integral are small businesses to the economy of TikTok that the platform launched an annual TikTok Ad Awards for this specific group of merchants. In 2024, Brett Armstrong – general manager of global business solutions for the Australia and New Zealand market for TikTok – announced TikTok's 'Greatest Small Business Award' to celebrate 'the 350,000 small businesses of all shapes and sizes on TikTok that are making a significant impact through paid advertising'.[6] In his press release, Armstrong underscores how small businesses are some of the most important partners for TikTok and that they 'continue to push the boundaries of creativity, delivering outstanding campaigns'.[6] TikTok has also since launched various initiatives like the 'TikTok SME campaign' and 'TikTok means business' campaign in the UK market where 'almost half of TikTok users… purchas[e] a product or service seen on the platform'.[7] In Canada, TikTok launched the 'TikTok SmallBiz Pop-Up' to celebrate small businesses in the country and to acknowledge the platform's growing importance as a 'launchpad for emerging and established brands'.[8] In these various press releases and initiatives, the corporate discourse continues to emphasise that small businesses benefit the most from TikTok as the format of short videos, together with the options provided through features like TikTok Live and TikTok Shop, 'enables entrepreneurs to showcase their products authentically, without the need for polish or filters'.[8]

Despite the promises of TikTok's integrated features for small businesses, it is important to remember that these options are only unlocked for businesses who are officially partnered with TikTok or officially onboarded on the app as a business account. In the opening of this Chapter, I noted how commercial activities on the likes of Instagram and Tumblr often proliferate outside of the formal commercial features afforded by the app. It is for this reason that businesses find not just a *low* cost to entry, but a *no* cost to entry as they are able to publicise their businesses on such platforms for free – all they have to do is to sign up for a free account on the platforms, and pursue their word-of-mouth marketing. However, fieldnotes from my digital ethnography in the infancy of TikTok dating back to 2018/2019 already point to businesses speculating that posts overtly promoting products and services or posts that contain links that overtly redirect users to other subscription-only or e-commerce platforms were shadowbanned or deranked on the FYP (see Chapter 3). In other words, promotional contents are gatekept on TikTok, and it is difficult to simply instigate a free hashtag publicity campaign or viral trend with overtly commercial ends. Instead, TikTok For Businesses invites brands to create and register their 'advertiser accounts' through which ads can be placed on the platform and advertorials can be taken on by TikTok creators through formal channels.

As such, small businesses who do want to advertise on TikTok without investing in the formal 'advertiser accounts' have to do so through creative means that focus the narration on the creator's lifestyle and their craft rather than appear 'hardsell' or overly commercial in the first instance. It is in this spirit that the rest of this Chapter considers the visual-narrative 'templates' adopted by small businesses on TikTok and some of their shared ethos and issues. We then delve into three case studies of popular TikTok trends that have been adapted to constitute or challenge commercial contents and commercialism on the platform: Morning routines, TikTok hauls, and De-influencing and Underconsumption core.

SMALL BUSINESS 'TEMPLATES'

Many of the small businesses on TikTok engage in the small-batch, hand-crafted highly personalised creation and consumption of artisanal goods, making TikTok a digital flea market of sorts. Popular goods include accessories like hair adornments and press-on nails, fashion items like hand sewn clothes and jewellery, paper goods like stickers and notebooks, art like paintings and pottery, toys like plushies and plastic figurines, novelty items like slime and glitter, and miscellaneous snacks and food items.

Production/Creation Process

Businesses who peddle hand-made items tend to showcase the production and creation process of their goods. Many of such TikToks focus on either the creation of raw materials, such as curing clay or blowing glass to make beads for jewellery, or the curation of these products, such as travelling to markets or overseas destinations to source for fabrics or paint. If these handicrafts do not involve a very high level of technical skill, such as the assembling of beads into necklaces, the small businesses introduce elements into the video that subtly underscore their professionalism: Sanitising all surfaces and tools before use; using hand sanitiser then wearing gloves before touching any objects; deploying tools like tweezers and magnifying glass stands to improve the precision of their craft (see Fig. 43); organising their materials and tools neatly into impressively upkept compartments; and showcasing their work environment such as a dedicated bedroom or table in a room designated just for their craft work. Despite being home based businesses, all of these elements serve to emphasise the professionalism of the small businesses and to boost confidence that great care has been taken in producing the handicraft that consumers are being encouraged to purchase.

For products that require technical knowledge, TikToks tend to focus on the skill and labour that goes into making the item. Here, the effort and time invested may be underscored through the use of creative narrative formats including time lapse snippets, before and after juxtapositions, or multi-parted TikToks that focus on the minutiae in each stage of production. A popular example of the last narration, which takes the form of a chronological diary, is when pottery makers curate a series of TikTok videos focused on the forming, sculpting, painting, glazing, firing, and polishing of their pieces, respectively. Unlike the pristine and clean environment of the small

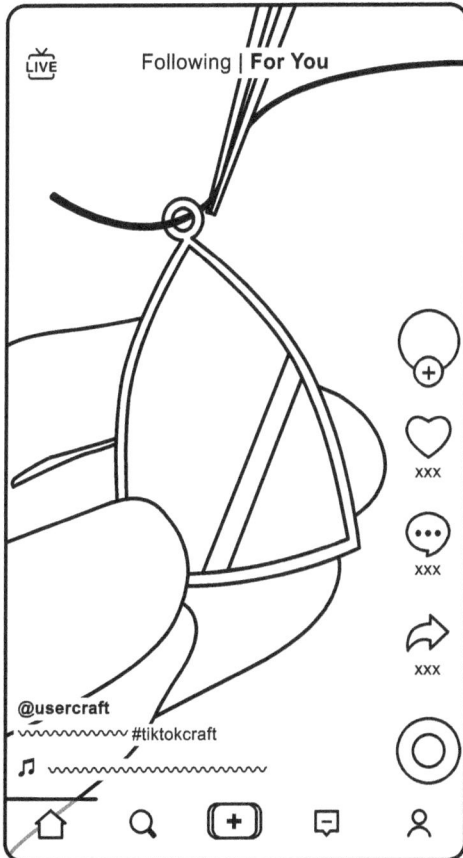

Fig. 43. Artist's Impression of a Small Business Showcasing the Production of Craft in a TikTok Post. Image Commissioned by and Copyrighted to Crystal Abidin. Art Provided by Phoebe Tan.

businesses aiming to elevate their mundane craft with professionalism, the TikToks focused on the expertise and labour of the creators is more likely to reveal behind-the-scenes snippets of the messiness of the bedroom or garage to point to the scale of their efforts, the perspiration of the creator signalled through beads of sweat on their foreheads or of t-shirts soaked in the armpit and back areas, and the clean-up process after a piece is completed.

In both instances, the purpose of production and creation TikToks are meant to underscore not just the pecuniary value of the handicraft but also its artisanal value of being made by human hands in the intimate setting of a home that feels effortful and relatable. This is unlike the products mass produced in a mechanised mode or in factory faraway that feels commonplace and blasé.

Packing

Another popular TikTok template spotlights the process of small business packing and packaging orders for customers. The most basic of these videos focus on how small business owners streamline the process of processing orders, revealing their inventory of packing materials, honing their organisational skills, and pointing to the volume of orders they may be receiving for every collection as a mark of success. A subset of small business packing videos also tend to intersect with the genre of Autonomous Sensory Meridian Response (ASMR) contents, with special sonic emphasis on the jingling of metal tools, the bounce of plastic beads, the wispy movements of paper and wrapping being folded, or the tapping sounds of stickers and tape being peeled and adhered to surfaces. In general, packing videos take a leaf out of the book of small art businesses on YouTube, which have long popularised the genre of 'packing bulk order' videos through time lapses. Given the very short runway for a TikTok video, packing videos focus less on such batch-work and more on the highly personalised and customised packaging for individual orders.

In these videos, small business owners usually begin with a narration or on-screen caption that announces an order, like 'pack an order with me', or 'pack order #184 with me', or 'packing an order for [name of customer]'. They generally reveal the order list from the customer, concealing personal details and taking the opportunity to thank them for their support, before displaying all the goods to be wrapped and packed (see Fig. 44). For many customers, witnessing their order being packed enhances the feelings of parasociality they feel with the small business owners, and the experience of personalisation underscores the satisfaction of having purchased from a small business that is intimate in its communication with customers and that takes pride in the smallest of

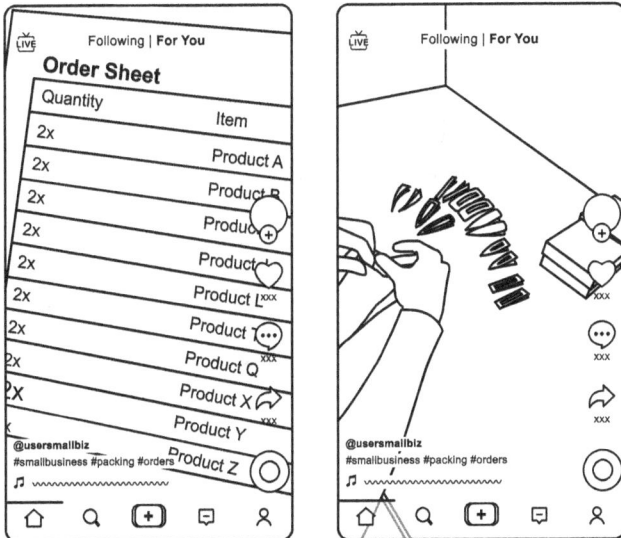

Fig. 44. Artist's Impression of a Small Business Demonstrating the Packing Process for an Order in a TikTok Post. Image Commissioned by and Copyrighted to Crystal Abidin. Art Provided by Phoebe Tan.

details, such as handwritten addresses on the envelopes or handwritten thank you notes on postcards.

To further emphasise their dedication to customers who support small businesses, many owners also showcase the array of freebies that they include in each package, ranging from stickers and postcards to candy and stationery. This underscores the importance of 'shopping small' on TikTok, where customers prize the experience of receiving and opening their parcels rather than simply being content with receiving the actual product purchased. This draws on the psychology of homemade gifts being interpreted as being more sincere, and the long-term cultivation of goodwill from the generosity of small businesses assists in fostering loyal relationships between the customer and the business.

However, for some small businesses that curate rather than create their products, packing videos serve an even more crucial purpose: To deflect from the mass produced nature of their goods and redirect prospective consumer attention to the rebranding, repackaging, and revaluation work undertaken by the small business, this highlighting their curatorial and sourcing efforts. Comments sections sighted in some of these packing videos indicate an appreciation of said efforts: 'I know this I can get this from [name of wholesaler] but I appreciate your dedication and care towards packing each order!'; 'I can get this cheaper [elsewhere online] but your customer service and cute packaging is next level!' Packing videos have become so central to small businesses on TikTok that those that just are starting out will often stage or role-play successful businesses, by simulating the packing of sizeable or bulk orders, while explicitly stating in the text overlay or captions that 'maybe someday [they] will actually get a large order like this'; while they are still on their aspirational journeys towards growing their small businesses, such Tik-Tokers commence their practice of small business narrative templates on TikTok for personal inspiration and also in the hopes that participating in the trend will encourage the platform's algorithm to disseminate their videos on more FYPs.

'Gambling'

TikTok's Community Guidelines explicitly state that TikTok Shops are prohibited from gambling and gamification strategies to boost customer engagement. However, both elements continue to be very present among small businesses on TikTok through a variety of user experiences that introduce an element of chance to the shopping experience. This includes 'scoops' where customers purchase a certain number of portions of items – usually crystals, beads, small capsule toys or candy – which the small business owner then portions out from a giant bucket or tray of goods prior to packaging. A variant of this is dice rolls, capsule draws, and scratch tickets, where customers pay for a certain number of 'turns'. The owner then rolls the dice or draws a capsule or scratches a ticket from their collection, and the number indicated corresponds with a pre-labelled item that the customer has 'won' akin to arcade games. Combined with the template of packing videos, the videos comprise the owners announcing who the customer is, what they have ordered, and the special items that their 'scoops' or 'draws' had 'incidentally' included like rare crystals, expensive beads, exclusive toys or special candies. Lucky dips and blind boxes are also popular customer engagement strategies among small businesses on TikTok, where customers purchase mysteriously packaged parcels only to have the owner unbox them in videos for the big reveal.

Common across these strategies is the sense of anticipation, the allure of speculation, and the thrill of suspense in the lead up to witnessing the actual item they have purchased and what possible 'bonuses', 'rewards' or 'freebies' might be thrown into the mix. Such TikTok videos and livestreams invite viewers to watch on to gauge the range of possible products – and the fleeting opportunities to secure said products – availed by the small business, generating also the experience of co-presence to witness the wins of fellow customers in the shop's community.

SMALL BUSINESS ETHOS AND ISSUES

Underscoring the visual and discursive templates of small business strategies is the embedded messaging of their ethos. This section will consider the strategies of anti-corporation messaging and guilt-tripping that small business owners on TikTok use to instigate interest, loyalty, and sales and the resulting issues of dropshipping and greenwashing exposed by TikTok audiences in their assessments of said businesses.

Anti-Corporation

Small businesses on TikTok often draw on the discourse of 'responsible consumption' and 'anti-brand movements'[9] to promote their wares. The various audio memes that have trended on TikTok to promote small businesses have variously underscored how prospective customers are not just supporting a business owner, but also directly supporting their families and securing their welfare. A popular trend that I noted in my fieldnotes during the course of digital ethnography sees small business owners tallying up their sales for the week, thanking customers for their support, then talking through their domestic 'bills' or 'grocery haul', listing the cost of each item that would sustain their family. An iteration of the trend sees small business owners combining this with 'packing videos', as they hold a parcel to be posted in one hand and a recently purchased grocery item in the other hand, to viscerally underscore how a sale 'out' enabled them to bring a necessary resource 'in' for their families. Common refrains would include 'I made [amount of money] this week, which paid our grocery bill for next week. Thank you, everyone!' and 'Thank you [name of customer]! Your order of [item] paid directly for this [grocery item] that my kids needed for their lunch boxes this week!' This discourse of responsibilisation accentuates the agency of consumers and their decision-making, where every act of choosing to 'shop small' is framed as being disruptive to the status quo, resistive to capitalism, activist in action, and charitable in outcome.

An instance of such anti-corporation discourse is evidenced in a well-written undergraduate Honours Thesis, by Media and Communication student Skyllar Capuno,[10] who studied what they called an 'ethnicised hustle' by Asian American artists and small businesses on TikTok during the time of the pandemic. During this period of economic crisis, Capuno found that TikTok owners of art businesses tended to intentionally draw attention to the 'intersection and collapse' of their personal ethnic-cultural identities and of their professional business owner/entrepreneurship activities. They conveyed their marginalised Asian American status in their artwork and in their marketing efforts to solicit the empathy and sympathy of prospective customers who were called upon to rally around the ethnic community. That is, while Asian American customers were being courted to support 'one of their own', demographically diverse customers were being invited to be reflexive about their ethos of inclusivity by supporting small Asian American businesses during a moment where anti-Asian racism was widespread in the country.

The anti-corporation discourse also proved to be useful for small businesses that peddled in pre-loved, second-hand, thrifted or vintage goods, where the branding invited customers to be generous with blemishes, small defects, and minor inconveniences of shopping small. Yet, many of these small businesses also exhibited some contradictions between their ethos and their actions, as the discussion later in this section raises the issues of waste and greenwashing.

Guilt-Tripping

Guilt-tripping is a staple narrative in small businesses messaging on TikTok. Dozens of audio memes call upon users to 'stop scrolling', 'take a pause', 'think for a moment' and assess whether or not they were willing to donate a few minutes of their time to engage with small business contents and boost the visibility of their marketing efforts, as a form of 'algorithmic mutual aid'.[11] In these instances, small business owners attempt to rally a sense of the commune and of community (see Chapter 2), calling upon the goodwill of fellow TikTokers to generously share their 'free' resource of time. Often, this pleading as a sales tactic goes so far as to position the small business as an 'underdog' to solicit support.

Scholars from the field of business studies tell us that underdog brand *positioning* is when brands willingly 'occupy a state of inferiority in contests and are expected to fail against their powerful competitors' in a bid to 'elicit favourable consumer responses'.[12] Further, an underdog brand *biography* describes when brands tend to spotlight their 'humble origins, lack of resources, and determined struggle against the odds'.[13] This has proven to be effective in increasing purchase intentions and fostering brand loyalty, as the discourse solicits within consumers feel-good sentiments about having facilitated a brand in overcoming an 'external disadvantage' from the start.[13] As such, this underdog *affect* sees consumers' support for businesses grow as they wish to invest in the journey and 'heritage' of the company.[14] The anti-corporation discourse discussed above evidenced this procedural thinking. However, scholars have also cautioned that when consumers prioritise 'quality' of goods over the 'self-indulgence' of activist consumption, top brands tend to be preferred and trusted.[14] It is on this note that we consider the issue of 'dropshipping' among small businesses on TikTok.

Dropshipping

Although many small businesses on TikTok focus on small-batch, handmade products, many shops simply engage in dropshipping wherein business owners engage third-party suppliers to provide pre-produced inventory, which the small businesses then rebrand, repackage or 'private label' – that is, to add one's branding to a product despite it being entirely conceptualised, constructed or manufactured by a wholesaler – for sale. Loyal consumers of genuine small businesses have accused dropship TikTok shops of being incongruous to the community's ethos of being anti-corporation and that the reliance on mass producing factories and warehouses defeats the purpose of 'shopping small'. This rising phenomenon of dropshipping among TikTok shops has negatively impacted the reputation of the businesses, which were previously marketed as being run by small business owners and families who took pride in their craft. It has also resulted in the homogeneity of goods available on TikTok shops, as the business model of dropshipping sees 'similarly-profiled businesses… intensively working on acquiring customers to sell goods delivered by the same distributors'.[15]

TikTok customers have pointed to incidents of receiving poor-quality products, and even knock-offs and counterfeits, when dropshipping manufacturers plagiarise the work of small businesses and mass produce copies at a much lower production cost for other merchants to sell. Such accusations of product plagiarism are rampant among small business TikTok communities, with original owners and artists calling upon prospective customers to report such errant design theft and to boycott these shops and creators, in the absence of formal redress outside the purview of TikTok's Community Guidelines. In fact, tutorials from the official press releases by Shopify – the e-commerce platform in partnership with Tik-Tok – even outline the positives and practices of dropshipping with tutorials like 'How to Dropship With TikTok Shop'.[16]

However, experts interviewed in an academic study point to some degree of effort and skill required by dropshippers, who still ultimately need to 'develop a brand that people recognise and value' and 'create a thematic web shop'[17] for consumers to access. Dropship TikTok shop owners themselves have defended their business models in various comments sections of viral TikTok posts calling them out. They emphasise that customers were still supporting 'small' as they were small-time, independent entrepreneurs engaging in the import of mass produced goods at a very small scale, unlike major brands and corporations who were doing the same for larger corporate margins on a much wider scale.

Regardless of the lukewarm stance towards dropshipping by TikTok and e-commerce experts, my digital ethnography evidenced an increasing awareness of dropshipping as prevalent among TikTok shops, with dedicated TikTok accounts focused on calling out such businesses, plagiarism, and other forms of design theft. Such posts see attentive customers using the green screen, stitch, and duet features to juxtapose the small business product against listings by major dropshipping platforms, like Aliexpress and Temu, or e-commerce platforms, like Amazon. It is also common for these TikTok posts to appeal to pedestrian TikTok viewers outside of the small business community by exposing the 'actual value' of the goods purchased; they do so by using overlay text to tally the total cost of the products on screen and to underscore the very cheap value of the mass manufactured product and the high profit margins of dropship TikTok shops.

Greenwashing

Greenwashing describes the practice of using misleading environmental claims or misframing charitable efforts such that businesses are perceived to be much more environmentally friendly that their actual practices reflect. It has been studied as a story-telling technique where businesses may adopt an 'educational' stance to 'heavily emphasise sustainability issues and seek to directly influence the audience's values' or an 'inspirational' stance for 'highlighting and romanticising one's own sustainable consumption to the audience'.[18] Academic research has found that interest in greenwashing peaks during key events, like 'Earth Day' and 'COP26', is widely rampant across social media other than TikTok and usually focuses on the 'issues of sustainability, climate change, and other environmental concerns'.[19]

On a corporate scale, oil companies have reportedly engaged TikTokers to promote 'petrol stations, fuel rewards and club cards' or hired them in paid partnerships to promote 'low-carbon products' like electric car-charging apps.[20] This is despite the poor track record of such oil companies who have variously been embroiled in controversies for oil spills and the degradation of the environment in their oil mining initiatives.

On a small business scale, attentive customers have accused TikTok shops of placing disproportionate emphasis on the environmental value of shopping small, especially when the elaborate packaging that is a signature of such TikTok shops is in reality contributing to material wastage. While there are unboxing videos from TikTok shop customers displaying appreciation for the care and personalisation that goes into the packaging, my digital ethnography has also evidenced a pushback against this expectation, with customers calling attention to the excessive amount of plastic wrap, styrofoam cushioning, and plastic-coated paper insulation in similar unboxing videos.

On a creator scale, 'green influencers' have become especially popular among Gen Z, including those on TikTok,[21] even though many of such creators have been found to 'preac [h] sustainability while hawking fast fashion',[22] evidencing a contradiction of their alleged values and their actual actions. However, like the growing resistance towards dropshipping, there is a growing literacy on how to identify greenwashing, as TikTokers are deeply engaged in peer education and learning through call-out posts[23] that call for further awareness of, education about, and caution towards such narrative discourses.

CASE STUDY: MORNING ROUTINES

On TikTok, morning routine videos are diary-like videos that showcase the sequence of motions or tasks undertaken by TikTokers to help them start their day 'on the right foot'. The discourse embedded in the videos often underscore focus and motivation, productivity and efficiency, and independence and agency. Morning routine videos promote 'productivity as an idealized form of empowerment',[24] framing success as an individualised responsibility that can be achieved through the careful selection of everyday habits to produce the optimal self. Like the above discussion on greenwashing, it deflects commentary from the more hard-hitting issues of structural inequity to scapegoat the personal responsibilisation of one's well-being and achievement.

While scholarship on the phenomenon on morning routine posts is still emerging, an early scholarly study on the topic underscores the overt commerciality and the homogenous patterns of consumption among creators: Waking up early in clean bed linen; wearing matching workout clothes; eating a colourful and healthy breakfast; hydrating oneself in a beautiful cup or an branded water bottle; using body-care products in a multi-step shower; using a repertoire of skincare products in an elaborate routine; wearing a coordinate lounge set, partaking in mindful journaling and then heading out the door to school or work.[24] News reports state that there were over 15 billion views on #MorningRoutine videos on TikTok in 2013.[25] Also known as 'GRWM' or 'Get Ready With Me' videos, these posts imply that the optimal and productive use of mornings are 'more virtuous' and 'more important' than 'any other time of day'.[26]

Calling back to the earlier discussion on dropshipping, many TikTokers seem to feature similar products in their 'morning routine' videos, such as exercise headbands, glass jars for drink supplements, and reusable straws. We can think of these items as symbols or emblems that are loaded with ideology – a shorthand to indicate a certain identity affiliation or a self-proclaimed belonging to specific communities. The glass jars, which are also really common in cafes, hints at someone who might be concerned about the environment, which is why they are reusing an old jar. Similarly, a reusable straw suggests that they have taken steps to procure a metal or glass straw for multiple uses to reduce the wastage caused by disposable plastic straws (see Fig. 45).

But of course, these are mere suggestions that the TikTok audiences read into the visual symbols, as the TikTokers could have very well purchased these items from major corporate

Fig. 45. Artist's Impression of a Small Business Using Lifestyle Marketing, Using the Aesthetic Genre of Slow Living to Advertise Metal Straws. Image Commissioned by and Copyrighted to Crystal Abidin. Art Provided by Ardine Keyla.

companies with poor environmental track records. Our belief in the ethos of these TikTokers is constructed, projected, and limited at the level of visual ideology rather than having a deeper understanding of their actual beliefs and practices. Indeed, some TikTok users have pondered in the comments sections if the overt placement of these items is in reality for virtue-signalling. More crucially, this discourse and thought-process continues to individualise the responsibility for environmental destruction, sidestepping the more challenging effort of holding major corporations responsible.

As a practice adopted by owners of small businesses on TikTok, many morning routine videos are brand-heavy, with TikTokers redirecting viewers to the links in their bio that invite prospective customers to view their shopfronts or Amazon recommendations and similar. They also often depict self-care activities such as meditation, juice and supplement drinks, and skincare routines that adopt lifestyle marketing strategies to appeal to followers. Lifestyle marketing is a hallmark of influencer cultures, where business owners – and/or the creators with which they partner – promote their businesses in attempts to cultivate connections between the products on offer and specific lifestyle ethos across target demographics of consumers. They tend to position products hawked to appeal to the everyday activities and interests of specific consumers, framing them as necessary and appealing items that are already congruent with their current consumption habits and consumer preferences to enhance both their market and social value. Morning routine videos thus present a helpful narrative template for demonstrating how the recommended products can be spontaneously integrated into everyday practices, and the advertising message comes across as more natural and casual and thus more genuine and credible. In other words, the discursive template of morning routine videos can serve to play down the centricity of commerciality in what would otherwise be overtly promotional videos and helps small businesses and creators appear less 'hard sell' to viewers.

Frequent watchers of morning routine videos, whether on TikTok or other platforms, will be quick to notice that these creators tend to hail from similar demographics – 'young, white or white-passing, thin, able-bodied, cisgender, and whose gender performance abides by heteronormative expectations of femininity'.[24] Subcultural trends within morning routine videos – like the 'That Girl' persona on TikTok – have also been found to espouse 'white supremacist views of beauty and productivity'.[24] This reminds us that despite the promotion of virtuous feminine forms of domesticity, the personal continues to be political as everyday routines – however curated, selected, and performed – are emblematic of wider social beliefs and systems of cultural value.

CASE STUDY: TIKTOK HAULS

TikTok hauls are the phenomenon of users purchasing multiple items in a single go, then displaying all the items conspicuously through unboxing videos, try-ons, and talk-throughs. Often, the discourse focuses on sheer numbers: The amount of money spent, the number of items purchased and the weight of the parcel. The sheer volume and fascination with numbers is intended to shock or surprise viewers, especially as haul videos have become a staple across visual social media like TikTok and YouTube. On TikTok, haul videos tend to focus on fast moving consumer goods like cosmetics and fashion items, stationery and household items, and food and drink items.

TikTok hauls are a successor to YouTube hauls, where 'fast fashion and its connection to digital platforms' raises concerns for sustainability.[27] They have deeper roots in early fashion blogging cultures of the 2000s, where many bloggers and influencers would swear by a 'one photo expiration date', meaning that fashion items that they have already been pictured or photographed in should not be reworn. Those who committed this faux pas were often subject to scrutiny and criticism in fan forums and hate blogs, pointing to the pressure to keep up with exclusive wears of exclusive items. This 'one-time use' culture thus saw the quick accumulation of fashion items in excess and the shortening of fashion trend cycles where styles and designs are quickly declared to be 'obsolete' to promote the next iteration of a collection.

Articles in lifestyle magazines report that TikTok hauls have extended to other consumer verticals like grocery shopping in supermarkets. Such TikTokers would showcase 'the outlandish foods that most people in the country do not have'[28] and combine the visual templates of TikTok haul videos with fridge and pantry restock videos to underscore their cultural capital and wealth. In response, brands have leveraged on these vernacular trends by partnering with TikTokers in 'back-to-school hauls', with campaigns inviting prospective child and teen customers to use the new schooling season to 'experiment with their identity'[29] through the mass purchase of consumer goods. In these instances, the adage 'new year, new me' was literally being rebranded as 'new year, new everything'.

The haul format works especially well on TikTok as the posts are relatively easy to produce compared to the longer formats that are popular on YouTube. Unlike the long narrations and detailed captions on YouTube, on TikTok clothing haul videos simply feature creators wearing each item for a few seconds – perhaps dancing to catchy, trendy music – before transitioning to the next look. TikTok posts that do not feature very much information about the items featured bait engagement by inviting queries in the comments section; some TikTokers do feature this information, but only in very brief and cursory displays of text on screen so as to encourage viewers to rewatch or reloop their videos to look out for these details (see Chapter 2). Further, many TikTokers simply tag the brand's official TikTok handle in their captions, and thank them for sponsoring the haul, rather than expending much more effort on narrating details of the brand's campaign.

As a small business strategy, TikTok hauls contradict the ethos of environmentalism as they encourage excess and waste. Some TikTokers also use the strategy to promote brands whose ethos are incongruous to the format, such as the odd promotion of online vintage shops that originally aimed to promote reuse and mindful consumption. While it has become trendy for fashion TikTokers to promote capsule wardrobes – a modest but curated collection of fashion items that can be used in different permutations and combinations to create different looks – my digital ethnography has sighted many of them who have also turned to TikTok hauls to promote the concept, such as purchasing 50 brand new items to start a new capsule wardrobe, thus defeating the original intention of minimalism and minimising consumption.

CASE STUDY: DE-INFLUENCING AND UNDERCONSUMPTION CORE

In response to the popularity of product-laden morning routines and the excesses of TikTok hauls, 'de-influencing' and 'underconsumption core' have emerged as two trends that promote more careful and mindful consumption habits.

Scholars have described de-influencing as 'a new movement aiming not to consume in the consumer society',[30] which sees TikTokers criticising the practices and promotion of over-consumption on the platform, while raising awareness and providing education about how to be more thoughtful and strategic about accumulating material goods. Lifestyle magazines and news commentary report that both trends emerged on TikTok in early-2023, with over 230 million views on #deinfluencing,[31] and raking up to 1.5 billion views by mid-2024 when the trends were at their peak.[32]

'De-influencers' have been described as having 'built a brand on buying nothing',[33] as their contents focus on persuading viewers not to buy specific items, pointing out how specific viral-at-the-moment items don't actually function well, calling out excessive kitchen restocks and shopping hauls through TikTok stitches and duets or promoting low-waste and carbon-neutral alternatives to products that are trending on the app. In general, they tend to adopt the same communicative models and strategies as regular influencers. For example, a study on how TikTokers de-influence travel contents has found that they use the narrative strategies of pointing out the 'hype' of trends, explaining how 'unnecessary' consumption trends are, showing 'alternative[s]' to the unsustainable promotions, calling out 'unreliable influencer content', reminding users how 'overprice[d]' specific items or experiences are, calling out 'over consumerism', reminding users about 'sustainability', sharing tips for resisting 'impulsive buying', encouraging followers to 'save money' or by simply 'complaining' about over-consumption.[30] A similar study of de-influencers and luxury brands sees them providing 'authentic and honest negative review[s] of a brand' – such as low quality products despite the high pricing – so as to dissuade excessive spending.[34]

However, other emerging scholarship highlights that de-influencing is ultimately still a practice of influencing or 're-influencing', as it functions as 'just another marketing strategy' when de-influencers recommend 'affordable and environmental friendly alternatives'.[35] They simply borrow from the aesthetic of minimalism to 'romanticis[e] a life of reduced materialism and consumption'.[18] Yet, de-influencers often peddle in the marketing of 'dupes' – 'duplicates' or replicas of original products at a cheaper price and (usually) lower quality – which still encourages mass consumption, thus 'undermining the original goal' of resisting over-consumption.[35] An article in a lifestyle magazine also observes a new paradoxical subculture ushered in by underconsumption core trends, which sees TikTokers promoting 'luxury minimalism' comprising designer goods that are alleged to last a 'lifetime'.[36] Yet, the discourse on TikTok sees de-influencers promoting multiple luxury goods for every occasion, which similarly defeats the original ethos of mindful consumption.[36]

Despite the early promises of de-influencing and underconsumption core initiatives, popular commentary provides an important stocktake by reminding us that over-consumption on TikTok has become so extensive that any pushback at all is immediately assumed to be activist and advocacy, regardless of the principles behind the optics and regardless of how 'normal' the new ethos of consumption is (Valko, 2024).[37] A line from lifestyle magazine *Elle Australia* best encapsulates this in the rhetorical question: 'Is it really "underconsumption core" or are we just... normal?'.[36] Indeed, any resistance to consumerism on social media is so rare that the discourse on de-influencing and underconsumption core have been perceived to be 'unnatural' to the point of becoming 'viral' as a fad itself.[38] On a structural level, de-influencing videos appear to criticise the 'platforms' architectures that further fuel these

processes' while simultaneously using these very same platforms and their viral affordances to promote their messaging.[39]

CONCLUSION

The first season of the Netflix series Squid Game was launched
on the platform in September 2021 to global fanfare and
instant virality. I remember walking through the shopping
mall in my neighbourhood during that season and being very
surprised to see pop-up stalls already selling the iconic red suit
and black mask – bearing circle, triangle or square shapes – in
time for Halloween. This really brought home how rapid viral
cycles, production cycles, and consumption cycles were, and I
was taken aback by just how quickly mass manufacturers
were working to keep up with pop culture. My fieldnotes from
digital ethnography on TikTok also noted several viral trends
that simulated memorable scenes and that reused the iconic
suspenseful music from the series, and it was not long before
the DIY Squid Games uniforms were replaced by the mass
produced replicas that became widely available for sale.

A few months later, during my afternoon walk in the
comfort of the same shopping mall with my newborn, I saw
multiple pop-up stalls catered to young children over the
school holiday season. It was January 2022, when reversible
plushies and pop-it fidget toys were viral on TikTok. I knew
this from my digital ethnography of TikTok, but the banners
covering the displays of these pop-up stalls also reminded me
of the fact: 'As seen on TikTok' (see Fig. 46). After noticing
that I had snapped a photo of their stall, a friendly shopkeeper
asked if I knew what TikTok was and told me that it's the
latest app that all the young people were now on. Having
begun my study of TikTok in 2018, I had already known this

Fig. 46. Example of a Stall Marketing Products as 'As Seen on TikTok'. Image by Author.

but feigned ignorance to learn more For Science. I asked what TikTok was, how they knew what products were popular, and how they were able to act so quickly. In Chinese-accented English, the shopkeeper told me that these products had long trended on Douyin, and so they were able to source and import these goods with the knowledge that they would soon be viral on TikTok as well. I switched to Mandarin and told the shopkeeper I was impressed with their knowledge of both

platforms and made a mental note that it was not only platform features (see Chapter 1) but also marketplace cultures
that carried over from Douyin to TikTok.

A year later, during the same school holiday season in
December 2023, my afternoon walk with my second newborn
in the same mall brought me back to these same pop-up stalls.
This time, the viral products on TikTok were rubber and
plastic 'charms' to customise the Crocs brand of footwear and
an assortment of crystals, also promoted as 'As seen on Tik-
Tok'. Throngs of preschoolers were crowding the stalls, and
as I hung around to observe the situation as an interested
customer, I overheard unacquainted parents commiserating
over how TikTok was the new TV, and that it was impossible
to keep their young children away from ads these days. I
mused in my head that this was true, but it was not just young
children who were susceptible to the advertising tentacles of
TikTok.

I had just walked past a physical bookstore that had a
similar poster promoting a wall of books as being 'As recommended by BookTok'; they were a combination of fiction
and non-fiction for adult readers. My recent transits and
stopovers at several airports around the world also saw books
being promoted as being endorsed by TikTokers (see Fig. 47),
but these tended to focus on cross-cultural literature – the
'TikTok viral' books on 'TikTok viral' Japanese concepts like
Ikigai and *Wabi-sabi*, and later on the 'TikTok viral' books by
'TikTok viral' Japanese and Korean authors who had their
fiction works translated into the English language.

By then, I was several years into my longitudinal digital
ethnography of TikTok, and had also observed many fashion
brands that had dedicated 'TikTok viral' tabs on their websites for ease of filtering and access for customers who had
found them specifically through TikTok posts. In the course of
2 years (and two newborns), marketplace cultures on TikTok

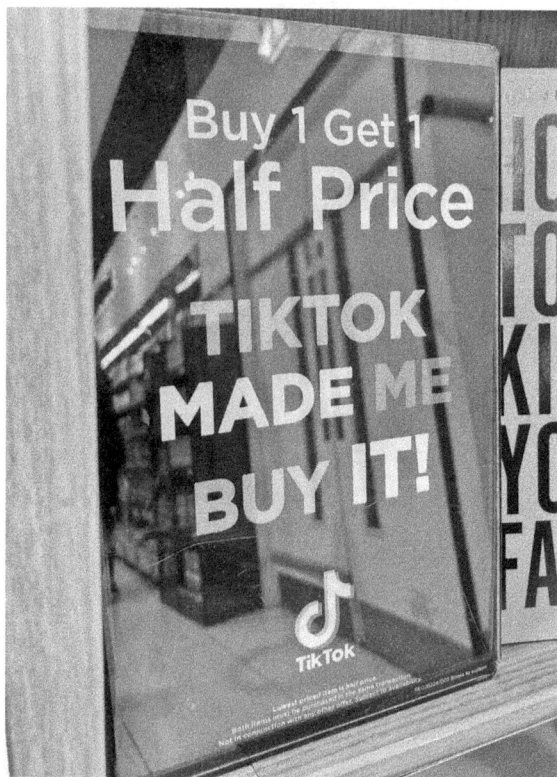

Fig. 47. Example of a Bookstore at an Airport Marketing Books as Being 'Endorsed' by TikTok. Image by Author.

had expanded to accommodate cross-platform promotions on two fronts: From online to offline, and from TikTok to a plethora of other platforms.

In wrapping up the writing for this book, I thought it was good measure to take a final walk in my neighbourhood shopping mall during another school holiday season. It is December 2024 and with two toddlers in tow, I returned to the same pop-up stalls. Alongside 'TikTok viral' toys for young children were an assortment of 'TikTok viral' household products for adults. Like myself, many parents armed with young children were supervising the grubby hands experimenting with the demonstration toys while eyeballing the candle warmers, mini waffle makers, foaming wall cleansers, and veggie choppers on display. The marketplace cultures of TikTok are no longer novel, unique to the platform, or confined to digital platforms. Buying an item that is 'As seen on TikTok' or purchasing an item because 'TikTok made me buy it' is as commonplace as succumbing to any variety of traditional advertising strategy. The same shopkeeper was tending to the stall, and while I was unsure if they recognised me, they opened with the same question: 'So, do you know TikTok now?'. This time, I reveal a little bit more than in the past years: 'Actually, I just wrote a book about TikTok'

EPILOGUE

I write this epilogue on my mobile phone. Specifically, I am on a plane ride home after a long restful holiday with my family, and am naptrapped under two toddlers in cramped aeroplane seats, so the only thing I can do with one mobile arm for the remaining duration of this flight is to type on my phone. I first conceptualised this book before incubating my Shy little Frog, and now my cute little Num Num Cat is snoring by my ear. After some pauses across my recent reproductive years, this book is finally entering the final stages of production. But several days ago, I urgently contacted my editors asking if I could please append an epilogue to the end of it, because the present state of matters is too epic, and I have been occupied with logging them.

Word on the street is that TikTok is about to be banned in the United States, and my TikTok feeds (I have more than one) are in various states of frantic disbelief.

My brain is on holiday mode and I don't necessarily want to deep dive into serious writing for a few more days. I make a note-to-self to email a collaborator in a few days' time, to discuss how we can theorise the notion of 'curtain calls' or 'platform evacuation'. My father was a military officer and my spouse is an engineer, so by default, I am always looking out for fire escape doors and evacuation routes every time we enter an enclosed space. I am also presently enveloped in this atmosphere of a tin can flying through the endless sky, and am the variety of passenger who always reads the in-flight safety cards. All of these seem to converge at once and call out to me to write about 'evacuation' from TikTok, or platforms more generally, as a concept.

I open the notes app on my iPhone and scroll through the stream-of-conscious fieldnotes I have been tapping into life, thumb by thumb, across several similar naptrapped sessions in the past few weeks. I connect to the in-flight Wi-Fi and scroll through my FYP once more. It seems the American TikTokers are now calling themselves 'TikTok refugees'.

CURTAIN CALLS

There are the beginnings of various grand announcements of departure, but already there are patterns. Various creator genres are saying goodbye in their own vernacular (see Chapter 4): TikTokers who broke into the scene for their viral talents are reenacting the song, the dance, the skit that first made them 'internet famous'; Reactors are reacting to the impending TikTok ban, although it is no longer quite so clear if they are still in character or reacting sincerely; POV actors and role-players have broken character all together to offer genuine gratitude to their audience, and I am taken aback by hearing their actual accents, their diction, their tone of voice for the first time, even seeing many of them out of costume and drag, perhaps for the first and last time.

It is a time of farewells, eulogies, and bereavement, of space, time, and community. But this is TikTok, and memes are our capital (see Chapter 3). My favourite meme of the moment is the 'Chinese spy'. TikTokers are cheeky with a wicked sense of humour. Chinese (local and diaspora) Tik-Tokers are using exaggerated Chinese-accented English and sending farewell messages to the Americans: 'Hello, this is your Chinese spy speaking. Thank you for letting me spy on you for the last few years...'. They are being sartorial about the granular level of detail that the US government believes TikTok has collected about its citizens. 'George' is being called out for his poor posture while scrolling on TikTok for hours a day. 'Stacy' has been instructed to please improve her grammar and to stop spamming comments. 'Michael' is advised to get off his bum and find a job. 'David' is assured that his contentious TikTok genre preferences are safe with his Chinese spy, for now. And the Americans are responding. 'Goodbye to my Chinese spy', begins the farewell speeches in response, as if a parasocial relationship has formed between them over time. I am taking dozens of screengrabs of TikToks which collate scenarios from various war movies; they all similarly feature two soldiers from opposite camps, exchanging solemn but knowing glances with teary eyes, in the knowledge that they are about to part ways upon the enactment of ceasefires. 'Me and my Chinese spy on 18 January at midnight', the captions read.

As the comedy is masking and lubricating some of this grief, other TikTokers are reminiscing with recaps and rewinds of their best moments and best posts on TikTok. 'TikTok couples' who have long since broken up are even playing old footage of happier times, igniting some excitement in the comments section over whether reunions are in order. A popular audio meme sees a voiceover announce 'And with that, the TikTok era comes to an end. Goodnight', before seamlessly transitioning to the bittersweet coda of alternative rock band Green Day's 'Good Riddance' (1997): 'I hope you have the time of your life~~~'.

There are also the more visceral POVs of everyday Tik-Tokers revealing themselves to be employees of TikTok, showing themselves switching off the lights on their floor, and tapping out of the office building, perhaps for the last time. There are very real conversations in the comments section about the implication of the US TikTok ban on job losses. This jarring juxtaposition reminds us that it is not all 'first world problems' and ~memes~, actual livelihoods and real world implications are at stake.

There is some schadenfreude, but the gentler segments of schadenfreude-Tok are of folks showing off the Canadian passports that will 'save' them from the rapture; of folks clarifying that they are American but have actually been living in Europe the whole time so the rapture will not reach them; of folks demonstrating their ability to code switch accents, revealing that they've been catfishing us the whole time and are not actually American at all, so the rapture will exclude them. Nationality and citizenship and place of residence are suddenly all so important in these self-identification exercises.

There is anticipatory loss of community, negotiation of community maintenance, and continued appeals to migrate together. This has been a recurring sentiment in the past week.

THE MIGRATION

I toggle my phone screen back to my fieldnotes, which remind me that it was around 13 January that TikTokers began to speak of 'the migration'. It seems like thousands of users were flocking towards Xiaohongshu, except they were now calling it 'RedNote'. I recall how the app used to be translated as 'Red' and 'Little Red Book' before, and made another note-to-self to write another collaborator about conceptualising the mutation of this cross-platform discourse.

Self-proclaimed TikTok refugees who are early adopters of Xiaohongshu are documenting the first few days of their immersion on the new app for old audiences on TikTok. They are variously staging skits where they are clad in rags, lugging heavy suitcases, and asking to be 'rescued'. I quickly text a friend to muse over how distasteful some of this discourse was, given the backdrop of ongoing war and conflict and actual refugee displacements happening in the world.

There are some similar features between Xiaohongshu and TikTok that would have no doubt facilitated the mass migration of 'TikTok refugees', as I wonder if this is the next battleground for 'platform wars' again (see Chapter 1). The posts from already established TikTokers reveal their efforts in wanting to carry over some of their legacies and reputation onto Xiaohongshu, but not all of these legacy practices appear to appeal to their new audience (see Chapter 2). Those who have quickly adapted know to post pictures of their pet cats and dogs as their 'tax' for joining Xiaohongshu, and cross-platform creators (see Chapter 3) are posting tutorials and quick tips for how to acclimatise to the new environment.

THE SETTLING IN

The song Jin Sheng Yuan (今生緣) by Chinese artist Chuan Zi (川子) is being heralded as the OST to TikTok's 'grand finale'. The strong and firm rhythm, the string of minor chord progressions, and the artist's hoarse tone are being interpreted as carrying nationalist and patriotic overtones. American Tik-Tokers are using the song as an audio meme and saluting emoji of the Chinese flag, demonstrating their attempts to learn the Chinese language speedily, showcasing their ability to dress in all-red attires – apparently signifying Chineseness – to 'blend in' with the locals on Xiaohongshu. The orientalism continues in another TikTok meme of users narrating what it is like after 'one day', 'one week', 'two weeks', and 'one month on Red-Note', as their dressing is progressively 'Chinese' and their command of English deteriorates with exaggerations of a pseudo-Chinese accent.

The more reflexive TikTokers announce that in one fell swoop, the US government has literally 'delivered' its citizens into the arms of the CCP, as more and more people flock to Xiaohongshu. Days later, several news reports claim that

there have been more than half a million downloads of the
Xiaohongshu/RedNote across app stores, and that over
700,000 new users have joined the platform over 2 days.

And then there are the call outs. Just as American TikTokers
were previously accused of 'digital colonialism' when tens of
thousands of them joined Douyin very suddenly, Chinese diaspora and migrant creators who have long been active across
different platforms (see 'cross-platform curators' in Chapter 4)
report that Americans on Xiaohongshu are behaving 'badly'.
Screengrabs of comments and screen recordings of posts show
them to be insisting that livestreamers speak in English,
demanding that the Xiaohongshu posts offer more cultural
context for their unlearned eye, and imposing their ethnocentric
worldviews on various Xiaohongshu posts focused on specific
subcultures or niche topics. It is all a little exhausting, but my
digital ethnography continues.

THE BAIT

On this day, there appears to be the emergence of a new
meme, which essentially serves to hook and bait TikTok
audiences into following creators as they cross over to other
platforms. The audio meme template, lifted from an episode of
the animated sitcom Family Guy, sets the scene between two
interlocutors:

> *Person A*: 'Since we're all going to die, there's one more secret
> I feel I have to share with you'.
>
> *Person B*: [silence]
>
> *Person A*: 'I did not care for the godfather...'
>
> *Person B*: 'What?!' [in disbelief]
>
> *Person A*: 'Did not care for the godfather...'

Accompanying this audio are TikTokers confessing 'mic drop' moments, 'big reveals', 'industry secrets' about their craft: This TikTok couple's romantic relationship was faked for views; this viral moment that slingshot a TikToker into overnight fame was actually preplanned and staged; the content for which I am known is actually not original to me, I have been plagiarising; I am not actually blonde. *mic drop*

Then there are the conspiracy theories, so aliterate, so deliberate and so proliferate that the genre is an exercise in memetic publics in itself: Follow this specific TikTok account to be excluded from the ban; repost this TikTok to retain all your posts and followers even after the ban; Facebook will buy over TikTok and save us from the ban. It is a field day for communication researchers.

THE RAPTURE

Just before the turn of midnight going into 19 January 2025, TikTok was no longer accessible in the United States.

THE REMAINS

It is past midnight on 19 January 2025. The Americans are asleep, offline and off TikTok. Despite the persuasions of Hollywood movie plots, the rest of the world continues to exist in time and on TikTok. The remains, the remnants, the left-behind folk post-rapture are discovering each other in new ways. There are new names for the emergence of continental and regional TikTok contents that, according to the lore, are suddenly visible on our FYPs overnight. We are #CommonwealthTok, #EuroTok, #AfricaTok and the like. In a cheeky bit to underscore the ethnocentrism and dominance of American discourse – in Hollywood, on TikTok, in our everyday lives – we are also now calling ourselves #GlobalTok and #WorldTok. In academia, we used to muse over this type of framing as Rest of World Studies, and RestOfWorld-Tok had a lot to say:

> ... *it's like the loud bully is finally absent from school and the quiet kids are bonding and coming out of their shells...*

> *Wow guys, my FYP is so calm and pleasant today...*

> *... there are these whole other worlds and societies that exist and I am finally getting to see you all on my FYP because the Americans are no longer here.*

> *Is this what world peace feels like?*

And my personal favourite:

> *COLOUR NEIGHBOUR HUMOUR*
> *BEHAVIOUR KILOMETERS METERS*
> *CENTIMETERS KILOGRAMS CELSIUS.*

As an ethnographer, the minutiae of everyday life from around the world is so beautiful and glorious to witness, and by the looks of the hundreds of thousands of TikTok posts in various hashtag streams, people around the world concur. I personally consider my FYPs across different accounts to already be quite diverse; I am after all literally an expert in curating my feed through the social science of digital ethnography. But chancing upon TikTok posts of Swedes vlogging in *my* local ICA store during the years I lived in Jönköping, accompanying tourists on the very *same* walk I took down a specific stream in Tartu over three research visits, and witnessing locals in Riga recommend the *exact* lychee wine that I enjoyed over past family reunions was a romantic experience.

It was beautiful, glorious, romantic, but all too short-lived.

THE RETURN

On 20 January 2025, after 14 hours of darkness, Americans returned to TikTok. All day, in-app prompts inform us that the app was back in the United States as a result of 'President Trump's efforts'. The future of the app is still uncertain, but services are restored from now. But the post-rapture returnees were not all met with warmth.

An old .gif meme that was last trending in 2020 was back in vogue, this time as an audio meme: 'Hey… hey… how y'all doing…' utters the uncertain voice in a trembling timbre. It is a line from the reality TV series 'Little Women: Atlanta', in a scene where the antagonist awkwardly reunites with cast members after an earlier disagreement. Here on TikTok, the voice exudes embarrassment, as returnees reveal themselves again, still fresh in the wake of mic drop revelations and the dramatic farewells lasting weeks until the day prior.

Some Rest Of World TikTokers were glad to have the Americans back: 'What was TikTok like without Americans? No fights, no controversies, no dramas! Boring!' But for the most part, there was already rampant nostalgia for the brief moment of solace over the 14 precious hours, where different types of contents fast accumulated new capital (see Chapter 3) and small business cultures in corners of TikTok and around the world (see Chapter 5) appear to have enjoyed a rejuvenation:

> Remember those few crazy moments when it was just us…

> It was nice experiencing a world without American drama… where we can all celebrate our cultures…

> I am so grateful for everyone who has seen my TikToks and supported my small home business. Thank you so much…

> *My FYP was great, and now that you're back, it's*
> *sh*t*
>
> *. . . you guys tend to take up all the spotlight and suck*
> *up all the air. . .*

It seems RestOfWorldTok is on an ad hoc mission to restore the vestiges of their brief time together. Folks are using country flag emojis in their handles to indicate their membership in the short-lived GlobalTok, and as a handy tool for 'telling each other apart' when they appear on the FYPs of pedestrian TikTokers. 'Please follow to stay connected; I have enjoyed all of you', some say. 'Please interact to stay on the international "side" of TikTok!' It seems visibility and engagement strategies (see Chapter 2) were key to preserving the United Nations of TikTok.

THE AFTERMATH

It is a few days post-grief, post-migration, post-strategy, post-rapture, post-diversity, post-return. I really really have to finalise and send this epilogue off now. The latest update is that President Donald Trump appears to be leveraging on the 'reinstallation' of TikTok in his victory rallies as returning president of the United States – all the broadsheets tell me so. There is much chatter about the various 'potential buyers' for TikTok to divest in the United States, talks of 'tariffs', conspiracy theories about 'bidding wars', discussions about a 'potential sale'.

I do a final scroll on my FYP to confirm what my fieldnotes already tell me: Life on TikTok has mostly been reinstated to the status quo. The 14-hour TikTok ban is no longer the trendy topic of the moment. A new wave of memes has taken over (my FYPs cannot seem to escape the 'Nishiyama Daddy Daddy' chant, but that is another story for another time).

TikTokers and small local businesses and places of interest in corners across the world have each experienced their transient time in the limelight with an international audience, but transient as this may be, the real lesson is that many Tik-Tokers finally have first-hand experience in how to hone their FYP to their liking, how to use algorithmic and interactive practices to surface the types of contents and creators that they want, how to deploy engagement strategies to retain the attention of their new-found audiences (see Chapter 2).

In other words, our palettes have been suddenly exposed to a new buffet of content – now we know how to yearn, and now we know how to learn. The bar for algorithmic, plat-formed and digital literacies has been raised significantly en masse in a very short span of time, and TikTokers are benefitting from the experience... until the next curtain call.

Appendix

TIKTOK INTERFACE AND FEATURES

For the unacquainted, TikTok's interface opens on a 'For You Page' (FYP) by default (Fig. A1), as indicated by the bold text on the top of the screen. The information presented on an FYP can generally be divided into four segments: feed, engagement options, post information, and account information.

Fig. A1. Artist's Impression of TikTok Interface on 'FYP' Mode. Image Commissioned by and Copyrighted to Crystal Abidin. Art Provided by Ardine Keyla.

FEED

The top of any FYP indicates two stream options, and the selected stream is indicated when the text is in bold and underlined. The default is 'For You' feed, which is a curated stream of TikTok posts offered by TikTok's proprietary algorithmic recommender system, offered as an endless scroll of content. This interface shows one post at a time, whether a video post, a carousel of image posts or a live video post.

Swiping to the right allows users to switch to the 'Following' feed, which is a curated stream of TikTok posts by users that a user has subscribed to or followed. In this feed, the top row usually shows a string of round buttons featuring profile pictures of users who are currently 'Live' or who have posted 'Stories'. 'Live' posts are livestreams (see below), while 'Stories' are transient updates of photos or videos that only appear for 24 hours. Below these 'Live' and 'Stories' updates is an endless scroll of content from accounts that a user has followed.

Apart from the two streams indicated in the centre, on the top left corner of the screen is a 'Live' 'button' which allows users quick access to an endless scroll of livestreamed content.

The top right corner of the screen is a 'Search' button. A search bar allows users to enter any keyword to search for content (see Fig. A2), and there is also an option to conduct a 'Sound search' or search by voice or audio, as indicated by a microphone button. Search results can be filtered by several options. A scrolling top bar enables results filtered by content type, including: Top, Users, Videos, Sounds, LIVE, Places, and Hashtags. Below that is a row of bottoms that enables results filtered by user activity, including: All, Unwatched, Watched, and Recently uploaded. Thereafter, select results are offered by content type, including Users, Hashtags, Posts, and 'Others searched for' suggestions of related search terms. These four search result options continue to alternate down the long

Fig. A2.   Artist's Impression of TikTok Interface on 'Search' Mode. Image Commissioned by and Copyrighted to Crystal Abidin. Art Provided by Ardine Keyla.

scroll, presenting a variety of content format options. Note also that even prior to entering any search terms, TikTok also offers a suggested list of 'You may like' key words and phrases based on user activity and current trends on the app.

ENGAGEMENT OPTIONS

On the right-hand side of an FYP are engagement options, showing the display picture of the creator of the post, a 'like' button, a 'comment' button, a 'share' button, and a rotating vinyl showing the display picture of the creator of the audio accompanying the post (see Fig. 19). Clicking on the creator button allows users to view the profile of the creator or sub-scribe to the creator's contents. Clicking on the 'like' button allows users to like a post and add it to their library of 'liked' posts. Clicking on the 'comment' button allows users to view the comments appended to the post, and to add to the con-versation. Clicking on the share button allows users to send the post to another user, repost the content on their own account, copy a URL to the post, or share the post on a variety of external platforms. In late-2022, TikTok added a 'favourites' button, allowing users to add posts to their library of 'favourited' content. While 'liked' content is sorted into a single stream on a user's profile, 'favourited' content is organised by default into different formats and uses including: Posts, Collections, Sounds, Effects, Products, Places, Playlists, Movies and TV, Comments, Add Yours, Hashtags, Series.

For video posts, the 'share' button also offers several actions, including:

- Report: Flagging the post as violating community guidelines.
- Not interested: Indicating desire to see less of similar contents.
- Save video: Downloading the post as a saveable document on your device.
- Promote: Paying a fee to disseminate the post more widely to other users.
- Captions: Viewing the subtitles appended to the post.
- Duet: Using the post as source content to create a 'duet' (see below).
- Stitch: Using the post as source content to create a 'stitch' (see below).
- Create sticker: Creating an animated sticker from the post for use in direct messages.
- Playback speed: Changing the pace of the video to 2x, 1.5x, normal or 0.5x.
- Live Photo: Converting the post into a live photo saveable on your device.
- Share as GIF: Creating a GIF from the post for use in direct messages.

For image carousel posts, the 'share' button offers a smaller range of additional actions, including:

- Report: Flagging the post as violating community guidelines.
- Not interested: Indicating desire to see less of similar contents.
- Promote: Paying a fee to disseminate the post more widely to other users.
- Save photo: Downloading the post as a saveable document on your device.

Occasionally, some video and image carousel posts also offer a 'Why this video' button, which informs users that they are seeing the post because content on the feed has been personalised for them based on a combination of factors. While this list of reasons changes per post, an example of one such 'Why this video' pop-up is:

Why you're seeing this post

- Your feed is personalised and there are many reasons why a post shows up on your feed. For this post, reasons may include:
- You shared similar pots.
- You are following [name of user].
- This video is longer, and you seem to like longer videos.
- You have viewed this creator's profile and posts.

For live posts, a preview of the livestream is shown with white text prompting users to 'Tap to watch event'. Doing so enters users into a livestream, where the top of the screen shows the livestream video, and the bottom of the screen shows a cascading feed of comments in real time. A line of icons line the top most bit of the screen, indicating the streamer's user handle, a follow button, the number of viewers in the stream, and flags indicating the stream's ranking in various charts like 'Gaming' or 'Daily'. A line of icons also line of the bottom most bit of the screen, allowing users to subscribe to the streamer, add a text comment, add an emoji comment, give virtual gifts like roses and other digital stickers or share the stream.

POST INFORMATION

On the bottom left corner of the screen contains post information (see Fig. 19), where users can view the username of the post creator; captions including text, emoji, and hashtags; and a running title of the sound appended to the post.

ACCOUNT INFORMATION

The bottom row on the screen shows a user's account information (see Fig. 19). Five buttons allow for various actions:

(1) Home: Shortcut to the Feed.
(2) Friends: Endless scroll stream of content from users who are one's mutual followers.
(3) Plus: Shortcut to the interface to create TikTok content, whether Post, Story, or Templates.
(4) Inbox: Notifications of new followers; Activity updates from followed accounts; and direct messages exchanged with other users.
(5) Profile: User's profile page, including their profile picture; their metrics including the number of accounts they follow, the number of followers they have, the total number of likes accrued across all their posts; options to edit profile, share profile, and add other users; a brief bio; and five streams of post content including 'all' posts, 'locked' posts, 'reposts', 'favourited' posts, and 'liked' posts.

In their excellent review of how TikTok encourages creativity among users, Kaye et al. (2022, pp. 59–78) offer a schema of feature categories including: For You Algorithm, Socially creative, Creation and editing, Social media platform, and Accessibility. Across these five categories, the authors further surmise 17 features of TikTok (Kaye et al., 2022, pp. 59–78) but have not yet defined each one. Adapting from this schema, I offer succinct definitions of the key TikTok features below:

For You Algorithm features

- Content discovery: Receipt of recommended content on feed.
- Personalisation: Algorithmically curated content based on user profile and activity.
- Spreadability: User initiative to share and distribute content.

Socially creative features

- Duet: Select existing video to embed beside own new video in a split screen format; usually used to respond, react, or relate to existing content.
- Stitch: Select segment of existing video to embed before own new video in a consecutive format; usually used as a preamble before own new content.
- Video Reply To Comments: Select comment on own existing video to reply to with a new video; usually used to append new content to previously published content.
- Use This Sound: Select existing audio meme as backtrack for own new video.

Creation and editing features

- Effects and filters: Select existing visual or audio template to superimpose on own new video.

- Live-streaming: Broadcast own new video in real time.

Social media platform features

- @mentioning: Create hyperlink to another user's handle, and also to send them a notification to the post being commented on to redirect their attention.
- Hashtags: Create hyperlink to streams of related content that have used the same keyword, and also to archive the post under the streams to acquire greater visibility.
- Likes: Indicate favour or endorsement, to archive post to a library of 'liked' content, and also to send a notification to the owner of the post.
- Comments: Text replies to a post; usually can be organised into tiered mother/child threads for multiple strands of conversation.
- Shares: Distribute post either to other users on the same platform, or to others across external platforms.

Accessibility features

- Closed captions: Text transcription synchronized to audio of the post.
- Text to speech: Audio rendering of text on the post.
- Trigger warnings: Statement flagging the description of content to alert users of potential distress.

ENDNOTES

CHAPTER 1

(1) Wong, Wilson. 2022. "A look back at Vine – the six-second video app that made us scream, laugh and cry." *NBC News,* January 17. Last accessed 24 February, 2025 from https://www.nbcnews.com/pop-culture/pop-culture-news/look-back-vine-six-second-video-app-made-us-scream-laugh-cry-rcna10910

(2) Newton, Casey. 2016. "Why Vine died." *The Verge,* October 28. Last accessed 24 February, 2025 from https://www.theverge.com/2016/10/28/13456208/why-vine-died-twitter-shutdown

(3) LaFrance, Adrienne. 2016. "Is Vine Dying?" *The Atlantic,* May 26. Last accessed 24 February, 2025 from https://www.theatlantic.com/technology/archive/2016/05/vines-death-knell-gets-louder/484301/

(4) O'Connell, Brian. 2020. "History of Snapchat: Timeline and Facts." *The Street,* February 28. Last accessed 24 February, 2025 from https://www.thestreet.com/technology/history-of-snapchat

(5) Langford, Sam. 2019. "Junk Explained: What The Hell Is TikTok, And Is It The New Vine?" *Junkee,* January 7. Last accessed 24 February, 2025 from https://junkee.com/tiktok-app-vine-challenge/188567

(6) Garrity, Katie. 2020. "Some of the Best Viners Have Made Their Way Onto TikTok." *Distractify,* April 15.

Last accessed 24 February, 2025 from https://www.distractify.com/p/best-viners-on-tiktok

(7) O'Hear, Steve. 2015. "Video Selfie App Dubsmash Proves To Be A Smash Hit." *Tech Crunch,* January 14. Last accessed 24 February, 2025 from https://techcrunch.com/2015/01/13/dubsmash/

(8) Constine, Josh. 2020. "How Dubsmash revived itself as #2 to TikTok." *Tech Crunch,* February 1. Last accessed 24 February, 2025 from https://techcrunch.com/2020/01/31/dubsmash-songs/

(9) Reuters. 2021. "Reddit to shut down Dubsmash app, integrate video tools with platform." *Reuters,* November 24. Last accessed 24 February, 2025 from https://www.reuters.com/technology/reddit-shut-down-dubsmash-app-integrate-video-tools-with-platform-2021-11-23/

(10) Malik, Aisha. 2021. "Reddit is shutting down Dubsmash and integrating video tools into its own app." *Tech Crunch,* November 24. Last accessed 24 February, 2025 from https://techcrunch.com/2021/11/23/reddit-is-shutting-down-dubsmash-and-integrating-video-tools-into-its-own-app/

(11) Brown, Abram. 2020. "Dubsmash, A Home For Black And Latino Teens, Is Figuring Out How To Turn Its Influencers Into Paid Stars." *Forbes,* November 19. Last accessed 24 February, 2025 from https://www.forbes.com/sites/abrambrown/2020/11/19/dubsmash-a-home-for-black-and-latino-teens-is-figuring-out-how-to-turn-its-influencers-into-paid-stars/?sh=9192ee7c0857

(12) Anand, Priya. 2022. "Dubsmash, No Match for TikTok, Dies Quietly After a Run at Viral Fame." *Bloomberg,* February 22. Last accessed 24 February, 2025 from https://www.bloomberg.com/news/articles/2022-02-22/dubsmash-no-match-for-tiktok-dies-quietly-after-its-acquisition-by-reddit

(13) Carson, Biz. 2016. "How a failed education startup turned into Musical.ly, the most popular app you've

probably never heard of." *Business Insider,* May 28. Last accessed 24 February, 2025 from https://www.businessinsider.com/what-is-musically-2016-5

(14) Jennings, Rebecca. 2019. "TikTok, explained." *Vox,* July 12. Last accessed 24 February, 2025 from https://www.vox.com/culture/2018/12/10/18129126/tiktok-app-musically-meme-cringe

(15) Mozur, Paul. 2017. "Musical.ly, a Chinese app big in the US, sells for $1 billion." *CNBC,* November 10. Last accessed 24 February, 2025 from https://www.cnbc.com/2017/11/10/musical-ly-app-sells-for-1-billion.html

(16) Newlands, Murray. 2016. "The Origin and Future Of America's Hottest New App: musical.ly." *Forbes,* June 10. Last accessed 24 February, 2025 from https://www.forbes.com/sites/mnewlands/2016/06/10/the-origin-and-future-of-americas-hottest-new-app-musical-ly/?sh=7d15916b5b07

(17) Kaye, D. Bondy Valdovinos, Xu Chen, and Jing Zeng. 2020. "The co-evolution of two Chinese mobile short video apps: Parallel platformization of Douyin and Tik-Tok." *Mobile Media & Communication* 9(2):229–253. https://doi.org/10.1177/2050157920952120

(18) Cole, Samantha. 2018. "RIP Musical.ly: A Very Brief History." *Vice,* August 4. Last accessed 24 February, 2025 from https://www.vice.com/en/article/xwk4pw/musically-shut-down-tiktok-memes

(19) Law, Tara. 2020. "Vine Has a New Successor: The 6-Second Video App Byte." *Time,* January 26. Last accessed 24 February, 2025 from https://time.com/5771854/vine-byte-app-launch/

(20) Kastrenakes, Jacob. 2021. "Byte, Vine's successor, has been purchased by another TikTok clone." *The Verge,* January 26. Last accessed 24 February, 2025 from https://www.theverge.com/2021/1/26/22250926/clash-buys-byte-vine-successor-dom-hofmann

(21) Singh, Manish. 2020a. "Facebook is shutting down Lasso, its TikTok clone." *TechCrunch,* July 2. Last accessed 24 February, 2025 from https://tech-crunch.com/2020/07/01/lasso-facebook-tiktok-shut-down/

(22) Santora, Jacinda. 2021. "What Is Triller? | Here's the Triller Guide You've Been Waiting For." *Influencer Marketing Hub,* 6 July. Last accessed 24 February, 2025 from https://influencermarketinghub.com/what-is-triller/

(23) Blum, Jeremy. 2014. "Meet Weishi, Tencent's version of Vine." *South China Morning Post,* February 26. Last accessed 24 February, 2025 from https://www.scmp.com/lifestyle/technology/article/14 35758/meet-weishi-tencents-version-vine

(24) Liao, Rita. 2018. "How Douyin became one of China's top apps in 500 days." *Tech in Asia*, April 11. Last accessed 24 February, 2025 from https://www.techinasia.com/douyin-rise-in-china

(25) Cuyugan, Emmanuel. 2023. "Compare Xigua Video vs Tiktok vs Youtube: China Marketing Guide." *Chinafy,* August 30. Last accessed 24 February, 2025 from https://www.chinafy.com/blog/compare-xigua-video-vs-tiktok-vs-youtube-china-marketing-guide

(26) Mahendran, Lavanya, and Nasser Alsherif. 2020. "Adding clarity to our Community Guidelines." *TikTok Newsroom,* January 8. Last accessed 24 February, 2025 from https://newsroom.tiktok.com/en-us/adding-clarity-to-our-community-guidelines

(27) Vigdor, Neil. 2020. "U.S. Military Branches Block Access to TikTok App Amid Pentagon Warning." *The New York Times,* January 4. Last accessed 24 February, 2025 from https://www.nytimes.com/2020/01/04/us/tiktok-pentagon-military-ban.html

(28) Kharpal, Arjun. 2020. "A security flaw in China's tik-Tok app was found. It lets hackers use text messages to control accounts." *CNBC,* January 9. Last accessed 24 February, 2025 from https://www.cnbc.com/2020/01/

09/tiktok-security-flaw-found-that-allowed-hackers-to-access-accounts.html

(29) Kelly, Makena. 2020. "TSA bans employees from using TikTok." *The Verge,* February 24. Last accessed 24 February, 2025 from https://www.the-verge.com/2020/2/24/21150667/tsa-tiktok-employee-ban-bytedance-chuck-schumer-homeland-security

(30) Matney, Lucas. 2020. "Reddit CEO: TikTok is 'fundamentally parasitic'." *TechCrunch,* February 27. Last accessed 24 February, 2025 from https://tech-crunch.com/2020/02/26/reddit-ceo-tiktok-is-funda-mentally-parasitic/

(31) TikTok Newsroom. 2020a. "TikTok Taps Leading Cyber Security Expert as Chief Information Security Officer." *TikTok Newsroom,* March 6. Last accessed 24 February, 2025 from https://newsroom.tiktok.com/en-us/tiktok-taps-leading-cyber-security-expert-as-chief-information-security-officer

(32) TikTok Newsroom. 2020b. "WHO to livestream on TikTok." *TikTok Newsroom,* March 17. Last accessed 24 February, 2025 from https://news-room.tiktok.com/en-us/who-to-livestream-on-tiktok

(33) Hern, Alex. 2020a. "TikTok 'tried to filter out videos from ugly, poor or disabled users'." *The Guardian,* March 18. Last accessed 24 February, 2025 from https://www.theguardian.com/technology/2020/mar/17/tiktok-tried-to-filter-out-videos-from-ugly-poor-or-disabled-users

(34) TikTok Newsroom. 2020c. "Our commitment to COVID-19 relief efforts." *TikTok Newsroom,* April 9. Last accessed 24 February, 2025 from https://newsroom.tiktok.com/en-us/our-commitment-to-covid-19-relief-efforts

(35) Collins, Jeff. 2020. "TikTok introduces Family Pair-ing." *TikTok Newsroom,* April 16. Last accessed 24 February, 2025 from https://newsroom.tiktok.com/en-us/tiktok-introduces-family-pairing

(36) TikTok Newsroom. 2020d. "TikTok Youth Portal and our commitment to digital literacy." *TikTok Newsroom,* May 14. Last accessed 24 February, 2025 from https://newsroom.tiktok.com/en-us/tiktok-youth-portal-and-our-commitment-to-digital-literacy

(37) TikTok Newsroom. 2020e. "ByteDance Names Kevin Mayer Chief Operating Officer." *TikTok Newsroom,* May 19. Last accessed 24 February, 2025 from https://newsroom.tiktok.com/en-us/byte-dance-names-kevin-mayer-chief-operating-officer

(38) Singer, Natasha. 2020. "TikTok Broke Privacy Promises, Children's Groups say." *The New York Times,* May 14. Last accessed 24 February, 2025 from https://www.nytimes.com/2020/05/14/technol-ogy/tiktok-kids-privacy.html

(39) Reuters Staff. 2020a. "House Republicans press TikTok on use of kids' data, ties to Beijing." *Reuters,* May 22. Last accessed 24 February, 2025 from https://www.reuters.com/article/us-tiktok-pri-vacy-children-republicans/house-republicans-press-tiktok-on-use-of-kids-data-ties-to-beijing-idINKBN 22X26P?edition-redirect=in

(40) BBC. 2020. "Google deletes millions of negative TikTok reviews." *BBC,* May 26. Last accessed 24 February, 2025 from https://www.bbc.com/news/technology-52808177

(41) Keenan, Cormac, Jeff Collins, and Arjun Manjunath. 2020a. "TikTok joins WePROTECT Global Alliance to combat online child sexual exploitation and abuse." *TikTok Newsroom,* June 22. Last accessed 24 February, 2025 from https://newsroom.tiktok.com/en-us/tiktok-joins-weprotect-global-alliance

(42) Lomas, Natasha. 2020a. "TikTok joins the EU's Code of Practice on disinformation." *TechCrunch,* June 22. Last accessed 24 February, 2025 from https://techcrunch.com/2020/06/22/tiktok-joins-the-eus-code-of-practice-on-disinformation/

(43) Shead, Sam. 2020a. "TikTok apologises after being accused of censoring #BlackLivesMatter posts." *CNBC*, June 2. Last accessed 24 February, 2025 from https://www.cnbc.com/2020/06/02/tiktok-blacklives matter-censorship.html

(44) Evelyn, Kenya. 2020. "Trump 'played' by K-pop fans and TikTok users who disrupted Tulsa rally." *The Guardian*, June 22. Last accessed 24 February, 2025 from https://www.theguardian.com/us-news/2020/jun/21/trump-tulsa-rally-scheme-k-pop-fans-tik tok-users

(45) Roy, Rajesh, and Shan Li. 2020. "India Bans TikTok, Dozens of Other Chinese Apps After Border Clash." *Wall Street Journal*, June 30. Last accessed 24 February, 2025 from https://www.wsj.com/articles/india-blocks-dozens-of-chinese-apps-including-tiktok-following-border-clash-11593447321

(46) Pappas, Vanessa. 2020. "Introducing the $200M TikTok Creator Fund." *TikTok Newsroom*, July 23. Last accessed 24 February, 2025 from https://news-room.tiktok.com/en-us/introducing-the-200-million-tiktok-creator-fund

(47) Pathak, Sushmita, and Lauren Frayer. 2020. "'Tiktok Changed My Life': India's Ban On Chinese App Leaves Video Makers Stunned." *NPR*, July 16. Last accessed 24 February, 2025 from https://www.npr.org/2020/07/16/890382893/tiktok-changed-my-life-india-s-ban-on-chinese-app-leaves-video-makers-stunned

(48) Liao, Rita. 2020. "After India and US, Japan looks to ban TikTok and other Chinese apps." *TechCrunch*, July 29. Last accessed 24 February, 2025 from https://techcrunch.com/2020/07/28/japan-pro-poses-tiktok-ban/

(49) Perez, Sarah. 2020a. "Triller sues TikTok over patent infringement." *TechCrunch*, July 31. Last accessed 24 February, 2025 from https://tech-crunch.com/2020/07/30/triller-sues-tiktok-over-pat-ent-infringement/

(50) Perez, Sarah. 2020b. "TikTok launches a new information hub and Twitter account to 'correct the record,' it says." *TechCrunch,* August 18. Last accessed 24 February, 2025 from https://techcrunch.com/2020/08/17/tiktok-launches-a-new-information-hub-and-twitter-account-to-correct-the-record-it-says/

(51) TikTok Newsroom. 2020f. "TikTok announces deal with UnitedMasters, the first distributor to be fully integrated into the TikTok platform." *TikTok Newsroom,* August 17. Last accessed 24 February, 2025 from https://newsroom.tiktok.com/en-us/tiktok-announces-deal-with-unitedmasters-the-first-distributor-to-be-fully-integrated-into-the-tiktok-platform

(52) TikTok Newsroom. 2020g. "Why we are suing the Administration." *TikTok Newsroom,* August 24. Last accessed 24 February, 2025 from https://newsroom.tiktok.com/en-us/tiktok-files-lawsuit

(53) Kolodny, Lora. 2020. "Trump orders ByteDance to divest from its U.S. TikTok business within 90 days." *CNBC,* August 14. Last accessed 24 February, 2025 from https://www.cnbc.com/2020/08/14/president-trump-orders-bytedance-to-divest-from-its-us-tiktok-business-within-90-days.html

(54) Microsoft Corporate Blogs. 2020. "Microsoft to continue discussions on potential TikTok purchase in the United States." *Official Microsoft Blog,* August 2. Last accessed 24 February, 2025 from https://blogs.microsoft.com/blog/2020/08/02/microsoft-to-continue-discussions-on-potential-tiktok-purchase-in-the-united-states/

(55) Allyn, Bobby. 2020. "Class-Action Lawsuit Claims TikTok Steals Kids' Data And Sends It To China." *NPR,* August 4. Last accessed 24 February, 2025 from https://www.npr.org/2020/08/04/898836158/class-action-lawsuit-claims-tiktok-steals-kids-data-and-sends-it-to-china

(56) Choudhury, Saheli Roy. 2020. "Trump issues executive orders banning U.S. transactions with WeChat and TikTok in 45 days." *CNBC,* August 6. Last accessed 24 February, 2025 from https://www.cnbc.com/2020/08/07/trump-issues-executive-orders-to-ban-us-transactions-with-wechat-tiktok.html

(57) Lomas, Natasha. 2020b. "TikTok is being investigated by France's data watchdog." *TechCrunch,* August 11. Last accessed 24 February, 2025 from https://techcrunch.com/2020/08/11/tiktok-is-being-investigated-by-frances-data-watchdog/

(58) Cohen, Max. 2020. "Meet The Politician Who Lives on TikTok." *Politico,* August 14. Last accessed 24 February, 2025 from https://www.politico.com/news/magazine/2020/08/14/politicians-using-tiktok-matt-little-395620

(59) Nassauer, Sarah, Georgia Wells, and Cara Lombardo. 2020. "Walmart Joins Microsoft's Pursuit of TikTok." *Wall Street Journal,* August 27. Last accessed 24 February, 2025 from https://www.wsj.com/articles/walmart-joins-microsofts-pursuit-of-tiktok-11598544354

(60) TikTok Newsroom. 2020h. "That's a wrap! A look back at the first-ever #TikTokFashionMonth." *TikTok Newsroom,* October 14. Last accessed 24 February, 2025 from https://newsroom.tiktok.com/en-us/thats-a-wrap-a-look-back-at-the-first-ever-tiktokfashionmonth

(61) TikTok Newsroom. 2020i. "Introducing TikTok's Marketing Partner Programme for advertisers." *TikTok Newsroom,* September 3. Last accessed 24 February, 2025 from https://newsroom.tiktok.com/en-us/introducing-tiktok-marketing-partner-program-for-advertisers

(62) Wadhwa, Tara. 2020. "Coming together to support body positivity on TikTok." *TikTok Newsroom,* September 23. Last accessed 24 February, 2025 from https://newsroom.tiktok.com/en-us/coming-together-to-support-body-positivity-on-tiktok

(63) Keenan, Cormac, Arjun Narayan Bettadapur Man-
     junath, and Jeff Collins. 2020b. "TikTok proposes
     global coalition to protect against harmful content."
     TikTok Newsroom, September 22. Last accessed 24
     February, 2025 from https://newsroom.tiktok.com/en-
     us/tiktok-proposes-global-coalition-to-protect-against-
     harmful-content

(64) Beckerman, Michael. 2020. "TikTok launches in-app
     guide to the 2020 US elections." *TikTok Newsroom,*
     September 29. Last accessed 24 February, 2025 from
     https://newsroom.tiktok.com/en-us/tiktok-launches-in-
     app-guide-to-the-2020-us-elections

(65) Hern, Alex. 2020b. "'Dark web' responsible for Tik
     Tok suicide video, says company." *The Guardian,*
     September 23. Last accessed 24 February, 2025 from
     https://www.theguardian.com/technology/2020/sep/
     22/dark-web-responsible-for-tiktok-suicide-video-
     says-company

(66) SCMP Reporters. 2020. "Here's what you need to
     know about Oracle's deal to buy TikTok in the US from
     China's ByteDance." *South China Morning Post,*
     September 19. Last accessed 24 February, 2025 from
     https://www.scmp.com/tech/big-tech/article/3102144/
     heres-what-you-need-know-about-oracles-bid-buy-tik
     tok-us-bytedance

(67) TikTok Newsroom. 2020j. "TikTok and OpenSlate
     partner to bring TikTok brand safety solution to
     advertisers." *TikTok Newsroom,* October 15. Last
     accessed 24 February, 2025 from https://news-
     room.tiktok.com/en-us/tiktok-and-openslate-partner-
     to-bring-tiktok-brand-safety-solution-to-advertisers

(68) TikTok Newsroom. 2020k. "Adding clarity to content
     removals." *TikTok Newsroom,* October 22. Last
     accessed 24 February, 2025 from https://newsroom.
     tiktok.com/en-us/adding-clarity-to-content-removals

(69) TikTok Newsroom. 2020l. "Connecting Shopify mer-
     chants with the TikTok community." *TikTok News-
     room,* October 27. Last accessed 24 February, 2025

from https://newsroom.tiktok.com/en-us/connecting-shopify-merchants-with-the-tiktok-community

(70) Shahzad, Asif. 2020. "Pakistan blocks social media app TikTok for 'immoral and indecent' content." *Reuters,* October 9. Last accessed 24 February, 2025 from https://www.reuters.com/article/pakistan-tik-tok-idUSKBN26U1AT

(71) Singh, Manish. 2020b. "Pakistan lifts ban on Tik-Tok." *TechCrunch,* October 19. Last accessed 24 February, 2025 from https://techcrunch.com/2020/10/19/pakistan-lifts-ban-on-tiktok/

(72) Kastrenakes, Jacob. 2020. "TikTok ban once again blocked by judge, this time thanks to three influencers." *The Verge,* October 30. Last accessed 24 February, 2025 from https://www.theverge.com/2020/10/30/21542641/tiktok-ban-commerce-department-blocked-november-12-influencers

(73) TikTok Newsroom. 2020m. "TikTok announces agreement with Sony Music Entertainment." *TikTok Newsroom,* November 2. Last accessed 24 February, 2025 from https://newsroom.tiktok.com/en-us/tiktok-announces-agreement-with-sony-music-entertainment

(74) TikTok Newsroom. 2020n. "Amplifying Black-owned businesses on TikTok." *TikTok Newsroom,* November 3. Last accessed 24 February, 2025 from https://newsroom.tiktok.com/en-us/amplifying-black-owned-businesses-on-tiktok

(75) Goodman, Joshua. 2020. "Making TikTok more accessible to people with photosensitive epilepsy." *Tik-Tok Newsroom,* November 24. Last accessed 24 February, 2025 from https://newsroom.tiktok.com/en-gb/tiktok-introduces-photosensitivity-feature-in-uk-ireland-providing-greater-controls-and-protections-for-people-with-photosensitive-epilepsy

(76) Shead, Sam. 2020b. "ByteDance has been given another week to sell off TikTok's U.S. business." *CNBC,* November 26. Last accessed 24 February,

2025 from https://www.cnbc.com/2020/11/26/byte-dance-gets-another-week-to-sell-tiktok-us.html

(77) Thalen, Mikael. 2020. "Drug cartels have taken over TikTok." *Daily Dot,* November 30. Last accessed 24 February, 2025 from https://www.dailydot.com/debug/drug-cartels-tiktok/

(78) Reuters Staff. 2020b. "Appeals court holding Dec 14 hearing on blocked U.S. TikTok new user ban." *Reuters,* December 3. Last accessed 24 February, 2025 from https://www.reuters.com/article/usa-tiktok/appeals-court-holding-dec-14-hearing-on-blocked-u-s-tiktok-new-user-ban-idUKL1N2II287

(79) Tippett, Elizabeth C. 2020. "How TikTok is upending workplace social media policies – and giving us rebel nurses and dancing cops." *The Conversation,* December 9. Last accessed 24 February, 2025 from https://theconversation.com/how-tiktok-is-upending-workplace-social-media-policies-and-giving-us-rebel-nurses-and-dancing-cops-151269

(80) Newton, Kamilah. 2020. "Viral TikTok video calls out how social media trends 'colonized and whitewashed' Black culture." *Yahoo! News,* December 5. Last accessed 24 February, 2025 from https://sg.news.yahoo.com/viral-tik-tok-video-calls-out-how-social-media-trends-colonized-and-whitewashed-black-culture-224054602.html

(81) Abidin, Crystal, and Jin Lee. 2023. "K-pop TikTok: TikTok's expansion into South Korea, TikTok Stage, and platformed glocalisation." *Media International Australia* 188(1): 86–111. https://journals.sagepub.com/doi/10.1177/1329878X231186445

(82) Grey, Joanne Elizabeth. 2021. The geopolitics of "platforms": The TikTok challenge. *Internet Policy Review* 10(2): 1–26. https://doi.org/10.14763/2021.2.1557

(83) Ahn, Ha-neul. 2019. "고려대서 '홍콩 시위 대자보' 훼손 中 유학생과 한국 학생 충돌" ["At Korea Uni, Tension between domestic students and Chinese students become intense around the damaged 'Free

Hong Kong' posters"]. *Hankuk Ilbo*, November 12. Last accessed 24 February, 2025 from https://www.hankookilbo.com/News/Read/201911121471094037

(84) Jang, Yoon-jeong. 2018. "[중국 한류 모방| 예능◆] 중국 도넘은 한국예능 표절, '대응책 시급'." ["China's mimicry of Korean wave: Entertainment. China's plagiarism of Korean variety shows becomes intense, needs 'urgent response'."] *Aju Business Daily*, June 22. Last accessed 24 February, 2025 from https://www.ajunews.com/view/20180622105822721

(85) Choi J. 2019. "'반중 넘어 혐중'.. 중국인 혐오, 도 넘은 수준까지?" ["Anti-Chinese sentiment develop into Chinese-hate...even at the extreme level"]. *Financial News*, June 13. Last accessed 24 February, 2025 from https://www.fnnews.com/news/201906131104460296

(86) Vizcaíno-Verdú, Arantxa, and Crystal Abidin. 2022. "Music Challenge Memes on TikTok: Understanding In-Group Storytelling Videos." *International Journal of Communication* 16(2022): 883–908. https://ijoc.org/index.php/ijoc/article/view/18141

(87) Kriegel, Elana R., Bojan Lazarevic, Christian E. Athanasian, and Ruth L. Milanaik. 2021. "TikTok, Tide Pods, and Tiger King: Health Implications of Trends Taking Over Paediatric Populations." *Current Opinion in Paediatrics* 33(1): 170–177. https://doi.org/10.1097/MOP.0000000000000989.

(88) Instagram. 2020. "Introducing Instagram Reels." *about. instagram.com,* August 5. Last accessed 24 February, 2025 from https://about.instagram.com/blog/announcements/introducing-instagram-reels-announcement

(89) Alexander, Julia. 2020. "Instagram launches Reels, its attempt to keep you off TikTok." *The Verge,* August 5. Last accessed 24 February, 2025 from https://www.theverge.com/2020/8/5/21354117/instagram-

reels-tiktok-vine-short-videos-stories-explore-music-effects-filters

(90) Aldred, Johnny. 2021. "The evolution of Instagram Reels: one year on." *Performance Marketing World,* September 7. Last accessed February 24, 2025 from https://www.performancemarketingworld.com/article/1739993/evolution-instagram-reels-one-year

(91) Jaffe, Chris. 2020. "Building YouTube Shorts, a new way to watch & create on YouTube." *blog.youtube,* September 14. Last accessed 24 February, 2025 from https://blog.youtube/news-and-events/building-you-tube-shorts/

(92) Spangler, Todd. 2020. "Instagram Reels, a Copycat of TikTok, Lands in 50-Plus Countries." *Variety.com,* August 5. Last accessed 24 February, 2025 from https://variety.com/2020/digital/news/instagram-reels-launches-tiktok-copycat-1234725509/

(93) Instagram for Business. 2024. "Stories." *business.instagram.com,* –n.d. Last accessed 24 February, 2025 from https://business.instagram.com/instagram-stories?locale=en_GB

(94) Wagner, Kurt. 2018. "'Stories' was Instagram's smartest move yet." *Vox,* August 8. Last accessed 24 February, 2025 from https://www.vox.com/2018/8/8/17641256/instagram-stories-kevin-systrom-facebook-snapchat

(95) Kaye, D. Bondy Valdovinos, Jing Zeng, and Patrik Wikstrom. 2022. *TikTok: Creativity and Culture in Short Video.* Cambridge: Polity Press. https://www.wiley.com/en-br/TikTok%3A+Creativity+and+Culture+in+Short+Video-p-9781509548927

(96) Hiebert, Alexa, and Kathy Kortes-Miller. 2021. "Finding home in online community: exploring TikTok as a support for gender and sexual minority youth throughout COVID-19." *Journal of LGBT Youth* 20(4): 800–817. https://www.tandfonline.com/doi/full/10.1080/19361653.2021.2009953

(97) Bhandari, Aparajita, and Sara Bimo. 2022. "Why's Everyone on TikTok Now? The Algorithmised Self and the Future of Self-Making on Social Media." *Social Media + Society* January-March 2022: 1–11. https://journals.sagepub.com/doi/full/10.1177/20563 051221086241

(98) Maris, Elena, Robyn Caplan, and Hibby Thach. 2024. "Taking back and giving back on TikTok: Algorithmic mutual aid in the platform economy." *New Media & Society* Online first: 1–19. https://journals.sagepub.com/doi/full/10.1177/14614448241 238396

(99) Maddox, Jessica. 2023. "More Real, or Just More Surveillance? Panopticism and Shifting Authenticity Paradigms in BeReal." *Convergence: The International Journal of Research into New Media Technologies* 29(5): 1183–1198. https://doi.org/10.1177/ 13548565221151027

(100) Abidin, Crystal. 2021. "From "Networked Publics" to "Refracted Publics": A Companion Framework for Researching "Below the Radar" Studies." *Social Media + Society* January-March 2021: 1–13. https://doi.org/10.1177/2056305120 984458

(101) Hafeez, Yumna. 2023. "Instagram Reels vs TikTok – The Battle for Videos Supremacy 2023." *Social Champ,* July 19. Last accessed 24 February, 2025 from https://www.socialchamp.io/blog/instagram-reels-vs-tiktok/

(102) Dass, Camilla. 2023. "Metrics rundown: Why exactly are Instagram Reels more popular than TikTok videos?" *Marketing Interactive,* August 4. Last accessed 24 February, 2025 from https://www.marketing-interactive.com/metrics-rundown-why-exactly-are-instagram-reels-more-popular-than-tiktok-videos

(103) Mileva, Geri. 2024. "Instagram Reels vs. TikTok: Which Is the Better Platform for Brand Marketing?" *Influencer Marketing Hub,* September 4. Last

accessed 24 February, 2025 from https://influen-cermarketinghub.com/reels-vs-tiktok/

CHAPTER 2

(1) Abidin, Crystal. 2020. "Mapping Internet Celebrity on TikTok: Exploring Attention Economies and Visibility Labours." *Cultural Science Journal* 12(1): 77–103. https://doi.org/10.5334/csci.140.

(2) Abidin, Crystal. 2016. "Visibility Labour: Engaging with Influencers' Fashion Brands and #OOTD Advertorial Campaigns on Instagram." *Media International Australia* 161(1): 86–100. https://journals.sagepub.com/doi/abs/10.1177/1329878X16665177

(3) Alexander, Julia. 2020. "TikTok's For You Page Algorithm Sides with Engagement, Not Data Creators." *The Verge*, June 18. Last accessed 27 February, 2025 from https://www.theverge.com/2020/6/18/21296044/tiktok-for-you-page-algorithm-sides-engagement-data-creators-trends-sounds

(4) Bucher, Taina. 2017. "The Algorithmic Imaginary: Exploring the Ordinary Affects of Facebook Algorithms." *Information, Communication & Society* 20(1): 30–44.https://doi.org/10.1080/1369118X.2016.1154086

(5) Bishop, Sophie. 2019. "Managing Visibility on YouTube through Algorithmic Gossip." *New Media & Society* 21(11–12): 2589–2606. https://doi.org/10.1177/1461444819854731

(6) Bishop, Sophie. 2020. "Algorithmic Experts: Selling Algorithmic Lore on YouTube." *Social Media + Society* January-March 2020: 1–11. https://doi.org/10.1177/2056305119897323

(7) Cortés, Michelle Santiago. 2020. "The Creator Of #August27 Wants You To Know It's Not That Serious." *Refinery29*, August 28. Last accessed 27

February, 2025 from https://www.refinery29.com/en-us/2020/08/9991869/august-27-tiktok-twitter-meme-explainer

(8) Haasch, Palmer. 2020. "TikTokers Have Been Mysteriously Counting Down to August 27 for Months, Posting Cryptic Messages About the Date." *Business Insider*, August 27. Last accessed 27 February, from https://www.businessinsider.com/tiktok-august-27-explained-manifesting-countdown-2020-8.

(9) Kang, Hyunjin, and Chen Lou. 2022. "AI agency vs. human agency: understanding human–AI interactions on TikTok and their implications for user engagement." *Journal of Computer-Mediated Communication* 27(5): 1–13. https://academic.oup.com/jcmc/article/27/5/zmac014/6670985?login=true

(10) Brandy, Jack, and Nicholas Diakopoulos. 2020. "#TulsaFlop: A Case Study of Algorithmically-Influenced Collective Action on TikTok." *arvix.org,* December 14. Last accessed 25 February, 2025 from https://arxiv.org/abs/2012.07716

(11) Davis, Jason P. 2019. "The TikTok Strategy: Using AI Platforms to Take Over the World." *Knowledge Insead,* June 19. Last accessed 25 February, 2025 from https://knowledge.insead.edu/entrepreneurship/tiktok-strategy-using-ai-platforms-take-over-world

(12) Su, Yiran, Bradley J. Baker, Jason P. Doyle, and Meimei Yan. 2020. "Fan Engagement in 15 Seconds: Athletes' Relationship Marketing During a Pandemic via TikTok." *International Journal of Sport Communication* 13(3): 436–446. https://doi.org/10.1123/ijsc.2020-0238

(13) Das, Rishub K., and Brian C. Drolet. 2021. "Plastic Surgeons in TikTok: Top Influencers, Most Recent Posts, and User Engagement." *Plastic and Reconstructive Surgery* 148(6): 1094e–1097e. https://journals.lww.com/plasreconsurg/fulltext/2021/12000/Plastic_Surgeons_in_TikTok__Top_Influencers,_Most.86.aspx

(14) Vizcaíno-Verdú, Arantxa, and Crystal Abidin. 2023. "TeachTok: Teachers of TikTok, micro-celebrification, and fun learning communities." *Teaching and Teacher Education* 123: 1–17. https://www.sciencedirect.com/science/article/pii/S0742051X22003535?via%3Dihub

(15) Cheng, Zicheng, and Yanlin Li. 2023. "Like, Comment, and Share on TikTok: Exploring the Effect of Sentiment and Second-Person View on the User Engagement with TikTok News Videos." *Social Science Computer Review* 42(1): 201–223. https://journals.sagepub.com/doi/full/10.1177/08944393231178603

(16) Abidin, Crystal. 2021. "Making Sense of Our Digital Lives." *Commonplace.* https://doi.org/10.21428/6ffd8432.e50956d8.

(17) Duffy, Clare. 2023. "TikTok is pushing longer videos. Some creators worry about the vibe shift." *CNN,* December 23. Last accessed 25 February, 2025 from https://edition.cnn.com/2023/12/16/tech/tiktok-pushing-longer-videos-creators-app-change/index.html

(18) Sato, Mia. 2024. "TikTok's longer videos are here to stay." *The Verge,* March 6. Last accessed 25 February, 2025 from https://www.theverge.com/2024/3/5/24090583/tiktok-creator-rewards-program-monetization-subscriptions

(19) Cai, Sophia. 2022. "If you know, you know." *Journal of Australian Ceramics* 63(1): 92–95. https://search.informit.org/doi/abs/10.3316/informit.779038860275998

(20) Dantzier, Jazmin, and Tolulope Taiwo. 2024. "IYKYK: Black Queer Womxn's Experiences at Religiously Affiliated Institutions." Pp.197–204 in *Perspectives on Transforming Higher Education and the LGBTQIA Student Experience*, edited by A. Herridge and K. Prieto. Hershey: IGI Global. https://www.igi-global.com/chapter/iykyk/337379

(21) Dodini, Meagan. 2023. "#IYKYK: TikTok as a Subversive Space: Democratising Dance and Shifting Artistic Paradigms." *MFA Dance,* Hollins University. https://digitalcommons.hollins.edu/dancetheses/25/

(22) Williams, Kori. 2022. "'IYKYK' Is Bringing Users Together on TikTok – but What Does It Mean?" *Distractify,* March 8. Last accessed 25 February, 2025 from https://www.distractify.com/p/what-does-iykyk-mean

(23) van der Nagel, Emily. 2018. "'Networks that work too well': intervening in algorithmic connections." *Media International Australia* 168(1): 81–92. https://journals.sagepub.com/doi/pdf/10.1177/1329878X18783002

(24) Burgess, Jean, and Joshua Green. 2018. *YouTube: Online video and participatory culture.* Wiley. https://www.wiley.com/en-us/YouTube:+Online+Video+and+Participatory+Culture,+2nd+Edition-p-9780745660196

(25) Shifman, Limor. 2011. "An anatomy of a YouTube meme." *New Media & Society* 14(2): 187–203. https://journals.sagepub.com/doi/full/10.1177/1461444811412160

CHAPTER 3

(1) Bogle, Ariel, and Farz Edraki. 2019. "Students are fighting climate change, one TikTok video at a time." *ABC,* September 19. Last accessed 25 February, 2025 from https://www.abc.net.au/news/2019-09-19/tiktok-youth-led-climate-activism-school-strike/11520474

(2) Kaye, D. Bondy Valdovinos, Jing Zeng, and Patrik Wikstrom. 2022. *TikTok: Creativity and Culture in Short Video.* Cambridge: Polity Press, p. 32. https://www.wiley.com/en-br/TikTok%3A+Creativity+and+Culture+in+Short+Video-p-9781509548927

(3) Ibid, p. 78.

(4) Ibid, p. 79–90.

(5) Zeng, Jing, and Crystal Abidin. 2021. "#OkBoomer, time to meet the Zoomers': Studying the Memefication of Intergenerational Politics on TikTok." *Information, Communication and Society* 24(16): 2459–2481. https://www.tandfonline.com/doi/full/10.1080/136911 8X.2021.1961007

(6) Vizcaíno-Verdú, Arantxa, and Crystal Abidin. 2022. "Music Challenge Memes on TikTok: Understanding In-Group Storytelling Videos." *International Journal of Communication* 16(2022): 883–908. https://ijoc.org/index.php/ijoc/article/view/18141

(7) Popielarz, Pamela A., and Zachary P. Neal. 2007. "The Niche as a Theoretical Tool." *Annual Review of Sociology* 33(2007): 65–78. https://www.jstor.org/stable/pdf/29737754

(8) Ibid, p. 69.

(9) Hannan, Michael T., Glenn R. Carroll, and László Pólos. 2003. "The Organizational Niche." *Sociological Theory* 21(4); 309–340. https://www.jstor.org/stable/1602329

(10) Kaye, D. Bondy Valdovinos, Jing Zeng, and Patrik Wikstrom. 2022. *TikTok,* p. 116.

(11) Ibid, p. 117.

(12) Thornton, Sarah. 1996. *Club Cultures: Music, Media, and Subcultural Capital.* Hanover: Wesleyan University Press.

(13) Tofalvy, Tamas. 2020. "Niche Underground: Media, Technology, and the Reproduction of Underground Cultural Capital." Pp. 59–76 in *Popular Music, Technology, and the Changing Media Ecosystem*, edited by T. Tofalvy and E. Barna. Cham: Springer. https://link.springer.com/chapter/10.1007/978-3-030-44659-8_4

(14) Gansinger, Martin A. M., and Kinda Al-Aridi. 2023. "Pseudo-Individualisation? An analysis of the incorporation of subcultures into commodified aesthetics

on Tiktok." Pp.222–245 in *Media technology in education: Uganda and beyond,* edited by M. A. M. Gansinger and A. Kole. Cambridge: Ethics Press. https://ethicspress.com/products/media-technology-in-education

(15) Ibid, p. 238.

(16) Abidin, Crystal. 2018. *Internet Celebrity: Understanding Fame Online.* Bingley: Emerald Publishing. https://www.emerald.com/insight/publication/doi/10.1108/9781787560765

(17) Yahoo! Life. 2021. "What Does the Chair Emoji Mean on TikTok and Why Is It So Popular?" *Yahoo Life!,* September 15. Last accessed 26 February, 2025 from https://www.yahoo.com/lifestyle/does-chair-emoji-mean-tiktok-202004039.html.

(18) Cavender, Elena. 2021. "What Is Going on with the Chair Emoji on TikTok? What Does It Mean!?" *Mashable,* September 15. Last accessed 25 February, 2025 from https://mashable.com/article/chair-emoji-meaning-explanation.

(19) West-Rosenthal, Lauren Brown. 2024. "Coquette, Cottagecore, and Preppy Explained – How to Decode Gen Alpha Fashion Trends." *Parents,* June 15. Last accessed 26 February, 2025 from https://www.parents.com/gen-alpha-style-explained-8661784.

(20) Gillespie, Katherine. 2020. "TikTok's Cottagecore Influencers Explain the Trend." *Paper Magazine,* April 24. Last accessed 25 February, 2025 from https://www.papermag.com/cottagecore-explained-tiktok-trend

(21) Pascoe, Alley. 2020. "I Lived Like a Cottagecore Influencer for a Week." *Marie Claire,* October 16. Last accessed 26 February, 2025 from https://www.marieclaire.com.au/latest-news/cottagecore-trend-challenge/

(22) Ellis, Emma Grey. 2020. "My Life Is Little House on the Prairie. I Blame TikTok." *Wired,* November 30. Last accessed 25 February, 2025 from https://www.wired.com/story/tiktok-homesteading/

(23) Lal, Kish. 2020. "What Is Cottagecore and Why Is It Taking Over TikTok?" *Dazed Digital,* April 1. Last accessed 26 February, 2025 from https://www.da-zeddigital.com/fashion/article/48609/1/cottagecore-tik tok-fashion-trend-gen-z-teen-subculture-country-life-social-media

(24) Lindsay, Valerie J., and Kathy Ning Shen. 2014. "Extending definitions on international entrepreneurs: the case of cross-cultural capital." *University of Wollongong in Dubai - Papers.* 20–35 https://ro.uow.edu.au/dubaipapers/668/

(25) Froese, Fabian Jintae, and Vesa Peltokorpi. 2013. "Organizational expatriates and self-initiated expatriates: differences in cross-cultural adjustment and job satisfaction." *The International Journal of Human Resource Management* 24(10): 1953–1967. https://www.tandfonline.com/doi/full/10.1080/09585192.2012.725078

(26) Bierwiaczonek, Kiga, and Sven Waldzus. 2016. "Socio-Cultural Factors as Antecedents of Cross-Cultural Adaptation in Expatriates, International Students, and Migrants: A Review." *Journal of Cross-Cultural Psychology* 47(6): 767–817. https://journals.sagepub.com/doi/10.1177/0022022116644526

(27) Harvey, Michael, Milorad M. Novicevic, and Garry Garrison. 2005. "Global virtual teams: a human resource capital architecture." *The International Journal of Human Resource Management* 16(9): 1583–1599. https://www.tandfonline.com/doi/full/10.1080/09585190500239119

(28) Lindsay, Valerie J., and Kathy Ning Shen. 2014. Extending definitions on international entrepreneurs, p. 21.

(29) Harvey, Michael, Milorad M. Novicevic, and Garry Garrison. 2005. Global virtual teams, p. 1591.

(30) Kubota, Samantha. 2020. "Meet the Real-Life Father Behind Viral 'Your Korean Dad' TikTok Account." *TODAY*, December 5. Last accessed 26 February,

2025 from https://www.today.com/parents/nick-cho-father-behind-viral-your-korean-dad-tiktok-t202839.

(31) Makalintal, Bettina. 2021. "Hey, It's Your Korean Dad." *Bon Appétit*, October 29. Last accessed 26 February, 2025 from https://www.bonappetit.com/story/nick-cho-tiktok

(32) Reneau, Annie. 2020. "'Your Korean Dad' Nick Cho Is Like a Modern Day Mr. Rogers, But for Grown-Ups." *Upworthy*, December 4. Last accessed 26 February, 2025 from https://www.upworthy.com/your-korean-dad-nick-cho

(33) Smith, Jacob Kenton, and Emily A. Mendelson. 2024. "Parasocial Parenting, Adoption, and Mone-tization of the 'Internet Parent' with the Griswolds on TikTok." *International Journal of Cultural Studies* 1–20. https://doi.org/10.1177/13678779241288619.

(34) King-O'Riain, Rebecca Chiyoko. 2022. "#Wasian Check: Remixing 'Asian + White' Multiraciality on TikTok." *Genealogy* 6(2): 55. https://doi.org/10.3390/genealogy6020055

(35) Angermuller, Johannes. 2018. "Accumulating discursive capital, valuating subject positions. From Marx to Foucault." *Critical Discourse Studies* 15(4): 414–425. https://www.tandfonline.com/doi/epdf/10.1080/17405904.2018.1457551

(36) Ibid, p. 415.

(37) Anspach, Whitney, Kevin Coe, and Crispin Thurlow. 2007. "The other closet?: Atheists, homosexuals and the lateral appropriation of discursive capital." *Critical Discourse Studies* 4(1): 95–119. https://www.tandfonline.com/doi/pdf/10.1080/17405906001149509

(38) Shugart, Helene A. 1997. "Counterhegemonic Acts: Appropriation as a Feminist Rhetorical Strategy." *Quarterly Journal of Speech* 83(2): 210–229. https://doi.org/10.1080/00335639709384181.

(39) 39.Ibid, p. 95.

(40) Zhao, Xinyu, and Crystal Abidin. 2023. "The 'Fox Eye' Challenge Trend: Anti-Racism Work, Platform Affordances, and the Vernacular of Gesticular Activism on TikTok." *Social Media + Society,* January-March 2023: 1–16. Last accessed 26 February, 2025 from https://doi.org/10.1177/20563051231157590

(41) Ibid, p. 6.

(42) Ibid, p. 3.

(43) Ask, Kristine, and Crystal Abidin. 2018. "My Life is a Mess: Self-Deprecating Relatability and Collective Identities in the Memification of Student Issues." *Communication & Society* 21(6): 834–850. https://doi.org/10.1080/1369118X.2018.1437204

(44) Christensen, Henrik Serup. 2011. "Political Activities on the Internet: Slacktivism or Political Participation by Other Means?" *First Monday* 16(2), February 7. https://doi.org/10.5210/fm.v16i2.3336

(45) Madison, Nora, and Mathias Klang. 2020. "The Case for Digital Activism: Refuting the Fallacies of Slacktivism." *Journal of Digital Social Research* 2(2). https://doi.org/10.33621/jdsr.v2i2.25

(46) Abidin, Crystal. 2021. "From "Networked Publics" to "Refracted Publics": A Companion Framework for Researching "Below the Radar" Studies." *Social Media + Society,* January-March 2021: 1–13. https://doi.org/10.1177/2056305120984458

(47) Bishop, Sophie. 2019. "Managing Visibility on YouTube through Algorithmic Gossip." *New Media & Society* 21(11–12): 2589–2606. https://doi.org/10.1177/1461444819854731

(48) Zhao, Xinyu, and Crystal Abidin. 2023. The 'Fox Eye' Challenge Trend, 11–12.

(49) Gregory, Karen, and Jathan Sadowski. 2021. "Biopolitical platforms: the perverse virtues of digital labour." *Journal of Cultural Economy* 14(6): 662–674. https://www.tandfonline.com/doi/full/10.1080/17530350.2021.1901766

(50) Ibid, p. 662.
(51) Maso, Giulia Dal, Shanthi Robertson, and Dallas Rogers. 2021. "Cultural platform capitalism: extracting value from cultural asymmetries in RealTech." *Social & Cultural Geography* 22(4): 565–580. https://www.tandfonline.com/doi/full/10.1080/14649365.2019.1601246
(52) Ibid, p. 565.
(53) Ibid, p. 572.
(54) Ibid, p. 568.
(55) Ibid, p. 574.
(56) Miyano, Miran. 2020. "TikTok Isn't in China, So Who's Posting All Those Chinese Street Style Videos?" *Vice*, July 30. Last accessed 26 February, 2025 from https://www.vice.com/en/article/chinese-street-style-tiktok-trend-fashion-viral-douyin/
(57) Allaire, Christian. 2020. "Chinese Street Style Is Taking Over TikTok." *Vogue*, July 22. Last accessed 25 February, 2025 from https://www.vogue.com/article/chinese-street-style-tiktok
(58) Ke, Bryan. 2019. "Chinese Designer and Her Sister Are Killing the Fashion Game on TikTok." *NextShark*, August 28. Last accessed 25 February, 2025 from https://nextshark.com/loora-wang-fashion-designer
(59) Klausner, Alexandra. 2024. "Gen Z Singing Praises for Karaoke-Based Weight Loss Technique That Could Burn 500 Calories in 1 Hour." *New York Post*, January 17. Last accessed 26 February, 2025 from https://nypost.com/2024/01/17/health/gen-z-singing-praises-for-karaoke-based-weight-loss-technique/
(60) Wang, Beverley. 2024. "Chinese Social Media, Translated for the Western World." *ABC Listen*, July 4. Last accessed 26 February, 2025 from https://www.abc.net.au/listen/programs/stop-everything/candise-lin/103944550
(61) Naqvee, Zeenia. 2024. "Most Unusual Chinese New Year Traditions and Superstitions: No Hair Cuts Allowed and Why You Shouldn't Be Cleaning the

House." *Daily Mail*, February 10. Last accessed 26 February, 2025 from https://www.dailymail.co.uk/femail/article-13047609/most-unusual-chinese-new-year-traditions-superstitions.html

(62) 62Slater, Jill. 2021. "Woman Shares Hilarious Meanings of Popular Names in Cantonese – And We Feel Sorry for Rosie!" *Mum's Lounge*, September 6. Last accessed 26 February, 2025 from https://mum-slounge.com.au/lifestyle/latest-news/woman-shares-hilarious-meanings-of-popular-names-in-cantonese-and-we-feel-sorry-for-rosie/

(63) Nyce, Caroline Mimbs. 2023. "How to Watch a Movie in 15 Easy Steps." *The Atlantic*, May 23. Last accessed 26 February, 2025 from https://www.theatlantic.com/technology/archive/2023/05/tiktok-movie-clips-scenes-12-feet-deep/674148/

(64) Rosenberg, Allegra. 2023. "TikTok's Viral Movie Clips Are Changing How I Watch Films." *Polygon*, May 10. Last accessed 26 February, 2025 from https://www.polygon.com/23716196/tiktok-movie-clips-turning-red-sully-arrival-streaming

(65) Horgan, Emily. 2024. "Viral TV and Movie Clips on TikTok Are Creating a Unique Problem for Streamers." *Observer*, January 17. Last accessed 25 February, 2025 from

(66) Heritage, Stuart. 2023. "Mean Girls in 23 Parts: The Rise of Movies and Shows Watched on TikTok." *The Guardian*, October 4. Last accessed 25 February, 2025 from

(67) Mattson, Anna. 2024. "Sludge Videos Are Taking Over TikTok – And People's Minds." *Scientific American*, January 10. Last accessed 26 February, 2025 from https://www.scientificamerican.com/article/sludge-videos-are-taking-over-tiktok-and-peoples-mind1/

(68) Ede-Osifo, Uwa. 2023. "'Sludge Content' Is the Latest Form of Escapism on TikTok." *NBC News*, April 27. Last accessed 25 February, 2025 from

https://www.nbcnews.com/tech/sludge-content-tik-tok-escapism-rcna77037

(69) Weaver, Jackson. 2023. "Sludge Content Is Consuming TikTok. Why Aren't We Talking About It?" *CBC News*, January 18. Last accessed 26 February, 2025 from https://www.cbc.ca/news/entertainment/sludge-content-1.6716185

(70) Snyder, Kristin. 2023. "Welcome to the World of Ambient 'Sludge' Content." *dot.la*, February 10. Last accessed 26 February, 2025 from https://dot.la/tik-tok-sludge-content-2659277126.html

(71) Castello, Jay. 2023. "TikTok's Sludge Content Isn't Just for Short Attention Spans: The Trend Has Only Grown in Popularity." *Polygon*, March 25. Last accessed 25 February, 2025 from https://www.poly-gon.com/23649389/tiktok-sludge-content-subway-surfers-attention-span-hasanabi

CHAPTER 4

(1) Abidin, Crystal. 2018. *Internet Celebrity: Understanding Fame Online*. Bingley: Emerald Publishing, pp. 88–97. https://www.emerald.com/insight/publica-tion/doi/10.1108/9781787560765

(2) Geeter, Darren. 2019. "Twitch Created a Business Around Watching Video Games – Here's How Amazon Has Changed the Service Since Buying It in 2014." *CNBC*, February 26. Last accessed 28 February, 2025 from https://www.cnbc.com/2019/02/26/history-of-twitch-gaming-livestreaming-and-youtube.html

(3) Browning, Kellen. 2021. "How Discord, Born From an Obscure Game, Became a Social Hub for Young People." *The New York Times,* December 29. Last accessed 27 February, 2025 from https://www.nytimes.com/2021/12/29/business/discord-server-social-media.html

(4) Nan, Lisa. 2022. "Bilibili Joins Double 11's Live-streaming Sales Battle." *Jing Daily*, October 26. Last accessed 28 February, 2025 from https://jingdaily.com/posts/bilibili-livestreaming-function-double-11

(5) BIGO LIVE Wiki. 2023. "BIGO LIVE Wiki: What is BIGO LIVE." *blog.bigo.tv*, April 11. Last accessed 27 February, 2025 from https://blog.bigo.tv/faq/what-is-bigo-live/

(6) Siegel, Joshua, and Christopher Hamilton. 2011. "YouTube Is Going LIVE." *YouTube Blog*, April 8. Last accessed 28 February, 2025 from https://blog.youtube/news-and-events/youtube-is-going-live/

(7) Hern, Alex. 2017. "Facebook Live Is Changing the World – but Not in the Way It Hoped." *The Guardian*, January 6. Last accessed 28 February, 2025 from https://www.theguardian.com/technology/2017/jan/05/facebook-live-social-media-live-streaming

(8) Constine, Josh. 2015. "Twitter Confirms Periscope Acquisition, and Here's How the Livestreaming App Works." *TechCrunch*, March 13. Last accessed 28 February, 2025 from https://techcrunch.com/2015/03/13/how-periscope-works/

(9) Chaykowski, Kathleen. 2016. "Instagram Launches Live Video, Makes Messaging More Ephemeral." *Forbes*, November 21. Last accessed 28 February, 2025 from https://www.forbes.com/sites/kathleenchaykowski/2016/11/21/instagram-launches-live-video-makes-messaging-more-ephemeral/

(10) Abidin, Crystal. 2017. "#familygoals: Family Influencers, Calibrated Amateurism, and Justifying Young Digital Labour." *Social Media + Society* 3(2): 1–15. https://journals.sagepub.com/doi/full/10.1177/2056305117707191

(11) BeReal n.d.a. "Time to BeReal. Notification." *help.bereal.com*, n.d. Last accessed 27 February, 2025 from https://help.bereal.com/hc/en-us/articles/15416869159197–Time-to-BeReal-Notification

(12) Minutiae. n.d.a. "Frequently Asked Questions." *Minutiae – Anti-Social Media App.* Last accessed 28 February, 2025 from https://minutiae-app.org/faqs

(13) Stinson, Liz. 2017. "Minutiae: The Curious App That Captures Your Unfiltered Life." *Wired*, May 26. Last accessed 28 February, 2025 from https://www.wired.com/2017/05/minutiae-curious-app-captures-unfiltered-life/

(14) Pangburn, DJ. 2017. "The 'Anti-Social Media' App for Sharing Your Mundane Moments." *Vice*, May 25. Last accessed 28 February, 2025 from https://www.vice.com/en/article/minutiae-anti-social-media-app-mundane-photos/

(15) BeReal. 2024. "Your daily dose of real life." *bereal.com,* n.d. Last accessed 27 February, 2025 from https://bereal.com/en/

(16) Minutiae. n.d.b. "One-Year Subscription to the iOS Version of Minutiae." *Minutiae – Anti-Social Media App.* Last accessed 28 February, 2025 from https://minutiae-app.org/minutiae-annualsubscription

(17) Minutiae. n.d.c. "Gift 360 Edition - One Year Book & Annual Subscription." *Minutiae – Anti-Social Media App.* Last accessed 28 February, 2025 from https://minutiae-app.org/gift-minutiae-360edition

(18) BeReal n.d.b. "RealPeople & RealBrands Intro." *help.bereal.com,* n.d. Last accessed 27 February, 2025 from https://help.bereal.com/hc/en-us/articles/16530938074141-RealPeople-RealBrands-Intro

(19) BeReal n.d.c. "RealFans." *help.bereal.com,* n.d. Last accessed 27 February, 2025 from https://help.bereal.com/hc/en-us/articles/16280722573341-RealFans

(20) BeReal n.d.d. "Bonus BeReal." *help.bereal.com,* n.d. Last accessed 27 February, 2025 from https://help.bereal.com/hc/en-us/articles/10388190752669-Bonus-BeReal

(21) Klasa, Adrienne, Stephanie Stacey, and Akila Quinio. 2024. "Photo-Sharing App BeReal Acquired by

Voodoo for €500mn." *Financial Times*, June 11. Last accessed 28 February, 2025 from https://www.ft.com/content/2c1d3fa8-e3a8-48e3-b252-9b40 59876412

(22) Maddox, Jessica. 2023. "More Real, or Just More Surveillance? Panopticism and Shifting Authenticity Paradigms in BeReal." *Convergence: The International Journal of Research into New Media Technologies* 29(5): 1183–1198. https://doi.org/10.1177/ 13548565221151027

(23) Taylor, Zari A. 2023. "Everyone Stop What You're Doing and BeReal: Live Networked Publics and Authenticity on BeReal." *Social Media + Society* October–December: 1–11. https://doi.org/10.1177/ 20563051231216959

(24) Duffy, Brooke Erin, and Ysabel Gerrard. 2022. "BeReal and the Doomed Quest for Online Authenticity." *Wired*, August 5. Last accessed 28 February, 2025 from https://www.wired.com/story/ bereal-doomed-online-authenticity/

(25) Snyder, Sarah J. 2024. "Always-On Authenticity: Challenging the BeReal Ideal of 'Being Real.'" *Media, Culture & Society* 46(2): 404–413. https:// doi.org/10.1177/01634437231209420

(26) Perez, Sarah. 2022. "Locket, an App for Sharing Photos to Friends' Homescreens, Hits the Top of the App Store." *TechCrunch*, January 11. Last accessed 28 February, 2025 from https://techcrunch.com/ 2022/01/11/locket-an-app-for-sharing-photos-to-friends-homescreens-hits-the-top-of-the-app-store/

(27) Forristal, Lauren. 2023. "Anti-Instagram Photo-Sharing App Daylyy Has No Vanity Metrics, Filters, or Algorithm." *TechCrunch*, October 24. Last accessed 28 February, 2025 from https://tech-crunch.com/2023/10/24/photo-sharing-social-app-day lyy-fosters-a-judgment-free-zone-with-its-hidden-likes-private-comments-and-zero-filters/

(28) Chen, Tanya. 2021. "I Am a Fan of TikToker Leenda-Dong. However..." *BuzzFeed News*, July 2. Last accessed 28 February, 2025 from https://www.buzzfeednews.com/article/tanyachen/i-am-a-fan-of-tiktoker-leendadong-however

(29) Sing, Nathan. 2021. "Leenda Dong Is Defying Asian Stereotypes, One Gut-Busting TikTok at a Time." *Complex*, May 28. Last accessed 28 February, 2025 from https://www.complex.com/pop-culture/a/nathan-sing/linda-dong-tiktok-star-feature

(30) Abidin, Crystal. 2016b. "Aren't these just young, rich women doing vain things online?: Influencer selfies as subversive frivolity." *Social Media + Society* 2(2): 1–17. https://journals.sagepub.com/doi/full/10.1177/2056305116641342

(31) Stackpole, Thomas. 2022. "What Is Web3? Your Guide to (What Could Be) the Future of the Internet." *Harvard Business Review*, May 10. Last accessed 28 February, 2025 from https://hbr.org/2022/05/what-is-web3

(32) Aghaei, Sareh, Mohammad Ali Nematbakhsh, and Hadi Khosravi Farsani. 2012. "Evolution of the World Wide Web: From Web 1.0 to Web 4.0." *International Journal of Web & Semantic Technology* 3(1): 1–10. https://airccse.org/journal/ijwest/papers/3112ijwest01.pdf

(33) Abidin, Crystal. 2015. "Communicative ♥ Intimacies: Influencers and Perceived Interconnectedness." Ada: A Journal of Gender, *New Media, & Technology* 8. https://espace.curtin.edu.au/handle/20.500.11937/79374

(34) Cunningham, Stuart, and David Craig, eds. 2021. *Creator Culture: An Introduction to Global Social Media Entertainment.* New York: NYU Press. https://nyupress.org/9781479817979/creator-culture/

(35) Ong, Jie Yee. 2023. "Inside the Bizarre World of TikTok Lives." *Gizmodo Australia*. (Link deleted). https://gizmodo.com.au/2023/08/bizarre-world-of-tiktok-lives/

(36) Fell, Julian, Teresa Tan, Ashley Kyd, and Matt Liddy. 2024. "What We Learnt Looking Inside TikTok's Live-Streaming Money Machine." *ABC News*, February 27. Last accessed 28 February, 2025 from https://www.abc.net.au/news/2024-02-27/what-we-learned-looking-inside-tiktok-money-making-machine/103487054

(37) Tenbarge, Kat. 2023. "YouTube's 'Cancelled' Stars Are Making Comebacks with TikTok, Podcasts, and Livestreams." *NBC News*, August 30. Last accessed 28 February, 2025 from https://www.nbcnews.com/tech/social-media/james-charles-tana-jeffree-youtube-influencer-podcast-video-rcna100977

(38) Turner, Graeme. 2013. *Understanding Celebrity*. London: SAGE Publications Ltd. Last accessed 28 February, 2025 from https://uk.sagepub.com/en-gb/eur/understanding-celebrity/book239014

(39) Abidin, Crystal, and Naomi Robinson. 2023. "A retrospect on young people and COVID-19 discourse on TikTok." *TikTok Cultures Research Network (TCRN), Centre for Culture and Technology (CCAT),* Curtin University. https://tiktokcultures.com/covid-19-report/

(40) Jarrett, Kylie. 2022. *Digital Labour*. Cambridge: Polity. Last accessed 28 February, 2025 from https://www.wiley.com/en-us/Digital+Labor-p-9781509545209

(41) Banks, John, and Mark Deuze. 2009. "Co-creative labour." *International Journal of Cultural Studies* 12(5): 419–431. https://journals.sagepub.com/doi/10.1177/1367877909337862

(42) Hardt, Michael, and Antonio Negri. 2001. *Empire*. Cambridge: Harvard University Press. https://www.hup.harvard.edu/books/9780674006713

(43) Hesmondhalgh, David, and Sarah Baker. 2011. *Creative Labour*. London: Routledge. https://doi.org/10.4324/9780203855881

(44) Sun, Ping, Julie Yujie Chen, and Uma Rani. 2023. "From Flexible Labour to 'Sticky Labour': A Tracking Study of Workers in the Food-Delivery Platform Economy of China." *Work, Employment and Society* 37(2): 412–431. https://doi.org/10.1177/09500170211021157

(45) Morgan, George, Julian Wood, and Pariece Nelligan. 2013. "Beyond the Vocational Fragments: Creative Work, Precarious Labour and the Idea of 'Flexploitation.'" *The Economic and Labour Relations Review* 24(3): 397–415. https://doi.org/10.1177/1035304613500601

(46) Rosenblat, Alex, and Luke Stark. 2016. "Algorithmic Labour and Information Asymmetries: A Case Study of Uber's Drivers." *International Journal of Communication* 10: 3758–3784. https://ijoc.org/index.php/ijoc/article/view/4892/1739

(47) Neff, Gina. 2012. *Venture Labour: Work and the Burden of Risk in Innovative Industries.* Cambridge: The MIT Press. https://doi.org/10.7551/mitpress/9780262017480.001.0001

(48) Warhurst, Chris, and Dennis Nickson. 2020. *Aesthetic Labour.* London: SAGE Publications Ltd. https://uk.sagepub.com/en-gb/eur/aesthetic-labour/book232313

(49) Neff, Gina, Elizabeth Wissinger, and Sharon Zukin. 2005. "Entrepreneurial Labor among Cultural Producers: 'Cool' Jobs in 'Hot' Industries." *Social Semiotics* 15(3): 307–334. https://doi.org/10.1080/10350330500310111

(50) Hardt, Michael. 1999. "Affective Labour." *boundary 2* 26(2): 89–100. https://www.jstor.org/stable/303793

(51) Baym, Nancy K. 2015. "Connect With Your Audience! The Relational Labour of Connection." *The Communication Review* 18(1): 14–22. https://www.tandfonline.com/doi/pdf/10.1080/10714421.2015.996401

(52) Wissinger, Elizabeth. 2015. "#NoFilter: Models, Glamour Labour, and the Age of the Blink." Pp. 1–20 in *Theorising the Web 2014*, edited by J. Davis and N. Jurgenson. *Interface* 1(1). https://www.academia.edu/20536708/_Nofilter_Models_Glamour_Labor_and_the_Age_of_the_Blink

(53) Abidin, Crystal. 2016a. "Visibility labour: Engaging with Influencers' fashion brands and #OOTD advertorial campaigns on Instagram." *Media International Australia* 161(1): 86–100. https://journals.sagepub.com/doi/10.1177/1329878X16665177

(54) Fast, Karin, Henrik Örnebring, and Michael Karlsson. 2016. "Metaphors of Free Labour: A Typology of Unpaid Work in the Media Sector." *Media, Culture & Society* 38(7): 963–978. https://doi.org/10.1177/0163443716643150

(55) Postigo, Hector. 2009. "America Online Volunteers: Lessons from an Early Co-Production Community." *International Journal of Cultural Studies* 12(5): 451–469. https://journals.sagepub.com/doi/pdf/10.1177/1367877909337858

(56) Duffy, Brooke Erin. 2016. "The Romance of Work: Gender and Aspirational Labour in the Digital Culture Industries." *International Journal of Cultural Studies* 19(4): 441–457. https://doi.org/10.1177/1367877915572186

(57) Gregg, Melissa. 2015. "FCJ-186 Hack for Good: Speculative Labour, App Development and the Burden of Austerity." *The Fibreculture Journal* 25: *Apps and Affect*. https://twentyfive.fibreculturejournal.org/fcj-186-hack-for-good-speculative-labour-app-development-and-the-burden-of-austerity/

(58) Kuehn, Kathleen, and Thomas F. Corrigan. 2013. "Hope Labour: The Role of Employment Prospects in Online Social Production." *The Political Economy of Communication* 1(1): 9–25. Last accessed 28 February, 2025 from https://polecom.org/index.php/polecom/article/view/9/116

(59) Valdovinos Kaye, D. Bondy, Jing Zeng, and Patrik Wikstrom. 2022. *TikTok: Creativity and Culture in Short Video*. Cambridge: Polity, p. 99–100. https://www.wiley.com/en-be/TikTok%3A+Creativity+and+Culture+in+Short+Video-p-9781509548941

(60) Ibid, p. 100.

(61) Ibid, p. 104.

(62) Ibid, p. 107.

(63) Ibid, p. 164–166.

(64) Jennings, Rebecca. 2020. "This Week in TikTok: And the Most Popular Video of the Year Is …" *Vox*, December 8. Last accessed 28 February, 2025 from https://www.vox.com/the-goods/2020/12/8/22160034/tiktok-top-100-bella-poarch

(65) Boffone, Trevor. 2021. *Renegades: Digital Dance Cultures from Dubsmash to TikTok*. Oxford: Oxford University Press. https://global.oup.com/academic/product/renegades-9780197577684

(66) Jennings, Rebecca. 2021. "The Blandness of Tik-Tok's Biggest Stars." *Vox*, May 18. Last accessed 28 February, 2025 from https://www.vox.com/the-goods/2021/5/18/22440937/tiktok-addison-rae-bella-poarch-build-a-bitch-charli-damelio-mediocrity

(67) Boffone, Trevor. 2024. *TikTok Broadway: Musical Theatre Fandom in the Digital Age*. Oxford: Oxford University Press. https://global.oup.com/academic/product/tiktok-broadway-9780197743676

(68) Abidin, Crystal, and D. Bondy Valdovinos Kaye. 2021. "Audio memes, Earworms, and Templatability: The 'aural turn' of memes on TikTok." Pp. 58–68 in *Critical Meme Reader: Global Mutations of the Viral Image*, edited by C. Arkenbout, J. Wilson and D. de Zeeuw. Amsterdam: Institute of Network Cultures. https://networkcultures.org/blog/publication/critical-meme-reader-global-mutations-of-the-viral-image/

(69) Horton, Adrian. 2022. "Hype House: Netflix Series Shows the Depressing Side of TikTok Fame." *The Guardian*, January 8. Last accessed 28 February,

2025 from https://www.theguardian.com/tv-and-radio/2022/jan/08/hype-house-netflix-series-shows-the-depressing-side-of-tiktok-fame

(70) Mercuri, Monica. 2024. "The Insane True Story Behind Netflix's 'Dancing for the Devil: The 7M TikTok Cult.'" *Forbes*, May 29. Last accessed 28 February, 2025 from https://www.forbes.com/sites/monicamercuri/2024/05/29/the-insane-true-story-behind-netflixs-dancing-for-the-devil-the-7m-tiktok-cult/

(71) Goodwin, Anastasia M., Katie Joseff, and Samuel C. Woolley. 2020. "Social Media Influencers and the 2020 US Election: Paying 'Regular People' for Digital Campaign Communication." *Centre for Media Engagement* 14. Last accessed 28 February, 2025 from https://repositories.lib.utexas.edu/server/api/core/bitstreams/2fa6ff00-f939-40af-b326-3b5c2de16490/content

(72) Goh, Emma Ashlee. 2024. "This TikToker's Videos on Toxic Work Environments Might Need a Trigger Warning." *Female*. June 18, 2024. Last accessed 28 February, 2025 from https://www.femalemag.com.sg/culture/singapore-tiktok-influencer-amanda-ang-hibyelovez-toxic-work-environment/

(73) Makalintal, Bettina. 2021. "Hey, It's Your Korean Dad." *Bon Appétit*, October 29. Last accessed 28 February, 2025 from https://www.bonappetit.com/story/nick-cho-tiktok

(74) Eddie M. 2010. "High Expectations Asian Father." *Know Your Meme*. Last accessed 28 February, 2025 from https://knowyourmeme.com/memes/high-expec-tations-asian-father

(75) Abidin, Crystal. 2018. *Internet Celebrity*, p. 38–44.

(76) Abidin, Crystal. 2018. *Internet Celebrity*, p. 45.

(77) Valdovinos Kaye, D. Bondy, Jing Zeng, and Patrik Wikstrom. 2022. *TikTok*, p. 2.

(78) TikTok. 2024. "Community Guidelines Overview." *TikTok*, April 17. Last accessed 28 February, 2025 from https://www.tiktok.com/community-guidelines/en

(79) TikTok Shop Academy. 2025. "Best Practices for Creating High-Quality Content." *TikTok Seller University*, January 2. Last accessed 28 February, 2025 from https://seller-us.tiktok.com/university/essay?knowledge_id=5846413191956226&default _language=en&identity=1

(80) TikTok. 2025. "Violence and Dangerous Activities." *TikTok Business Help Centre*. Last accessed 28 February, 2025 from https://ads.tiktok.com/help/article/tiktok-ads-policy-violence-and-dangerous-activities

(81) Abidin, Crystal. 2020. "Mapping Internet Celebrity on TikTok: Exploring Attention Economies and Visibility Labours." *Cultural Science Journal* 12(1): 77–103. https://sciendo.com/article/10.5334/csci.140

(82) Valdovinos Kaye, D. Bondy, Jing Zeng, and Patrik Wikstrom. 2022. *TikTok*, p. 150.

(83) Valdovinos Kaye, D. Bondy, Jing Zeng, and Patrik Wikstrom. 2022. *TikTok*, p. 15.

(84) Abidin, Crystal. 2020. Mapping Internet Celebrity on TikTok, p. 95.

(85) Maris, Elena, Robyn Caplan, and Hibby Thach. 2024. "Taking Back and Giving Back on TikTok: Algorithmic Mutual Aid in the Platform Economy." *New Media & Society*: 1–19. https://doi.org/10.1177/14614448241238396

(86) Elias, Michelle. 2022. "'Begging,' 'Colourism,' and Controversy: How Are Creators Making Money on TikTok Live Streams?" *SBS News*, October 18. Last accessed 28 February, 2025 from https://www.sbs.com.au/news/the-feed/article/begging-colourism-and-controversy-how-are-creators-making-money-on-tiktok-live-streams/84tsz7yub

(87) Gelbart, Hannah, Mamdouh Akbiek, and Ziad Al-Qattan. 2022. "TikTok Profits from Livestreams of Families Begging." *BBC News*. October 12, 2022. https://www.bbc.com/news/world-63213567

(88) The Guardian. 2019. "Young, Entitled and Over There: The Rise of the Begpacker." *The Guardian*,

July 23. Last accessed 28 February, 2025 from
https://www.theguardian.com/travel/shortcuts/2019/
jul/22/young-entitled-and-over-there-the-rise-of-the-
begpacker

(89) Yahoo7. 2017. "Locals Furious as Western 'Beg-
Packers' Hit Asian Streets to Fund Travel." *Yahoo News
Australia*, April 12. Last accessed 28 February, 2025
from https://au.news.yahoo.com/beg-packers-western-
backpackers-hope-asian-locals-will-fund-their-travels-
35011906.html

(90) Abidin, Crystal, and Naomi Robinson. 2023. A
retrospect on young people and COVID-19 discourse
on TikTok, p. 20.

(91) Lloyd, Andrew. 2023. "A TikTok Dad Asked for Help
Getting His Kids a New Home, Saying They'd Been
Living in a Car for a Year. Within Days, Viewers
Donated Double What He Needed." *Business Insider*,
April 12. Last accessed 28 February, 2025 from https://
www.businessinsider.com/tiktok-dad-viral-lives-in-car-
with-kids-raises-thousands-2023-4

(92) Tempesta, Erica. 2021. "Homeless Teen Reveals
How He Cooks Innovative Meals While Living in a
Car with His Mother and Surviving on as Little as
$1.25 a Day." *Daily Mail*, February 26. Last
accessed 28 February, 2025 from https://www.dai-
lymail.co.uk/femail/article-9300275/Homeless-teen-
reveals-cooks-meals-living-car.html

(93) Yuniar, Resty Woro. 2023. "Indonesia's TikTok Trend
of Begging for Money in Mud Sparks Backlash,
Exploitation Concerns." South China Morning Post,
January 31. Last accessed 28 February, 2025 from
https://www.scmp.com/week-asia/politics/article/3208
620/indonesias-tiktok-trend-begging-money-mud-spa
rks-backlash-exploitation-concerns

(94) Manggala, Irvan, Ismi Dwi Astuti Nurhaeni, and
Andre Rahmanto. 2023. "Commodification of the
Elderly in TikTok Live Streaming (TikTok Account
Case Study @intan_komalasari92)." Formosa

Journal of Social Sciences 2(4): 495–510. https:// doi.org/10.55927/fjss.v2i4.6995

(95) Shanana, Raisha, Maria Indriani K., and Detya Wiryany. 2023. "Analysis of Online Begging Phenomena in TikTok (Case Study of Changes in the Structure of Social Problems About Online Beggars)." *West Science Interdisciplinary Studies* 1(6): 346–352. https://doi.org/10.58812/wsis.v1i06.199

CHAPTER 5

(1) Jennings, Eliza Maria Pinto. 2022. "Short Video Marketing: A Good Strategy for Small Businesses on TikTok?" *Master's Dissertation*, Porto's School. http://hdl.handle.net/10400.26/41724

(2) Chen, Huan, Dalong Ma, and Bhakti Sharma. 2024. "Short Video Marketing Strategy: Evidence from Successful Entrepreneurs on TikTok." *Journal of Research in Marketing and Entrepreneurship* 26(2): 257–278. https://doi.org/10.1108/JRME-11-2022-0134.

(3) Zhang, Lingjun, and Emre Erturk. 2022. "Potential Lessons from Chinese Businesses and Platforms for Online Networking and Marketing: An Exploratory Study." *Social Sciences & Humanities Open* 6(1): 1–13. https://doi.org/10.1016/j.ssaho.2022.100274

(4) Jennings, Eliza, Fernando Pinto Santos, and Ana Paula Marques. 2022. "Does Your Business TikTok? Genuineness, Proximity to Customers and International Expansion with Short Video Marketing." Pp. 283–291 in *Marketing and Smart Technologies: Proceedings of ICMarkTech 2022, Volume 1*, edited by J. L. Reis, M. Del Rio Araujo, L. P. Reis and J. P. Marques dos Santos. Singapore: Springer Nature. https://doi.org/10.1007/978-981-99-0333-7

(5) Prilosadoso, Basnendar Herry, Ainun Nazriah, Johni Eka Putra, Eva Desembrianita, and Ainil Mardiah.

2024. "Socialization of the Use of the Live TikTok Shop Feature as a Marketing Method in Increasing House-wives' Home Businesses." *Journal of Human And Education* 4(4): 737–744. Last accessed 27 February, 2025 from https://doi.org/10.31004/jh.v4i4.1335

(6) Buaya, Alisha. 2024. "TikTok Ad Awards return with new small business award category." *Mediaweek*, October 3. Last accessed 27 February, 2025 from https://www.mediaweek.com.au/tiktok-ad-awards-return-with-new-small-business-award-category/

(7) TikTok. 2024a. "TikTok SME Campaign Highlights the Power of Discovery for Small Businesses." *TikTok Newsroom*, October 7. Last accessed 28 February, 2025 from https://newsroom.tiktok.com/en-gb/tiktok-means-business

(8) TikTok. 2024b. "Celebrating Small Businesses at the TikTok SmallBiz Pop-Up, Presented by TD." *TikTok Newsroom*, October 28. Last accessed 28 February, 2025 from https://newsroom.tiktok.com/en-ca/cele-brating-small-businesses-canada

(9) Arruda Fontenelle, Isleide. 2010. "Global Responsibil-ity through Consumption? Resistance and Assimilation in the Anti-Brand Movement." *Critical Perspectives on International Business* 6(4): 256–272. https://doi.org/10.1108/17422041011086841.

(10) Capuno, Skyllar. 2022. "Artist or Small Business Owner? Asian American Content Creators on Tik-Tok during the Early COVID-19 Pandemic and the #StopAsianHate Movement." *Undergraduate Media and Communication Honours Thesis*, Muhlenberg College. https://www.jstor.org/stable/pdf/community.33037097.pdf?acceptTC=true&coverpage=false&addFooter=false

(11) Maris, Elena, Robyn Caplan, and Hibby Thach. 2024. "Taking Back and Giving Back on TikTok: Algorithmic Mutual Aid in the Platform Economy." *New Media & Society*: 1–19. https://doi.org/10.1177/14614448241238396

(12) Tang, Yangyi (Eric), and Alex S.L. Tsang. 2020. "Inspire Me to Purchase: Consumers' Personal Control and Preference for Underdog Brand Positioning." *Journal of Business Research* 115: 101–109. https://doi.org/10.1016/j.jbusres.2020.04.031

(13) Paharia, Neeru, Anat Keinan, Jill Avery, and Juliet B. Schor. 2011. "The Underdog Effect: The Marketing of Disadvantage and Determination through Brand Biography." *Journal of Consumer Research* 37(5): 775–790. Last accessed 27 February, 2025 from https://doi.org/10.1086/656219

(14) Schmidt, Holger J., and Pieter Steenkamp. 2022. "Beware, an underdog may bite: Literature review and brand management framework in the context of underdog brands." *Journal of Brand Management* 29: 85–110. Last accessed 27 February, 2025 from https://doi.org/10.1057/s41262-021-00259-1

(15) Winiarski, Jacek, and Bartosz Marcinkowski. 2020. "e-Commerce Websites and the Phenomenon of Dropshipping: Evaluation Criteria and Model." Pp. 289–300 in *Information Systems. EMCIS 2020*, edited by M. Themistocleous, M. Papadaki and M.M. Kamal. Lecture Notes in Business Information Processing, vol. 402. Cham: Springer. https://doi.org/10.1007/978-3-030-63396-7_19

(16) Shopify Staff. 2024. "TikTok Dropshipping: How To Dropship With TikTok Shop." *Shopify*, May 21. Last accessed 28 February, 2025 from https://www.shopify.com/blog/tiktok-dropshipping

(17) Scott, Kellie. 2023. "Side hustles for the 'broke and lazy' are trending on TikTok. Are they really that simple?" *ABC News*, February 7. Last accessed 27 February, 2025 from https://www.abc.net.au/news/2023-02-07/why-tiktoks-side-hustles-arent-as-simple-as-they-seem/101892624

(18) Rouhesmaa, Emma. 2024. "Addressing The Promotion of Overconsumption among Beauty Influencers."

Bachelors thesis Science (Economics and Business Administration), Aalto University. https://aaltodoc.aalto.fi/server/api/core/bitstreams/11974cf9-6547-48a1-8c43-a7060a42f0b2/content

(19) Alperstein, Neil. 2022. "Greenwashing as grassroots or no roots social movement." *The Journal of Social Media in Society* 11(2): 4–28. https://thejsms.org/index.php/JSMS/article/view/1099

(20) The Straits Times. 2024. "Oil Firms Pay Instagram, TikTok Influencers for Ads." *The Straits Times*, November 15. Last accessed 28 February, 2025 from https://www.straitstimes.com/world/europe/oil-firms-pay-instagram-tiktok-influencers-for-ads

(21) Liskova, Adela. 2024. "Inspiring in a Realistic Way: Role of Authenticity in Gen Z's Perceptions of Green Influencers on TikTok." *Department of Strategic Communication Master's thesis*, Lund University. https://lup.lub.lu.se/student-papers/search/publication/9173150

(22) Manavis, Sarah. 2023. "Preaching sustainability while hawking fast fashion – meet the greenwashing influencers." *The Guardian*, December 11. Last accessed 27 February, 2025 from https://www.theguardian.com/commentisfree/2023/dec/11/sustainability-fast-fashion-greenwashing-influencer-trend-

(23) Nemiroff, Brianne. 2025. "Fashion educator shares 'red flags' for buying new clothing: 'Just need to be mindful.'" *The Cool Down*, January 19. Last accessed 27 February, 2025 from https://www.thecooldown.com/green-home/greenwashing-red-flags-online-shopping-tiktok/

(24) Sweeney-Romero, Katlin Marisol. 2022. "Wellness TikTok: Morning Routines, Eating Well, and Getting Ready to Be 'That Girl.'" Pp. 108–116 in Tik-Tok Cultures in the United States, edited by T. Boffone. London: Routledge. https://doi.org/10.4324/9781003280705

(25) Signer, Rachel. 2023. "Broadcasting Your Breakfast: Why TikTokers Obsess Over Morning Routines." *The Guardian*, February 19. Last accessed 28 February, 2025 from https://www.theguardian.com/lifeandstyle/2023/feb/19/broadcasting-your-breakfast-why-tiktokers-obsess-over-morning-routines

(26) Grady, Constance. 2024. "Why are we so obsessed with morning routines?" *Vox*, June 6. Last accessed 27 February, 2025 from https://www.vox.com/culture/353950/morning-routines-rituals-huberman-morning-pages-excercise-meditation-journaling-cold

(27) Cooney, Sarah, Mya Dang, Rebecca Jackson, and Sophia Perdoncin. 2024. "#Haul: An Analysis of YouTube Discourse Surrounding Over-Consumption and Sustainability in Haul Videos." *NordiCHI '24*, 13–16 October. https://dl.acm.org/doi/pdf/10.1145/3679318.3685373.

(28) Diamond, Krista. 2024. "The Influencers Going Viral in Aisle 8." *Cosmopolitan*, November 14. Last accessed 27 February, 2025 from https://www.cosmopolitan.com/lifestyle/a62671359/tiktok-trend-luxury-supermarket-hauls/

(29) Francombe, Amy. 2024. "Back-to-school hauls are flooding TikTok. Where do brands fit in?" *Vogue Business*, August 23. Last accessed 27 February, 2025 from https://www.voguebusiness.com/story/consumers/back-to-school-hauls-are-flooding-tiktok-where-do-brands-fit-in

(30) Kılıç, İlker, and Şevval Polat. 2024. "Monkey See, Monkey Do! De-Influencing Travel." *Current Issues in Tourism* 1–17. https://doi.org/10.1080/1368350 0.2024.2404998.

(31) Lai-Lim, Cheryl. 2023. "Under de-influence: What is the de-influencing trend that's taking over TikTok?" *Her World*, February 24. Last accessed 27 February, 2025 from https://www.herworld.com/life/deinfluencing-tiktok-trend-influencers

(32) Scott, Brianna. 2024. "'This is garbage': Step aside, influencers – we're now in the era of de-influencing." *NPR*, March 25. Last accessed 28 February, 2025 from https://www.npr.org/2024/03/25/1239897929/influencers-deinfluencing-tiktok-instagram-shopping-environment

(33) Gogarty, Josiah. 2024. "Meet the De-Influencers, Who've Built a Brand on Buying Nothing." *GQ*, November 6. Last accessed 27 February, 2025 from https://www.gq.com/story/meet-the-de-influencers

(34) Teheran, Faegheh, Abdolali (Ali) Mortazavi, and Veronica L. Thomas. 2024. "The Influence of De-Influencing: Examining the Effect of Negative Endorsements by Social Media Influencers." *Doctoral Presentation, Strome College of Business.* https://digitalcommons.odu.edu/gradresearch_achievementday/2024/business/1/

(35) Ekvall, Manda, and Ellen Mellberg. 2023. "'This is Crap': Consumers' Experience of De-Influencing on TikTok." *Bachelor Thesis International Business and Marketing*, Kristianstad University. https://people.southwestern.edu/~bednarb/capstone/capstone_materials/ouellette-reading.pdf

(36) Law, Angela. 2024. "Is 'Underconsumption Core' Really As Virtuous As It Claims?" *Elle Australia*, July 23. Last accessed 27 February, 2025 from https://www.elle.com.au/culture/underconsumption-core/

(37) Valko, Alana. 2024. "Thousands of Gen Z'ers Are Taking to TikTok to Share Everything They're Not Buying, and It's Kinda Refreshing to See." *BuzzFeed*, September 18. Last accessed 28 February, 2025 from https://www.buzzfeed.com/alanavalko/underconsumption-core-tiktok-trend-explainer

(38) Collins, Riyah. 2024. "When TikTok's underconsumption trend meets festive excess." *BBC News*, December 23. Last accessed 27 February, 2025 from https://www.bbc.com/news/articles/cx2p784ppzqo

(39) Bainotti, Lucia. 2023. "Trending Resistance: A Study
       of the TikTok #Deinfluencing Phenomenon." *AoIR
       Selected Papers of Internet Research*. https://doi.org/
       10.5210/spir.v2023i0.13392

ADDITIONAL RESOURCES

Here I provide a (non-exhaustive) shortlist of scholarly resources for the reader to peruse, created and curated by the TikTok Cultures Research Network (TCRN).

TCRN SPECIAL ISSUES

- **TikTok and Social Movements (2023)** by Jin Lee and Crystal Abidin. *Social Media + Society* 9(1). https://journals.sagepub.com/page/sms/tiktokandsocialmovements
- **Cultures of TikTok in the Asia Pacific (2023)** by Crystal Abidin, Jin Lee, and D. Bondy Valdovinos Kaye. *Media International Australia* 186(1). https://journals.sagepub.com/toc/miad/186/1
- **Research Perspectives on TikTok & Its Legacy Apps (2021)** by Jing Zeng, Crystal Abidin, and Mike S. Schäfer. *International Journal of Communication* 15(2021). https://ijoc.org/index.php/ijoc/issue/view/17
- **TikTok Methodologies (forthcoming 2025)** by Crystal Abidin and Jin Lee. *Cultural Science Journal.*
- **TikTok and Children (forthcoming 2025)** by Jin Lee, Crystal Abidin, and Tama Leaver. *International Journal of Cultural Studies.*

TCRN SYLLABI & CONCEPTUAL GLOSSARIES

- **A Retrospect on Young People and COVID-19 Discourse on TikTok (2023)** by Crystal Abidin and Naomi Robinson. *TikTok Cultures Research Network (TCRN), Curtin University.* https://tiktokcultures.com/covid-19-report/
- **TikTok Syllabus: Explorando la cultura pop y los movimientos sociales [TikTok Syllabus: Exploring Pop Culture and Social Movements] (2023)** by Arantxa Vizcaíno-Verdú and Crystal Abidin. *TikTok Cultures Research Network (TCRN), Curtin University.* https://tiktokcultures.com/spanish2023/
- **Social Justice Through Social Media Pop Cultures: Case Studies and Reading Resources on Influencers and TikTok (2022)** by Crystal Abidin and Jin Lee. *TikTok Cultures Research Network (TCRN) & Social Media Pop Cultures Programme, Centre for Culture and Technology (CCAT), Curtin University.* https://tiktokcultures.com/socialjustice2022/
- **TikTok Syllabus: Teaching Socio-Cultural Issues on TikTok (2021)** by Crystal Abidin and D. Bondy Valdovinos Kaye. *TikTok Cultures Research Network (TCRN), Social Media Pop Cultures Programme, Centre for Culture and Technology (CCAT), Curtin University.* https://tiktokcultures.com/syllabus2021/
- **TikTok Cultures Research Network Bibliography (updated every quarter).** *TikTok Cultures Research Network.* https://tiktokcultures.com/bibliography/

TCRN EVENTS & VIDEO RECORDINGS

- **TikTok & Grief (2025)** by Larissa Hjorth, Katrin Gerber, and Crystal Abidin. *Digital Ethnography Research Centre, RMIT University, and TikTok*

Cultures Research Network, Curtin University. https://tiktokcultures.com/tiktok-grief/

- **TikTok Cultures in Korea (2024)** by Crystal Abidin, Janey Umback, Faye Mercier, and Jin Lee. *TikTok Cultures Research Network, Curtin University.* https://tiktokcultures.com/tiktok-cultures-in-korea/
- **Latin American Cultures on TikTok (2023)** by Daniela Jaramillo-Dent, Tom Divon, and Natalia Orrego. *Media Change and Innovation Division at the University of Zurich, The Hebrew University of Jerusalem, and The Pontifical Catholic University of Chile, supported by Tik-Tok Cultures Research Network, Curtin University.* https://tiktokcultures.com/latin-american-cultures-on-tiktok/
- **TikTok Creators & Digital Economies (2023)** by Zoetanya Sujon, Sevil Yesiloglu, Irida Ntalla, Jonathan Hardy, Yue Qin, Yingwen Wang, and Richard Meng. *Digital Cultures and Economies Research Hub at London College of Communications, University of the Arts London, supported by TikTok Cultures Research Network, Curtin University.* https://tiktokcultures.com/tiktok-creators-digital-economies/
- **TikTok & Children Symposium (2023)** by Crystal Abidin, Jin Lee, and Tama Leaver. *TikTok Cultures Research Network, Curtin University. and ARC Centre of Excellence for the Digital Child, Curtin University.* https://tiktokcultures.com/tiktok-and-children/
- **TikTok & Asian Diaspora (2022)** by Jin Lee and Crystal Abidin. *TikTok Cultures Research Network, Curtin University.* https://tiktokcultures.com/tiktok-asian-diaspora/
- **TikTok Books Roundtable (2022)** by Trevor Boffone, D. Bondy Valdovinos Kaye, Jing Zeng, Patrik Wikström, and Crystal Abidin. *TikTok Cultures Research Network, Curtin University.* https://tiktokcultures.com/tiktok-books-roundtable/
- **TikTok and Social Movements (2021)** by Jin Lee, Crystal Abidin, and D. Bondy Valdovinos Kaye. *TikTok Cultures Research Network, Curtin University.* https://tiktokcultures.com/tiktok-and-social-movements/

- **TikTok Methodologies (2021)** by Crystal Abidin, Patrik Wikström, and D. Bondy Valdovinos Kaye. *TikTok Cultures Research Network, Curtin University.* https://tiktokcultures.com/tiktok-methodologies/
- **TikTok and Youth Cultures in the Age of COVID-19 (2021)** by Crystal Abidin, D. Bondy Valdovinos Kaye, and Xinyu (Andy) Zhao. *TikTok Cultures Research Network, Curtin University.* https://tiktokcultures.com/covid-19-event/
- **Cultures of TikTok in the Asia Pacific (2020)** by Crystal Abidin and Michael Keane. *TikTok Cultures Research Network.* https://tiktokcultures.com/cultures-of-tiktok-in-the-asia-pacific/

INDEX

www.ingramcontent.com/pod-product-compliance
Lightning Source LLC
Chambersburg PA
CBHW050644270326
41927CB00012B/2874